MW00575629

Also by James Ursini

David Lean and His Films
The Vampire Film
The Life and Times of Preston Sturges,
An American Dreamer
Film Noir (Third Edition)

Also by Alain Silver

David Lean and His Films
The Vampire Film
The Samurai Film
Film Noir
Robert Aldrich
The Film Director's Team
Raymond Chandler's Los Angeles

JAMES URSINI AND ALAIN SILVER

MORE THINGS THAN ARE DREAMT OF

MASTERPIECES OF SUPERNATURAL HORROR—FROM MARY SHELLEY TO STEPHEN KING—IN LITERATURE AND FILM

PREFACE BY WILLIAM PETER BLATTY

SPECIAL RESEARCH
DAVID DEL VALLE
ELIZABETH WARD

LIMELIGHT EDITIONS

NEW YORK

First Limelight Edition May 1994

Copyright © 1994 by Alain Silver and James Ursini

All rights reserved under International and Pan-American Copyright Conventions. Published in the United States by Proscenium Publishers, Inc., New York, and simultaneously in Canada by Fitzhenry & Whiteside, Limited, Toronto.

Library of Congress Cataloging-in-Publication Data

Silver, Alain, 1947-

    More things than are dreamt of : masterpieces of supernatural horror, from Mary Shelley to Stephen King, in literature and film / Alain Silver and James Ursini ; preface by William Peter Blatty, — 1st Limelight ed.

    p.   cm.

    Filmography: p.

    Includes bibliographical references and index.

    ISBN 0-87910-177-8

    1. Horror film—History and criticism.   2. Horror tales—Filmand video adaptations.   3. Horror tales—History and criticism.

I. Ursini, James. II. Title.

PN1995.9H6S64 1994

791.43'616—dc20

                                            94-1655

                                             CIP

This book is affectionately dedicated
to our mothers,
Christiane Andrée Coulon-Silver
and
Marie Ursini

Contents

CHAPTER FOUR: The Two Jameses

CHAPTER FIVE: Selected Modern Classics

Acknowledgements

This book was originally commissioned nearly twenty years ago, shortly after the first edition of our study of vampire films appeared. While work on it stopped after a few months, much of the research and the assistance which we received goes back to that period. Seeing the films in the days before VCRs would not have been possible without the help of David Bradley, the ASUCLA Film Commission, and the Film Screening Cooperative. In addition to providing most of the stills, David Del Valle loaned us viewing copies of several of the other films. The original filmography which was compiled by Elizabeth Ward was completed at the Academy of Motion Picture Arts and Sciences in Beverly Hills. Joel Argenti designed the illustrative scheme and produced the camera-ready pages. Other stills were provided by Timothy Otto, Ruth Kennedy at Dan Curtis Productions, and Glenn Erickson, who also proofread portions of the manuscript. Additional proofreading was done by Jim Paris and Christiane Silver. Linda Brookover also read portions of the manuscript and offered numerous perspicacious suggestions.

All photographs, including the cover illustration from *The Innocents*, are from the David Del Valle Archive and reproduced courtesy of Allied Artists, American International, Bryanston, Columbia–Sony–Tri-Star, Dan Curtis, Empire/Full Moon, Hammer, MGM/UA, Orion, Paramount, Realart, Scotti Bros., Twentieth Century-Fox, Universal, Vestron, and Warner Bros.

As with **The Vampire Film** a final thanks goes to Mel Zerman at Limelight.

Preface

I saw *The Haunting* by accident. I had gone to the theater to watch *Lonely Are the Brave*, and I decided to stay for the other half of the double bill. It turned out to be the most frightening movie I had ever experienced. The sequence with Julie Harris and Claire Bloom as Eleanor and Theo, huddled together in a bedroom as some unseen force pounds at the door, was heart-stopping. The sound effects, the subtle camera moves, the actresses emoting—it was a textbook case of how to make a truly terrifying film without blood or bogeymen. Every time Robert Wise cut back to that empty staircase, I shivered. By the time I came out of the theater, the impression of conscious artfulness left by Kirk Douglas' predestined encounter with a truck load of toilets in *Lonely Are the Brave* was gone. It had been completely displaced by *The Haunting* and a major case of the willies.

It was *Rosemary's Baby*, a few years later, that really started me in the supernatural genre. Ira Levin's novel and the bizarre creative combination of William Castle and Roman Polanski produced another chillingly effective movie. This time I came out of the theater wanting to create something as good as that. That may have been a presumptuous thought for an out-of-work comedy writer, but as I began to haunt the libraries of New York in search of inspiration, I discovered how rich and varied the history of horror fiction really was. I read everything from **Frankenstein** to Grimm fairy tales. Somehow, out of all that, **The Exorcist** took shape. Writing the novel and then making the movie with William Friedkin are among the most memorable and highly publicized events of my career, events which the authors of this book have vividly

xi

dissected. I never imagined then that I would become trapped in the genre as firmly as Eleanor is trapped in Hill House.

In the introduction to this book, the authors talk about suspension of disbelief and how that effect covers everything "from fairy tales to Freddy Krueger." From my position trapped inside this genre and trying to write my way out, I can vouch for how very true that is. Until **More Things Than Are Dreamt Of**, there were many movies and many scary sequences, like the arrogant professor's encounter with those forces in which he does not believe in *Burn, Witch, Burn*, that were buried in my memory. As I read about and remember these books and movies, I can see clearly that there is some part of many of these characters in Father Karras, my own character struggling to believe in **The Exorcist**. **More Things Than Are Dreamt Of** let me revisit those books and movies and remember those moments. And if I got a case of the willies, it was only a slight one.

William Peter Blatty

More Things Than
Are Dreamt Of

Above, an archetype of Gothic horror: Frankenstein's Monster (Boris Karloff) lurks in *Frankenstein* (1931).

Introduction

There are more things in heaven and earth, Horatio,
Than are dreamt of in your philosophy.

> William Shakespeare, "Hamlet"

In a new age or an old one, the very word supernatural has immediate connotations: spectral, occult, unearthly, mystical, frightening, perhaps even ghoulish. Any thesaurus will provide another score of terms, but only the experience can evoke the real meaning. We can only guess if any of you reading this have felt the hairs on the back of your neck bristle while you stood in a graveyard at midnight clutching a grimoire. If none of you have, a safer assumption might be that those hairs have stood on end, a shudder has coursed through your body, you may even have gasped, while sitting in bed at midnight reading or watching a work of supernatural fiction.

Most often in the history of fiction, the role of the supernatural in general and the horrific in particular has been isolated and ambiguous. Isolated, because the authors of "serious" fiction in the realm of the supernatural are always outside the mainstream. Laboring in a literary tributary alongside the cheap-jack and sensationalist, these authors risk having their work regarded as "low art" by readers conditioned to this point of view. Ambiguous, because at the core of supernatural fiction is the metaphysical, because it is rooted in man's questioning the unknown and unnameable.

3

In primitive societies, the unknown was a fertile ground for a process of mythic transformation. As the aspects of material reality which could not be scientifically understood were explained through folk tale and fable, the basis for all of supernatural literature was laid down. The conflicts established there between the deific and atavistic faces of man created the fundamental, pan-cultural myths of regression and rebirth. The difference between the reborn, transfigured God and Yeats' "rough beast" quickly became the heroes and monsters of supernatural fiction.

In a more modern and ostensibly more sophisticated context, the supernatural became a larger-than-life arena for the enactment of existential set pieces. It was sufficiently detached from fact, so as not to inhibit its authors with the need for verisimilitude. It was also sufficiently close to material reality so as not to break its audience's suspension of disbelief. The prosaic descriptions and use of brand names which typify everyday reality in the work of Stephen King, for instance, give his apparitions of horror a frightening context that has gripped millions of readers.

In many respects the supernatural is like any genre of fiction. It is defined by the narrative and iconic motifs held in common by a body of actual works. With the supernatural this generic superstructure, which individual authors may reconstruct and/or de-construct in their individual *oeuvre*, does not exactly parallel the broader or narrower constructs attached to other genres that may range from melodrama, to detective fiction, to novels about Hollywood.

Because the context of these other fictions is naturalistic, the process of extracting the generic markers from the works themselves is a traditional one. At some arbitrary point in the critical process, an induction is made: the key aspects, the indicators repeated within a given body of fiction come to be understood as the defining motifs of the genre. Because this induction necessarily takes place after a certain number of works themselves, it is independent of the works. In fact, when it is first formulated the abstraction, genre, must relate to the antecedent fiction in a descriptive rather than prescriptive manner. The practical result of this *ex post facto* process is that the earliest examples of a genre are least precise or conforming. Once established, however, either formally by commentators or informally between authors and audiences, the genre markers create an expectation.

With melodrama, detective fiction, or novels about Hollywood, these markers are well defined. With the supernatural, a single metaphysical moment can be the fulcrum point. If that moment should happen to be the sudden metamorphosis of a private eye into a werewolf, it can unravel the all the indicators found in a hundred pages of realistic description and hard-boiled dialogue with a single, "supernatural" sentence.

It is this power which can make the supernatural pan-generic. It is also this power which complicates the distillation of its iconic markers and genre expectations. On the one hand, what could be simpler? All that is required is a single event, something, anything, that is by definition supernatural, "above nature." On the other hand, from minotaurs to magicians, what concept could be broader? In this sense, the supernatural may be tragic, comic, melodramatic, or all of the above. Anything and everything are possible. At the same time, on a purely experiential level, the horrific aspects of the genre must allow for both a casual *frisson* and a profound catharsis.

II.

> ...we have our philosophical persons to make modern and familiar
> things supernatural and causeless. Hence is it that we make trifles of
> terrors, ensconcing ourselves into seeming knowledge when we
> should submit ourselves to an unknown fear.
>
> William Shakespeare, "All's Well That Ends Well"

In his study of **The Fantastic** the structuralist Tzvetan Todorov tries to isolate the defining moments of the genre based on two key concepts: hesitation and fear. Todorov asserts that "the fanstastic is that hesitation experienced by that person who knows only the laws of nature, confronting an apparently supernatural event. The concept of the fantastic is therefore to be defined in relation to those of the real and imaginary: and the latter deserve more than a mere mention." Later Todorov cites H.P Lovecraft's essay on "Supernatural Horror in the Literature": "A tale is fantastic if the reader experiences an emotion of profound fear and terror, the presence of unsuspected worlds and powers."

Like Northrup Frye and other formalist forebears, Todorov seaches for a model, an ideal of fantastic fiction separated from individual expressions *and* individual value judgments. In a sense, Todorov inverts the observations of Shakespeare. It is not those things in heaven and earth which cause the unknown fear. It is not those things on the page and on the screen. It is merely the possibility of those things for which Todorov searches. This is not the aim of our study. For the casual reader and viewer, fantastic literature and film is entirely self-evident. It is the texts themselves which are of interest here; but we have set some limits.

Because they are the themes of fiction in general, it is well beyond the scope of this study to explore the entire tradition of supernatural fiction. Like a Manichaean wheel, these themes revolve around good and evil, love and hate. While the heroes and villains of ordinary fiction must wrestle with these ponderous issues within the confines of material reality, characters in narratives of the supernatural are not shackled by the everyday. Freed from the strictures of material reality but also divorced from its security, sometimes invested with fantastic powers but probably still mortal, these characters are caught in an un-stable and ill-defined terrain. If there is one overriding impulse in su-pernatural fiction, it is to restore the natural order, to get away from a realm where unknown terrors lurk and back to solid ground. Not only does supernatural horror depend on a type of narrative or iconic motif—these merely invoke the genre without giving it substance—but also on a stylistic manipulation of these motifs to produce that sense of amazement, terror, or relief which the audience shares as those charac-ters try to regain that solid ground.

As we have said this study does not pretend to treat all the significant examples or to explicate the genre in an exhaustive manner. As viable and widespread as supernatural fiction is, not only would such an enterprise require multiple volumes but it would have to encompass works with which the casual reader is unlikely to be familiar. As it is, what follows is a survey of works which we regard as prototypical. Some such as Mary Shelley's promethean novel, **Frankenstein**, or Roman Polanski's film, *Rosemary's Baby*, are available at practically any library or video store. Others from D.W. Griffith's *The Avenging Conscience* to M.R. James' short story, "Casting the Runes," may re-quire a bit of searching. While some are unquestionably milestones in the genre and appropriate to any chart of its meandering course, others are, by the same analogy, seldom travelled side streams. In trying to survey the broad landscape of supernatural fiction, it is hoped that each example will offer a glimpse from a particular perspective.

As with most surveys, the tendency is to look first to those selected works which might loosely be termed "classics"; and we have followed that tendency. Inevitably, some readers will discover that a favorite novel or motion picture has been discounted or omitted entirely. In that regard, we must beg indulgence. Our study is restricted by the limita-tions of space and the vagaries of critical inclinations. To those who would disagree over the merits of the works which are included, we can only answer that the uncertain combination of historical significance, innovative approaches, and aesthetic value guided our selection. As Kim Newman points out in her book, **Nightmare Classics**, the earliest authors of studies of horror films looked back fondly on the productions of Universal in the 1930s and 40s as the foundation of the classic period and on the likes of directors Tod Browning and James Whale as firmly ensconced in the fantastic film pantheon. After the rise and fall of Hammer and AIP and the pioneering French critics at *Midi/Minuit Fantastique*, a new generation which has grown up with the ongoing, grisly depradations of *Friday the 13th* and *Nightmare on Elm Street* is addressing the concept of classic horror films from a different point in time.

Because this is a survey of both literature and film, our concept of a classic is necessarily bi-focal, beginning with the prose work and progressing to the film version. And since the works of Mary Shelley, Robert Louis Stevenson, Poe *et al.* have been repeatedly adapted with varying results, some of the lesser efforts rate scant comment. Our value judgments are part of the critical process; but with regards to any fiction where the impact on both authors (writers and filmmakers) and audiences alike was great, our personal like or dislike must be a secondary consideration. There are two completely arbitrary factors: (1) we have dealt only with original works written in English; and (2) we have excluded works in the vampire sub-genre, which we have already treated in a separate study.

None of this introduction is to say that we promise to be unemotional or maintain a rigorous, critical detachment. Indeed, almost all of the books and movies which we discuss were read and viewed long before any thought of writing a book transformed those experiences into "research." The interest which impels this writing is the same which impelled those readings and viewings which preceded it. It is quite simply that reader's and viewer's delight in the unearthly, the dreadful, the indescribable, that discovery of a metaphysical treatise with an agreeable shudder attached, which has impelled all those who ever have or ever will enjoy supernatural fiction.

Since it includes elements which are simultaneously realistic and fantastic and since it requires a willing suspension of disbelief at both levels, the primary consideration for distinguishing the supernatural from other genres may also be quite simple. From fairy tales to Freddy Krueger the key is the same. It is something above nature, the stuff of dreams and even more—more than is dreamt of.

Above, Peter Cushing in one of his many portrayals of Dr. Frankenstein in the Hammer series raptly studies a beating human heart in his laboratory tank in *The Evil of Frankenstein.*.

CHAPTER ONE

The Prometheans

I. The Haunted Summer:
Mary Wollstonecraft Shelley (1797-1851)

Did I request thee, Maker, from my clay
To mould me man? Did I solicit thee
From darkness to promote me?

John Milton, **Paradise Lost**

If any work fits the definition of a classic, it is surely Mary Shelley's **Frankenstein, or The Modern Prometheus.** Since its first publication in 1818 it has been issued in subsequent editions scores of times and in dozens of translations to other languages. Frankenstein and his unhappy creature have become part of our collective unconscious, with creator and created often conflated in later generations' minds. In theater, film, and television the Frankenstein story has become a staple, rivaling Bram Stoker's **Dracula** for the title of most adapted supernatural horror story. From *Frankenstein* (1931) to *Frankenhooker* (1990), from the sublime to the ridiculous, popular culture has made Mary Shelley's myth its own.

What is most amazing about this work is that it was written by a young woman in her teens. Mary Wollstonecraft Shelley, née Godwin, the daughter of radicals William Godwin and Mary Wollstonecraft, grew up in an atmosphere of freethinking, feminism, and revolutionary ideals. Like most intellectuals of her period she was profoundly in-

9

fluenced by two social forces, the French Revolution and the budding
Romantic movement.

When Mary was sixteen she met one of the prime architects of that
Romantic movement, Percy Bysshe Shelley. Falling in love with the
then-married Shelley, she ran off with the poet and formed a notorious
liaison with him, bearing him children out of wedlock. In 1816 she
finally married the poet after his wife's suicide.

Mary's freethinking also extended to the friends she kept, which included the already infamous Romantic poet George Gordon, Lord
Byron. It was, in fact, during the summer of 1816 when Mary, Percy,
Dr. John Polidori, and Byron's mistress, Claire Clairmont, were
vacationing in Switzerland on Lake Leman that her classic novel was
begun. Its inception is described by Mary herself in the introduction to
the 1831 edition of **Frankenstein,** "'We will each write a ghost story,'
said Lord Byron; and his proposition was acceded to. There were four of
us. The noble author began a tale, a fragment of which he printed at
the end of his poem **Mazeppa.** Shelley, more apt to embody ideas and
sentiments in the radiance of brilliant imagery, and in the music of the
most melodious verse that adorns our language, than to invent the

Below, "the Haunted Summer" as imagined by James Whale in *The Bride of Frankenstein* with
Mary Shelley (Elsa Lanchester) and Lord Byron (Gavin Gordon).

machinery of a story, commenced one founded on the experiences of his early life. Poor Polidori had some terrible idea about a skull-headed lady..." Her inspiration came later on, after a discussion of reanimation experiments between Percy Shelley and Byron. It was part-vision, part-dream. "[I saw] the pale student of unhallowed arts kneeling beside the thing he had put together. I saw the hideous phantasm of a man stretched out..."

Over the next month Mary worked on her novel while haunted by personal tragedies: the suicide of Shelley's wife as a result of Mary's affair with the poet; the suicide of her half-sister; and the death of her own newborn child. From a hotbed of poetic idealism, suicidal despair, and infant death, **Frankenstein** was born.

Mary Shelley's novel can be read on several different levels. The most superficial is a melange of science fiction and the Gothic novel. In fact, many commentators have asserted that Mary Shelley's **Frankenstein** is not a Gothic or horror novel at all, but one of the first instances of science fiction. To appreciate Shelley's influence in requires only a superficial look at the plethora of subsequent stories which feature scientists defying God and trying to create life. Stevenson's **The Strange Case of Dr. Jekyll and Mr. Hyde** and Lovecraft's **Herbert West—Reanimator** are but two. As pure science fiction, however, **Frankenstein** falls short as does its descendant **Dr. Jekyll and Mr. Hyde.** There is little scientific detail. The chapter dealing with the creation of the homonoid is noticeably obscure, supplying the reader with almost no information on the process. Victor Frankenstein, the young "father" of the monster, is more like a medieval alchemist than a 19th Century scientist. He refers to a secret he has stumbled upon in his study and experimentation which makes him "capable of bestowing animation upon lifeless matter" and to the "dissecting room and the slaughterhouse [which] furnished many of my materials." Beyond this, there is almost nothing which the reader can use to form a picture of how this eight-foot monstrosity was fashioned. For all the reader knows, the means of creation could have been magical.

As a Gothic novel the work is far more successful. It features many of the conventions and icons of that genre. As in Todorov's working definition, the mood is one of fear and terror, with the creature threatening Victor and his loved ones, and fulfilling that threat. He murders Victor's bride, Elizabeth, his brother, William, and his friend, Henry, and ultimately causes Victor's own death in the frozen Arctic. The settings are also typical of the genre: blasted expanses of terrain, like the Arctic locale at the beginning and end of the novel; primeval forests like the one in which the creature hides after he flees Frankenstein's laboratory.

Above, evolving visualizations of Frankenstein's science: at left, Dr. Pretorius (Ernest Thesiger) with one of his *homunculi* in miniature formal dress posed under glass on a shiny lab table in James Whale's *The Bride of Frankenstein*; at right, makeshift surgery as Frankenstein (Peter Cushing) holds an artery in his teeth while his assistant (Shane Briant) works on a hand bandaged in dirty rags in Terence Fisher's *Frankenstein and the Monster from Hell.*

The structure of **Frankenstein** also adheres to the Gothic model. The story is told largely through letters, journals, and flashback narrations rather than through a straightforward third person or first person narration. This narrative mode would also become a favorite among horror writers for decades to come, most notably J. Sheridan Le Fanu, Bram Stoker, and Robert Louis Stevenson.

Beyond the structural level, there is the psychological. Although **Frankenstein** may lack verisimilitude in its failure to construct a feasible scientific context, on a level of character interaction it is finely-tuned. As other critics have suggested, the thematic center of **Frankenstein** is the child's search for parental love and its inextricably linked corollary, parental responsibility. Mary Shelley, for most of her life, wrestled with family tragedies: Mary was already burdened with guilt over the death of her mother while giving birth to her before the suicides of Percy's wife and her own half-sister and the death of one of her own children. Not long after the Haunted Summer, two more children died of fever and her beloved husband drowned in Italy. It is not surpising that one of **Frankenstein**'s main themes should be the often calamitous nature of familial relations.

The creature Frankenstein brings forth is as much his child as if he had sired it naturally. When the creature accosts Victor in the mountains, demanding a mate to relieve his loneliness, he says, "Yet you, my creator, detest and spurn me, thy creature, to whom thou are bound by ties only dissoluble by the annihilations of one of us...Do your duty towards me." The creature rightly upbraids Victor for deserting him, for leaving him literally and figuratively like a "babe in the woods."

Because Victor refuses to acknowledge his responsibility and cravenly flees it, his own family is decimated. When he does choose to pursue the creature to the "ends of the world," it is only to wreak vengeance on an entity he calls "a devil." Only at the end of his life, when he is dying of fever aboard ship, does he admit his guilt: "In a fit of enthusiastic madness I created a rational creature, and was bound towards him, to assure, as far as was in my power, his happiness and well-being. This was my duty."

The final level of the novel is a mythological-supernatural one, as invoked by the subtitle, "The Modern Prometheus." The myth of Prometheus was crucial to the ideology of the Romantic Movement. Many Romantic writers referred to it in their works including Percy Shelley in his play, "Prometheus Unbound." The attraction of this myth for the Romantics is its affirmation of man's struggle to reach perfection, both spiritual and intellectual. The ancient Greek Prometheus, involved in the creation of humans and so enamoured of them that, without permission from Zeus, he gave them fire, is an archetype of Romantic idealism. His horrific punishment, chained to a rock where birds of prey peck at his entrails, embodies the Romantic Agony.

Victor is an obvious analog for Prometheus. He defies God by having the *hubris* to believe that he can create life on his own, an arrogance to which he clings even at his death. "Nor do I find it blameable," he says referring to his act of creation. He does repent his treatment of the creature but not the act of creation itself. Like Prometheus he defied the gods and must suffer his punishment.

The Romantics' basic distrust of science echoes through subsequent examples of popular supernatural fiction from Stevenson to Stephen King. Although they hoped that the industrial revolution and its fiery dynamos would liberate humanity, much as Prometheus' gift of fire did, from drudgery and poverty, the Romantics, taking their cue from mystic poet William Blake, reproached science and the Industrial Age. Clearly, one of Victor Frankenstein's flaws is his unshakable faith in a science which leaves little room for the spiritual side. He refuses, until the end, to take responsibility for his child/creature. Frankenstein's moral and spiritual dimensions are so underdeveloped, because this was, according to the Romantics, a characteristic of the 18th Century "Enlightened man."

The second myth invoked in Shelley's novel is that of Adam. Clearly Mary was influenced by Milton's epic poem **Paradise Lost.** The epigraph for the novel, reproduced at the head of this chapter, is from that mammoth work, as is the theme of man abandoned by God. The creature is a new Adam after the Fall, abandoned in a dark forest, searching desperately for warmth, comfort, and security. In one of the more poignant scenes in the novel, the creature comes upon a cottage in the woods. In it resides a blind man, De Lacey, and his family. Over a period of months the creature watches their interactions with intense interest, learning language and human behavior.

Wishing to share their love and warmth, the creature approaches the blind man, only to be repulsed by the returning family who is shocked by his gruesome appearance. His innocence is soiled, and so he burns the cottage in a fit of shame and fury. Cast out of his Eden, he becomes an alienated freak, hunted by any human who sees him even when he is bent on aiding them, as in the scene when he rescues the drowning girl. And so he searches for the only one who can help him, his creator, his "father," Victor Frankenstein.

While the creature appeared on film as early as 1910 in an Edison short, most of the conventions of future Frankenstein films would be established by James Whale in the first feature adaptation of Shelley's novel. *Frankenstein* (1931) introduced conventions only hinted at in the original work or not present at all. First, the physical terrain of Frankenstein's laboratory is visualized concretely by Whale. While Mary Shelley is vague about the look of this place, referring to a "solitary chamber, or rather cell" and a "workshop of filthy creation," Whale constructs an expressionistic, Gothic structure with steep, stone staircases, distorted angles, and chiaroscuro lighting. In this workshop Frankenstein has set up a vast laboratory of bubbling beakers, immense electrical devices, cantilevered operating tables, and lightning rod kites floating above a tower.

Frankenstein's method of reanimation is also made specific by Whale, in whose hands Frankenstein becomes a master surgeon who stitches dead bodies together and then electrifies them, using lightning as his source, recalling the Promethean allusions of the original. In a spectacular scene, Frankenstein raises the body of his creature to the pinnacle of the tower during a storm. Thunder roars on the soundtrack as blasts of lightning activate his transformers. Lowering the body, there is an anxious moment of silence as the camera moves in on the creature's

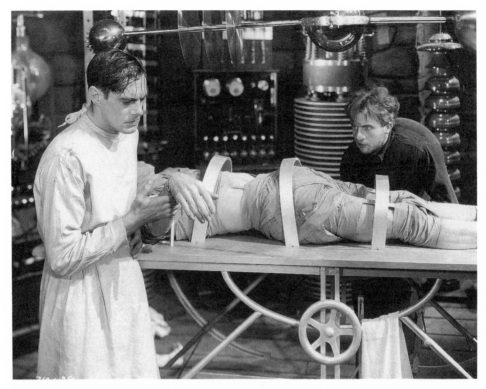

Two concerned creators: above Colin Clive as Frankenstein, Dwight Frye as his assistant, and a bandaged creature in *Frankenstein*; below, Christopher Lee as the Creature, Peter Cushing as Frankenstein, and Robert Urquhart as his assistant in *The Curse of Frankenstein*.

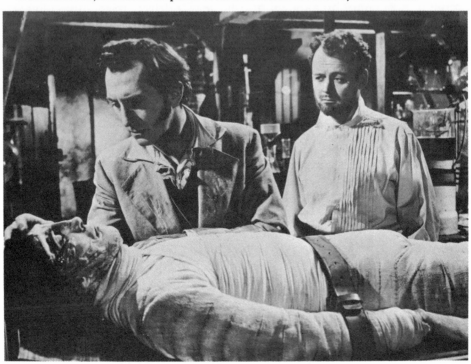

hand. At its barely perceptible movement, Frankenstein screams madly, "It's alive, alive, alive!"

Whale also created the look of the creature. Mary Shelley chose to rely on the reader's imagination and the other characters' terrified reactions to the monster to carry the effect. In Whale's film the audience first sees the creature in an Eisensteinian montage of three cuts, each one closer than the next and ending in a tight close-up of his scarred face. The creature is huge, as Shelley indicated; its movements are stiff and mechanical; its features cadaverous; and its verbal expressions guttural, as opposed to Shelley's creature who learns a perfect, very florid form of English.

In another departure from the novel, the "serious" moments, such as the early scene of body snatching where the camera lingers over the monomaniacal scientist and his assistant as they dig beneath a gibbet, are balanced by macabre humor in the antics of the old Baron and the occasional gleam in the eye of the deformed aide-de-camp, Dwight Frye. Whale does keep to the schizophrenic split of the original novel, however, and compels the audience to identify with both the creature and the creator. Dr. Frankenstein ("Henry" not "Victor" in this version) is more frenetic than his literary progenitor. While an associate observes that "Herr Frankenstein is a brilliant young man, yet most erratic," the camera tightens ominously from a medium three shot to a close-up. As played by Colin Clive, Henry Frankenstein seems to be always on the verge of a nervous breakdown and is nearly driven to mental collapse when his creature murders his assistant and turns on Frankenstein's own family and his new bride. While the audience is led to sympathize with Frankenstein's plight, particularly when his bride is attacked, the creature's childlike qualities also elicit empathy. This new Adam is persecuted and tortured from the moment of his "birth." Frankenstein's assistant chains him to the wall and torments him with a firebrand. Villagers shoot him and eventually burn him to death.

Ironically counterposed against the kinetic montage of the creature's animation is a scene cut from re-release versions for decades, where the creature plays gaily with a young child, happy for once, as they throw flowers in the lake and watch them float. There is an overtly lyric staging of this scene, suffused in sunlight, free of any ominous shadows. The grotesque giant is even smiling. There is only the merest suggestion, like the glistening ripples made by the flowers falling into the tranquil lake, of anything disruptive or deadly impending. Associating the beautiful flowers with the little girl, he picks her up gently and tosses her into the water. She does not float. Terrified, the creature runs away to meet his end, burned alive in a windmill whose blades resemble a fiery cross that became an iconic link with Whale's sequel four years later.

The Bride of Frankenstein is a much more ambitious film than its predecessor. It is also much more iconoclastic, as Whale gives free rein to his sardonic and sacrilegious impulses, from the brilliant prologue to the final orgiastic destruction. The tone is set in the prologue of the movie where the camera glides into a Gothic castle assaulted by torrential rain and lightning. Inside a cozy sitting room, the audience is introduced to three notable literary personages: Mary Shelley, her husband Percy, and Lord Byron, whose bursts of sarcasm and poetry presage the rest of the film. Both men inquire anxiously of the demure Mary if she will continue with her narrative of Dr. Frankenstein. She nods shyly as she passes her needle through the lace work on which she is concentrating. Slowly she begins the frightening sequel to **Frankenstein,** smiling and innocent-looking as she speaks of horrors to come. Lord Byron wonders, parenthetically, as did indeed generations to come, how such perversity and horror can rise full grown from the brain of this sedate young woman. Significantly Whale chose to have Elsa Lanchester play Mary Shelley as well as the creature's bride, possibly hinting at the attraction to the forbidden and perverse in Shelley herself.

The core of the film rests, however, not with these literary figures but with three others: Dr. Frankenstein, again played by Colin Clive; the creature with Boris Karloff reprising his pantomimic tour de force; and finally the ghoulish Dr. Pretorius (Ernest Thesiger). After Frankenstein's "hellish fall" and the supposed death of the creature, Frankenstein is nursed back to health by his devoted Elizabeth. Soon, though, this Prometheus-like figure is tempted again, this time by the mysterious Dr. Pretorius, whose "only vices," are, by his own admission, necrophilia, blackmail, and grave robbing. He inhabits crypts,

Below, Ernest Thesiger as Dr. Pretorius pays off his grave robbing cronies.

creates *homunculi*, and uses the coffins of beautiful female corpses as dining tables. Joining forces with the creature, Pretorius coerces Frankenstein into reanimating a "bride" for his lonely monster.

The sardonic attacks against religion and its myths, which appear in all of Whale's work, are particularly striking in two scenes. The first occurs when the creature is captured by the villagers and mounted on a cross in a parody of the Crucifixion, then he is transported to prison where the villagers abuse and taunt him.

The second scene is the interlude with the blind hermit in which the creature is taught to eat properly and to smoke. It is what Carlos Clarens called in his ground breaking **An Illustrated History of the Horror Film**, a "pastoral-grotesque interlude," which functions as satire of the novel's sentimental interaction between the creature and De Lacey. While the creature learned perfect English, indirectly, from De Lacey, here the creature learns the simple pleasures of life as he chants enthusiastically, "Drink is good. Smoke is good." When the hermit prays at night for protection, Whale adds irony by highlighting a crucifix with a bloody Christ as "Ave Maria" resounds in the background.

The sequence in which the "bride" is created also verges on parody as the canted camera angles, gliding movements, and "wedding bells" soundtrack confound the bathos of the scene. Frankenstein has created a mate for the lonely creature, but his bride prefers the handsome doctor to her monstrous betrothed. When the creature tries to touch her hand, she hisses and recoils like a cat. Disillusioned, the creature blows up the laboratory, permitting only Frankenstein and Elizabeth to escape. As he leans on the fatal lever, he intones to Dr. Pretorius and his "bride" the ominous words, "We belong dead."

Below, Elsa Lanchester as the Bride and Boris Karloff as the Creature in *The Bride of Frankenstein.*

Above, Bela Lugosi as Igor, Boris Karloff as the Creature, and Basil Rathbone as the title character in *Son of Frankenstein.*

The financial success of Whale's *Frankenstein* films led Universal to continue recycling Shelley's characters, most often the creature, in a hodgepodge series of films. The notable exception is Rowland V. Lee's *Son of Frankenstein* (1939), which is more concerned with the character of Frankenstein himself (or, actually, in this case, Frankenstein's son who is intent on vindicating his father's name) than with the creature. Frankenstein, Jr. is haunted by his father's disgrace, trying but unable to expiate for the past. When he arrives to take up residence at the family manor, he makes a conciliatory speech in the cold drizzle at the train station to the people of the village in which his father lived and worked; but they spurn him. The police inspector, who has lost his arm to the creature, watches him suspiciously from the crowd. With rain-dampened spirits and clothes Frankenstein Jr. takes refuge in the gloomy, expansive mansion, where the expressionistic shadows that loom over him and his family come to depress him as much as the hostility of his neighbors.

Before the atmosphere becomes too unbearable, Frankenstein meets the sardonic Igor, a crippled peasant who has survived hanging but been disfigured: "I scare him to death. I don't need to kill him to death." Igor introduces Frankenstein to his father's creature, who has survived once again, and the young scientist can no longer resist the call of the past.

The revitalization of the creature is a montage reminiscent of Whale's laboratory sequences. Unfortunately for Frankenstein, Igor has other, more devious plans for the creature. He sends it out on missions of vengeance against those who tried to execute him. As the dead bodies pile up, Frankenstein becomes frantic, sarcastically lashing out at anyone who accuses him of creating a new monster: "Am I supposed to have whipped one up as a housewife whips up an omelette?".

Besides the oppressive, expressionistic sets, what is memorable about this film version is the level of the performances. Basil Rathbone plays Frankenstein with a febrile energy which is especially evident in the scenes with Lionel Atwill, as the inspector. A simple dart game between the two men, during which Atwill lines up the darts on his wooden arm, becomes a cutting battle of wits. Bela Lugosi's Igor is equally subtle, combining a mocking sense of humor with a menacing facade. And, of course, Boris Karloff returns as the monster, this time with less sympathy and more murderous rage.

In 1957 director Terence Fisher made a film which would radically alter audiences' expectations of the Frankenstein story. Much as he would do the next year for Stoker's **Dracula,** Fisher deconstructed and reinterpreted Mary Shelley's mythical framework. *The Curse of Frankenstein* shifts the dramatic emphasis of Shelley's novel from the creature to Victor Frankenstein himself, energetically portrayed in all the Fisher films by Peter Cushing. Along with this seismic shift of focus came an equally momentous shift of tone. Up to this point Frankenstein's character had been a reflection of the image designed by Mary Shelley and based somewhat on her husband, a flawed human being who reached for the ideal, only to fall short like his archetype, Prometheus. With Fisher at the helm, the character was pulled back down from the stars and into the mud.

Fisher's Frankenstein is ruthless and amoral, exploiting everyone around him. He threatens and cajoles his tutor, Krempe, to whom he is indebted for much of his knowledge, in order to obtain his aid in his experiments. Finally Krempe is forced to break with him ("You can't see the horror of what you are doing."). His fiancée, Elizabeth, is ignored and then used as bait, so that Krempe will return and help him. The innocent maid, Justine, is seduced, impregnated, and abandoned. And the creature which he makes is chained to a wall to be taught tricks like a dog.

Frankenstein's machinations go far beyond any previous conception so that he becomes the villain of the piece. When Elizabeth returns to marry Frankenstein, she tells Krempe, "It's always been my dearest wish, his, too." Fisher then cuts to a two-shot of Frankenstein and the maid locked in an embrace. When Frankenstein needs a brain for his creature, he invites the "greatest mind of Europe," Professor Bernstein, to his house, dines him, murders him and blithely extracts his cerebrum. Even in the final scene of the film, Frankenstein's execution for murder, when Fisher has the opportunity at least to portray this manipulator as courageous, he opts instead to show Frankenstein whining and weeping, as he is dragged to the guillotine,

Fisher's naturalistic, unsentimental tone carries over to the look of the film. Gone are the chiaroscuro lighting, twisted angles, and expressionistic set design so typical of Universal. Frankenstein's laboratory is drably realistic. There are no elevators to the stars on which the body of the creature will be reanimated by lightning. There is no clutter of gadgets, no Jacob's ladders, glowing tubes, or guillotine switches, all

Below, two faces of the Creature: Boris Karloff, right, and Christopher Lee in *The Curse of Frankenstein*.

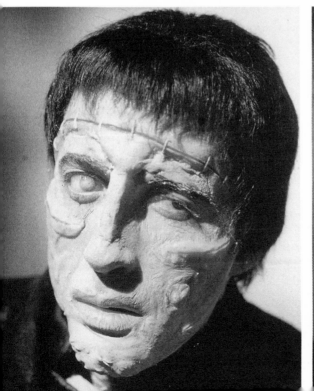

Above, display art from the U.S. release of *The Revenge of Frankenstein.*

housed in a Gothic chamber. This Frankenstein's claustrophobic workplace is simply that, a workplace. It often contains only a dingy surgical table, a chemical bath for the body of the creature, a crude transformer, and little else.

In *Revenge of Frankenstein* (1958) the reprehensible doctor is rescued from the guillotine and sets up shop in a clinic. Under the cover of treating the indigent, he amputates their healthy body parts for his new creature. In this sequel Frankenstein has become even more coldblooded. He shrugs his shoulders after appearing out of the night like a phantom and causing a gravedigger to die of a heart attack; with a mocking smile he chops off the limbs of patients; and when he transfers the brain of his crippled servant, Karl, to the handsome body of his new creature, he neglects to tell the painfully shy man that he will become a scientific specimen at which the world will gawk.

With this film Fisher begins to develop the audience's sympathy for the creature as a moral counterweight to the depraved Dr. Frankenstein. When the gentle Karl is given his perfect body, he is ecstatic; but when he finds out that he will be put on exhibit with his old body, he escapes, destroying his old frame in the process. In a fight with a guard, his brain is damaged and his old physical defects return.

Mad with grief and terror, he throws himself at the feet of Frankenstein at an elegant soirée and exposes him. Frankenstein returns to the clinic where, in an especially graphic scene, he is surrounded and beaten to a bloody pulp by the patients he had mutilated.

In *Frankenstein Created Woman* (1966) Fisher's recurring hypothesis that Frankenstein himself is the monster is restated when the audience first sees the doctor being revived from a cryogenic state, a fate reserved in most films for the creature. Frankenstein now believes in a more transcendental form of science: capturing the soul at the moment of death and transferring it to a sympathetic body. When his assistant, another Karl, is unjustly executed for murdering the father of his lover, who in turn commits suicide, Frankenstein seizes the opportunity to perform the switch.

This time around the creature is a beautiful temptress who seeks out the men responsible for Karl's conviction, communicating telepathically with his decapitated head which is seen mounted on her bed post at night. When she finds the men, she seduces and murders them. When her mission is complete the guilt-ridden creature leaps into the river and drowns.

Although other Hammer writers and directors were concurrently producing Frankenstein films, such as *The Evil of Frankenstein* (1964) and *Horror of Frankenstein* (1970), the psychological insight and moral

Below, as the series progresses, the operating rooms get smaller and dingier: in an attic Dr. Simon Helder (Shane Briant) prepares to remove a pair of eyes from a corpse in *Frankenstein and the Monster from Hell*

complexity of Fisher's films provided a through line eschewed by other Hammer filmmakers. Fisher's next installment in the saga was *Frankenstein Must Be Destroyed* (1969). Certainly the expectations of Fisher's audiences supported the sentiments of the title. In the opening sequence, a deformed "monster" confronts a thief, beheads him, and discards the body. It is no surprise when the "monster" rips off his mask and reveals the face of Dr. Frankenstein.

Whatever trace of humanity Frankenstein might have had in the earlier films, and there was very little, had now vanished. As he murders a night watchman, Cushing displays the trademark sardonic smile. The innocent, soft-spoken Anna and her lover, Karl, have been stealing drugs from the clinic and selling them to help her impoverished mother. Frankenstein blackmails her, so that he might turn out her boarders and convert the cellar into a laboratory. Later he rapes her for no other reason than to solidify his power over her. Eventually he kills her for damaging his newest creation. Karl, who has become the latest assistant, is, like all of his expendable, like-named predecessors, browbeaten and scorned.

In many ways *Frankenstein Must Be Destroyed* is the most fully realized film of the series. Two scenes demonstrate the range of Fisher's sure-handed staging. When Anna is home alone, the director uses suspense to increase viewer empathy: a pipe bursts, and a body which Frankenstein had buried in the garden of the boarding house is gradually unearthed. In a panic Anna struggles with the bloated corpse to hide it before the workmen arrive. Soaked by the torrent of water, she drags the corpse to the bushes, just as several officials appear.

The second scene is a tender interchange between the creature and his wife. Frankenstein has kidnapped a scientist who was an expert on brain transplants from an asylum. He restores his mind through a series of operations on his brain, then transfers it to a stronger body. When the scientist awakes to find himself in another's body, he is driven to despair. He visits his house and his beloved wife. In order not to alarm her, he hides behind a screen, speaking tenderly to her of his love and his tragedy. It is the only moment of human warmth in this otherwise unsentimental film. The film ends on an appropriately apocalyptic note with the creature burning his own house and then carrying a struggling Frankenstein back with him into the flames.

Frankenstein Must Be Destroyed would have been a fitting close to Fisher's cycle of Frankenstein films. *Frankenstein and the Monster from Hell* (1973) comes at the end of Fisher's long career and has little of the vigor of his former work. The decors are shabbier and less imaginative. The hirsute creature looks like someone in a cheap monster suit, nothing like the doomed creatures Fisher had envisioned before. Even Cushing, reprising Frankenstein, seems wan and feeble. While this is not entirely inappropriate to an "old man's film," it is an anticlimactic finale to Fisher's innovative treatment of the Frankenstein legend.

Long after *Frankenstein and the Monster from Hell,* the influence of Fisher's reinterpretation of the Frankenstein story on other filmmakers continues to be felt. Two diverse examples are the campy *Flesh for Frankenstein* (or *Andy Warhol's Frankenstein*, 1973) and Roger Corman's *Frankenstein Unbound* (1990).

In the first film Frankenstein is transformed into a proto-Nazi. This aristocratic Baron is creating a super race, a perfect Serbian man and woman who will mate and multiply. As he works in his laboratory, stitching together his ideal man and woman and pontificating to his servant ("I've always looked for beauty. In fact, I insist on it."), Wagner resounds on the soundtrack. Like Wagner's Siegmund this Baron Frankenstein is married to his voluptuous sister, played by the statuesque starlet, Monique Van Vooren, and has produced two mute children who spy on all that he and his sister do. The camera takes their points of view as they watch through decorative foregrounds while their mother seduces the new servant and their father disembowels bodies. It is then only fitting that this absolutist's dream of a master race is destroyed by an over-sexed, unkempt peasant who beds

Below, two more faces of the creature: at right, Bo Svenson in Dan Curtis' *Frankenstein;* at left, the monster as overstuffed teddy bear in *Frankenstein and the Monster from Hell* (inside the suit is David Prowse, better known for his performance inside the Darth Vader costume).

Above, Udo Kier as a blood-spattered Baron in *Flesh for Frankenstein*. Left, Susan Denberg as Christina portrays the creature as a vengeful temptress in *Frankenstein Created Woman*.

Frankenstein's sister-wife, then inspires the homosexual creature to destroy both the Baron and Baroness.

Frankenstein Unbound is far more serious and complex a work than *Flesh*. The film attempts to interweave three stories into one, that of the historical Mary Shelley, of her creation, Victor Frankenstein, and of Dr. Buchanan, a scientist with ethical shortcomings. It begins in the year 2031 as Buchanan in designing a new weapon has created "time slips" through which humans are being drawn into other time-space dimensions in the past and the future. On his way home in his computerized car, Buchanan himself is transported to the Switzerland of Mary Shelley's "haunted summer." There he finds himself face to face with the moral dilemmas with which he has never been able to grapple before.

A young woman, Justine, is scheduled to be executed for the murder of William Frankenstein, an incident from Shelley's novel which is rarely included in film versions. With his knowledge of the novel Buchanan knows that she is innocent and that the creature is guilty. He appeals to his brother scientist, Victor Frankenstein, but to no avail. He even appeals to Mary Shelley, whom he finds in the courtroom watching the trial, but her awareness is limited since she has not written the book as yet. All that she can tell him is, "I'm afraid you're here to stop Dr. Frankenstein." Through his meeting with Frankenstein, Buchanan comes to understand the immorality of his own work. Like Victor he had refused to consider the effects of his new, "monstrous" weapon. Like Victor he was single-minded in his pursuit of "pure science." When Victor involves him in an attempt to reanimate the body of Elizabeth, who has been killed by the creature, Buchanan finally revolts. Rigging his car's computer ("Meet my monster!") to Victor's power source atop his laboratory, Buchanan waits for the proper moment. Invoking in a single composition the Apocalyptic and the Gothic, the film sends Buchanan, Victor, the creature, and Elizabeth into the post-nuclear wastes of the future, for which, Buchanan discovers, he and his weapons are responsible. The Creature says to Buchanan, "This world you made is better than Victor's." Realizing that his science has turned the world into a barren landscape, Buchanan laments, "I am Frankenstein," while the monster whose spirit he cannot kill, even with lasers, screams out, "I'm with you forever. I am unbound." By invoking and reworking Mary Shelley's subtitle, **Prometheus Unbound,** Corman and writer Brian Aldiss have painted a bleak picture of science without limitations.

Television is the medium which has most assiduously readapted the original no less than four times. There are two British productions, *Frankenstein, the True Story* (1973) and *Frankenstein* (1984), and two American, Dan Curtis' *Frankenstein* (1973) and Turner Network Television's *Frankenstein* (1993). Curtis' version was relatively faithful yet staged like a soap opera. In the same year Yorkshire TV's adaptation emulated Masterpiece Theater, that is, prestigious actors, authentic period sets, and little innovation or Romantic horror. There are some notable elements, primarily David Warner's creature who is remarkable in his sensitivity. He is soft-spoken and often tender: begging William Frankenstein, a small boy, to be his friend and, unaware of his great strength, hugging him to death; crying as Justine falls to her death while fleeing him; or pleading on his knees with Frankenstein to make him a mate to assuage his loneliness.

Frankenstein, the True Story, as co-written by playwright Christopher Isherwood, is far from the "true story" but does capture much of the spirit of the original. The film revives the split-focus sympathy of Shelley's novel, going further than any previous version in establishing that Frankenstein and his creation are two sides of the coin. Isherwood posits a teacher/pupil relationship between man and creature. Where Shelley's scientist shunned his work, Isherwood's becomes the benevolent good parent. Of course, this creature is a much more attractive child than Shelley's as he is both innocent and handsome. Even the evil Dr. Polidori, a character unique to this version who combines the qualities of the historical Dr. Polidori with those of Whale's sardonic Dr. Pretorius, comments on Victor's sense of responsibility. When they agree to destroy the creature who has turned violent and begun to decay physically by tossing him into a vat of acid, Victor balks and Polidori observes sarcastically, "What a model parent you've been!" Victor, like so many movie Frankensteins before him, can never really free himself of his double. The decomposing creature crashes a party where his beautiful "bride," created by Frankenstein at the behest of Polidori and the creature, has become a "social darling." When she reacts to his advances with a catlike snarl, reminiscent of the "bride" in Whale's film, he rips off her head. Victor flees with his beloved Elizabeth aboard a ship, only to find the creature has tracked them there.

After murdering Elizabeth and strapping Polidori to a mast to be consumed alive by lightning, the creature kidnaps Victor and races off for the Arctic wastes. In the final scene creator and creation are reconciled as they never are in the novel, as Victor asks for the monstrous being's forgiveness. As they reach to embrace each other, an avalanche rolls through the mountain of ice, as if nature herself is reacting to their reconciliation, covering them in a blanket of purity.

The Turner *Frankenstein* is, at last, "The True Story." Of all the myriad versions of the classic, it follows the original's narrative line most closely. Like the novel, the story is told in flashback from aboard a ship traveling through the Arctic. A feeble Victor Frankenstein recounts his tale to the captain of the ship as the creature wanders over the ice packs surrounding them. The duality of the novel, merely emphasized in Isherwood's version, is laid out schematically in this film. From the first scenes of the making of the creature, the filmmakers intercut the two stories dialectically. The creature bursts violently through the confines of his womb-like tank filled with fluid, to be born disoriented and deformed. Suffering from birth trauma, he wanders out of the laboratory, stumbling down the darkened streets. Intercut with this sequence is Victor falling to the floor of his lab, a victim of fever and exhaustion, the palpable after effects of his own special form of labor.

Later when the creature is shot by a frightened villager, after he has saved the life of a drowning girl, a scene from the book rarely reproduced on film, the movie cuts to Victor in pain. A wound appears on his chest to mark his guilt, like the "scarlet letter" of Hawthorne's novel. Victor laments appropriately, "We are one. The guilt is mine, all mine." While Victor recuperates among his family and loved ones, the film interweaves the story of the creature finding companionship with the blind De Lacey.

In the final scenes of the film as Victor, after losing his brother, father, best friend, and wife to the vengeful creature, pursues him to the Arctic, the dialectic reaches its apex. As creator and created confront each other, the creature begs him, "Help me!" reinforcing his past accusation, "You made me and gave me nothing." Victor moves towards the creature, saying softly, as if soothing a disturbed child, "I will help us both," and in a violent embrace thrusts both of them into the freez-

Above, Mel Brooks' zipper-necked monster echoes the original and sports the formal dress of Pretorius' *homunculus.*

ing Arctic waters. The father has finally accepted his son as they return to the womb of the sea, the camera following their bodies beneath the surface as they float in the amniotic-like fluid of the ocean.

Following the success of *Bram Stoker's Dracula* (1992), producer Francis Ford Coppola has promised that *Mary Shelley's Frankenstein* (1994) will be a most faithful adaptation. With Kenneth Branagh directing himself as Frankenstein and Robert De Niro as the Creature on a $40 million budget, it will certainly be the costliest and likely a far cry from the imaginative but impoverished productions of Terence Fisher.

It is appropriate to end this section with Mel Brooks' satire *Young Frankenstein* (1974). As many observers know, one way to reveal the conventions and icons of a genre is to parody them. *Young Frankenstein* draws its material mainly from the earliest Universal films, *Frankenstein, The Bride of Frankenstein,* and *Son of Frankenstein.* From the first film *Young Frankenstein* parodies the notorious scene in which the creature tosses a small girl into the lake. In Brooks' version he cuts to a knowing smile on the face of the creature when the child finds out they have run out of flowers and wonders what to toss next. From *Bride* the film borrows the sequence with the blind hermit. In Brook's rendering the hermit becomes mildly lecherous ("You're a big one.") and instead of lighting the creature's cigar, lights his fingers. From *Son of Frankenstein* Brooks takes the general style of the film, with its expressionistic sets and chiaroscuro lighting. In the elaborate opening, for instance, a long travelling shot moves across the floor from a clock to a coffin. When the lid is thrown off, hands snatch a satchel from the grip of a decomposed corpse and an iris reveals an "F" cachet.

Comic actor Marty Feldman recreates Lugosi's Igor (pronounced "Eye-gor"), with a hump that keeps changing positions while Dr. Frankenstein (pronounced "Frankensteen"), in Gene Wilder's deft hands, comes to resemble the nervous, neurotic Basil Rathbone in physical aspect as well as psychology. Kenneth Mars duplicates Lionel Atwill's Germanic inspector with an often incomprehensible accent and a creaking wooden arm. The creature, played by Peter Boyle, combines Karloff's innocence and pantomimic skills with an intense sexual drive, to the delight of Frankenstein's fiancée, Elizabeth, who while making love to the creature breaks into a chorus of "Ah, Sweet Mystery of Life."

The tragedy of the original story is, of course, reversed here by the requirements of a comedy where "zipper neck" becomes a term of endearment. Frankenstein finds happiness with a voluptuous peasant girl while Elizabeth marries her potent "monster lover." Even the creature is treated more kindly. He becomes a dancing sensation on stage.

Below, the "classic" Hollywood creature: Boris Karloff mutely contemplates the twin mysteries of sex and death in *The Bride of Frankenstein*.

II. The Other Bram Stoker (1847-1912)

In the past, in the early days of the world, there were monsters who were so vast that they could exist thousands of years. Some of them must have overlapped the Christian era. They may have progressed intellectually in process of time. If they had in any way so progressed, or got even the most rudimentary form of brain, they would be the most dangerous things that were ever in the world.

Bram Stoker, **The Lair of the White Worm**

"Well, sir, I think it would hardly interest them. It was just the head and a few bones of a mummy. It may have been a thousand years old. But it wasn't there before."

Sir Arthur Conan Doyle, "Shoscombe Old Place"

While justly celebrated for the novel, **Dracula** (1897), which has never been out of print since its first appearance, Bram Stoker's other supernatural fiction is little read. Aside from the short story, "Dracula's Guest" (1914), which was originally written as a prologue to the novel and published with a collection of other tales shortly after Stoker's death, little else of his work is ever in print.

Stoker's other fiction includes several romances and a few novels with supernatural themes. **The Mystery of the Sea** (1902) has allusions to rune casting and **The Lady of the Shroud** (1909) has a female vampire who turns out to be an impersonator. **The Jewel of Seven Stars** (1903) and **The Lair of the White Worm** (1911) were in all likelihood adapted into motion pictures for the same reason that they occasionally appear in cheap paperback editions: Stoker's name and the association with **Dracula**. The former novel has actually been filmed twice, once by Hammer retitled, typically for them, as *Blood from the Mummy's Tomb* (1972) and more recently as *The Awakening* (1980). As with several of his short stories, Stoker's **Jewel** is a first person narrative, told from the point of view of Malcolm Ross, a young lawyer. Unlike **Dracula**, which uses alternating points of view in the form of letters, journals, and early dictaphone recordings, **The Jewel of Seven Stars**, is firmly planted in the perspective of Ross as colored by his infatuation with troubled Margaret Trelawney and her scientist father, Abel.

The prose style of **The Jewel of Seven Stars** shows scant progression from **Dracula**, which appeared six years earlier. Although Ross is the underlying story teller, other characters add their own histories as if in movie flashbacks. These may stretch over several chapters, as for instance, when Mr. Corbeck relates Trelawney's discovery of the mummy of Queen Tera in Egypt. Much of Ross' direct narrative also includes long exchanges of dialogue. As in **Dracula** many of these exchanges are lengthy recapitulations; and their mannered phrases without dramatic purpose quickly become tedious.

Unlike **Dracula**, Stoker does not use the occasional shift in narrative voice to set up conflicting viewpoints; and many descriptive passages, particularly the conclusion, are elaborate but essentially vapid. Stoker piles adverbs onto already overcharged or somewhat redundant adjectives, as in not merely "wearied and haggard" but "terribly wearied and haggard." In this regard, all the characters ultimately speak with the same voice, which is Stoker's.

Without real dramatic impact from its dialogue or subjective descriptions, all that remains to sustain reader interest in **The Jewel of Seven Stars** is the plot itself. In the early chapters, Stoker is content to mimic Conan Doyle. If Holmes' only encounter with a mummy cited at the beginning of this sub-chapter is any indication, he would likely find a reanimated corpse, like other quasi-supernatural events which Holmes confronts, worthy only of debunking. Conan Doyle wrote two stories dealing directly with Egyptian antiquity, "The Ring of Thoth" (1890) and "Lot No. 249" (1892). In the former, an Egyptian, who has doomed himself to immortality by devising an elixir, finds death at last through a deadly antidote entombed with the mummy of his beloved. The reanimation of a mummy in "Lot No. 249" is the likeliest inspiration for the celebrated introduction of the title figure in Karl Freund's *The Mummy* (1932). Stoker was almost certainly familiar with these stories.

There is nothing ostensibly supernatural in the mystery of who attacked Trelawney and tried to get into his safe. While not as compelling an opening as Harker's visit to Count Dracula, it gets the reader to point B, from where Stoker finally elaborates, two decades before the King Tut phenomenon, on Queen Tera: an ancient sorceress, whose seven-fingered hand was cut from her body by priests fearing her return. Led by the 17th Century manuscript of a Dutch explorer, Trelawney and Corbeck locate and open the tomb. At the same time in England, Trelawney's wife dies in childbirth. His daughter has a birthmark on her wrist that resembles the wound left when Tera's hand was severed. As in Tut's reputed curse, an unknown force eventually kills the members of the expedition and Margaret as well when they perform Tera's ceremony with the items from the tomb. The distraught Ross, the only survivor, is unable to tell for certain whether or not it was Tera who returned and what fearful apparition caused his associates' deaths.

Blood from the Mummy's Tomb is as much a part of Hammer's own series of "Mummy" films, begun with Terence Fisher's *The Mummy* (1959) and inspired by the Universal productions of the 1930s and 40s, as it is an adaptation of a particular novel. As it happens, the key premise which concerns Queen Tera's curse and her magic, so powerful that the priests of her own era cut off her hand to prevent from using it after death, bears considerable resemblance to the earlier films made by both Universal and Hammer.

Christopher Wicking's script for *Blood from the Mummy's Tomb* combines elements of Stoker, the "Mummy" genre, and the Tut legend. Stoker's novel and both versions of *The Mummy* hinged on an attempted transference of the soul of an ancient Egyptian princess into the body of a modern woman who physically resembled her. As the possessed daughter of Professor Trelawney, here called Fuchs, conspires with Corbeck, the associate from the novel, those holding the items from the tomb which must be ceremonially reunited are murdered. Fuchs' intervention and destruction of the mummy results in a less mysterious but catastrophic conclusion equal to that of the novel, except that Ross, here named Browning, dies and Margaret survives. Whether Margaret, pulled from the rubble but unable to speak with her entire body bandaged like a mummy, has become Tera is not certain. A

Below, Valerie Leon, center, as Queen Tera struggles with Andrew Keir as Trelawney and her own photo double, left, as Margaret in *Blood from the Mummy's Tomb*.

macabre side note: Seth Holt, the director of *Blood from the Mummy's Tomb*, died suddenly during filming.

The Awakening (1980) is a higher budget adaptation of **Jewel**, which is more in the tradition of the *The Exorcist* or *Wolfen* than the Universal or Hammer "mummy" films. From the perspective of genre expectation, *The Awakening* leaves no uncertainty about the identification of Tara, its version of Stoker's "nameless one," and Margaret Corbeck (Stoker's Corbeck and Trelawney are made into one). In a dynamic montage, the sound of Corbeck's sledge hammer striking the outer door of the tomb is first heard over a long shot of his pregnant wife as she doubles over in pain from premature labor. As if this were not explicit, when the sarcophagus is opened some days later, the comatose Mrs. Corbeck comes to with a scream in a hospital in Cairo. Rather than use the "flash-backs" from the novel, the film is linear. The characters fill in the background through expository dialogue; and 18 years after Corbeck's find, an eclipse of the sun coincides with cracking glass in the mummy's display case *and* a weird encounter between a grown Margaret and a jackal in the Central Park Zoo.

Jack Cardiff's photography of the archaeological prologue in Egypt and the odd, fatal accidents which befall two Egyptian officials and ultimately Corbeck's assistant, Jane, clearly evoke the milieu and sense of pre-destiny of *The Exorcist* and imitators such as *The Omen*. The manner of Jane's death, in particular, first thrown out of a window by an unseen force and then impaled by a piece of glass, seems a direct allusion to a sequence in *The Omen*. Although Stoker's Margaret Trelawney is marked by "Tera," she is unquestionably sympathetic to her plight. She even remarks that "to me, then, it is given to understand what was the dream of this great and far-thinking and high-souled lady of old." Margaret Corbeck is entirely possessed by "Tara." What drags Trelawney's form to his safe remains a mystery for Stoker and his narrator, Ross; in *The Awakening* it is the anguished Margaret who stands by convulsed with emotion while this same thing happens. Director Mike Newell uses repeated, slow side movements of the camera to suggest, in genre context, an unseen watcher; sometimes a figure is even revealed in the foreground, as with the jackal-shaped Anubis who seems to growl at Jane. Given that the viewer is already aware of how Tara manifests herself, the only real question is whether or not she will succeed in taking full possession of Margaret. In the end, she does, and Corbeck, whose feeble accusation of "Oh, you evil thing" as Tara/Margaret hisses and topples a wall to crush him, clearly seems to have been the last one to figure out all the obvious clues.

AWK-27

Above, Corbeck (Charlton Heston) and his daughter, Margaret (Stephanie Zimbalist) return to Tara's tomb to find the canopic jars in *The Awakening*; below, Corbeck prepares for the final ceremony.

Stoker died before **The Lair of the White Worm** was fully completed. That the draft manuscript was published without benefit of his copy editing is obvious from the prose style, which is rough even for Stoker. Sir Nathaniel, Adam Salton, and Mimi Watford, whom Salton marries, are the analogs of **Dracula**'s Van Helsing, Jonathan Harker, and Mina, as Stoker again tried to rearrange the elements of his great success. His initial description of the monster in this work, Lady Arabella March, echoes that of Count Dracula:

> ...he took a long look at her. She was certainly good to look at in herself, and her dress was sufficient to attract attention. She was clad in some kind of soft white stuff, which clung close to her form, showing to the full every movement of her sinuous figure. She was tall and exceedingly thin. Her eyes appeared to be weak, for she wore large spectacles which seemed to be of green glass. Certainly in the centre they had the effect of making her naturally piercing eyes of a vivid green. She wore a close fitting cap of some fine fur of a dazzling white. Coiled round her white throat was a large necklace of emeralds whose profusion of color quite outshone the green of her spectacles—even when the sun shone on them. Her voice was very peculiar, very low and sweet, and so soft that the dominant· note was of sibilation. Her hands, too, were peculiar—long, flexible, and white with a strange movement of waving gently to and fro.

"Peculiar," "white," "green"—Stoker's introduction of Lady Arabella is certainly flaccid compared to his classic evocation of the count. The encounter on a country road in broad daylight with Sir Nathaniel in tow has none of the menace of Harker's meeting with Dracula, which Harker himself described. While Stoker uses third person throughout **The Lair of the White Worm,** there is a clear implication here of Salton's point of view ("...he took a long look"). Behind the indirectness of "stuff" and "seeming," there is the possibility of Salton's attraction to Lady Arabella; but Stoker never follows up on this.

Coming fifteen years after **Dracula** and at the end of the Victorian era, aspects of the novel such as the crude sexual sub-text between Lady Arabella Marsh and Edgar Caswall's African servant, Oolanga, seem quite retrograde. Stoker's background research which produced the extensive invocation of legends from Eastern European history and Egyptian mythology in **Dracula** and **The Jewel of Seven Stars** respectively is much less detailed in **The Lair of the White Worm.** Sir Nathaniel briefly tells Adam of Roman Mercia, King Penda, early Christianity, and the philology of the word "worm," but there are none of Van Helsing's detailed discourses. The African Oolanga is variously a witch-finder, Voodoo priest, and one who can smell death. His dialect (e.g. "Much death here—big death. Many deaths. Good, good!") is in keeping with Stoker's overall racist characterization of the black man as a subhuman: "Oolanga...was pure pristine, unreformed, unsoftened savage, with inherent in it all the hideous possibilities of a lost, devil-ridden child of the forest and the swamp—the lowest and most loathsome of all created things which were in some form ostensibly human." A character named Adam and a serpent might have suggested other allusions, particularly since the name of Mimi's cousin, Lilla, resembles the biblical Lilith; but Lilla perishes in a bizarre sub-plot after a mesmeric conflict of wills with Caswall. Stoker's ending in which Lady Arabella in her guise as the white worm is blown to pieces with dynamite is a long way from facing Dracula in the Borgo Pass at sunset.

Ken Russell's adaptation of Stoker's novel is a fairly literal one and mostly a parody. Like Russell's early biographical films, *The Lair of the White Worm* has several dream sequences employing exaggerated optical effects; but where such effects were meant to be endistancing in the dramas, in the context of the supernatural genre, viewer expectation can readily accommodate such extreme visual treatments.

Russell's script does make a few plot changes: the events are reset to the present day; the egomaniacal Caswall becomes the sympathetic Lord D'Ampton, whose ancestor's slaying the Worm is memorialized in a family painting; Adam (Angus) is an archaeological student who does not need a Sir Nathaniel to tell him the background of the region; cousins Lilla and Mimi are sisters Eve and Mary Trent; and Lady Sylvia Marsh is not the Worm itself but a snakelike worshipper seeking a virgin sacrifice. None of these is significant; but they all permit Russell to make quick cross-references and broadly satirize Anglo-Christian myths. After a standard opening in which Angus Flint discovers the head of a dinosaur-like creature in his excavation of a roman site, Mary comes out to help. A cutaway to her legs entangled in a coiled, garden hose is accompanied by an ominous chord in the underscore in wry anticipation of the snaky menace to come.

At a dance at D'Ampton castle in honor of the lord's return, a folk/rock group sings about a fish thrown down a well which becomes a worm. A huge, white pantomime worm appears, a kind of Celtic-cum-Chinese Dragon, which when lit by strobes and chase lights becomes a weird mixture of old and new rituals, or as D'Ampton himself observes: "This year, which is my first as Lord of the Manor, as it were, I thought we'd hit the worm with a little rock."

As a Jaguar XKE drives by on the forest road, more ominous chords announce the arrival of Lady Sylvia. Russell takes Stoker's anemic, ophidian villainess to the limit. The first sight of her is, in context, understated. Costumed in elegant white suit and tricorn hat, Lady Sylvia helps the local constable who has been bitten by a snake. After enthusiastically sucking out the poison, she even daintily dabs at the edge of her mouth with a handkerchief. The next morning, in tight scarf and sunglasses for a truly reptilian look, Lady Sylvia slithers around the sisters' farmhouse and finds the skull. Russell uses more visual exaggeration in a wide angle shot of Angus' room with the skull on a table in the foreground, as she comes up to it, caresses, and carries it off. She does stop to bare her fangs and spit venom onto a crucifix on the way out. Russell defies genre convention by introducing the figure of supernatural evil quite early and quite casually. Unlike Stoker's novel, Eve Trent is given a name which clearly refers back to mankind's first fateful encounter with a serpent in Eden. When this namesake touches the venom left on the crucifix, the shock to her system sends her reeling backwards, falling over a vacuum cleaner hose (snake forms are everywhere), and into a solarized Jungian dream. It's a very mixed metaphor as Roman soldiers rape nuns dressed in white like vestal virgins, while a large snake coils around a crucified figure in an oversized, animated imitation of a caduceus. Lady S. in her metamorphosized, brightly colored and snake-eyed state, laughs and flashes her fangs. Russell may be a long way from *Altered States*, but he can't resist having D'Ampton remark after Eve has come to her senses and Angus and Mary have arrived that "Eve's had a bad trip."

Where Lady Arabella was somewhat discreet about her real nature, Russell's Lady Sylvia positively revels in hers; and Russell's dialogue

Below, Amanda Donohoe as Lady Sylvia confronts a crucifix in *The Lair of the White Worm*.

plays right along with the supernatural and sexual innuendo. "I'm not really into head banging," remarks the boy scout whom she picks up about the music on her car radio. What other riposte could there be but, "Are you into any sort of banging?" "I'm not bad on the mouth organ," says the boy scout; and, after Lady Sylvia invites him to a game of snakes and ladders at her place, he tries to serenade her with a harmonica transcription of Rimsky-Korsakov.

By the time the boy scout succumbs to a fanged fellatio, Russell has forsaken the supernatural for the just plain silly. While Lady Sylvia's snake puns (from "I practically hibernate for the winter" to "Name your poison") are at least somewhat appropriate to the subject matter, the movie allusions take the viewer beyond any suspension of disbelief. For whose benefit does Lady Sylvia say "Rosebud," as she burns her snakes and ladders board? The Méliès-like short that D'Ampton watches on television which features a snake charmer and a large worm that turns into a woman in a butterfly costume is a only a slight stretch compared to the lord of the manor's dream. While the Concorde jet which D'-Ampton boards in that dream is *The Lair of the White Worm*'s largest phallic symbol, the pen that he holds in his lap while watching Lady Sylvia and Eve dressed as flight attendants and wrestling on the floor in high heels and black hose is the smallest. There are plenty of others from the XKE to a loufa sponge. By the time Eve comes across Lady Sylvia sitting in a tree, Russell has already taken the viewer from the realm of plain horror to rocky horror.

Still Lady Sylvia's discourse from her tanning bed about Eve's false gods has a camp grandeur. Less amusing is the awkward satire of supernatural explication, as when D'Ampton observes sanguinely to Angus in the Trent's parlor that "It seems to me that there's some kind of conflict going on...a conflict between Christianity and some early pagan cult, possibly involving human sacrifice." Faced with such an eventuality, what else would one do but set up loudspeakers and spin some platters to charm the monster from her lair. In fact, Lady Sylvia is charmed right out of her basket and slinks across her own atrium. Saved by a power failure, Lady S. gets some earplugs. Her outfit for the final ritual is absolutely *de trop*: snakeskin cap and arm bands to accent her scaly, blue skin and a large dildo made of dragon horn. Any remaining subtlety is lost when Russell zooms back from this implement through Eve's legs.

Of course, Lady Sylvia herself becomes worm food. While Angus' condition is suspect in that he has taken the wrong serum, the worm itself is blown up as in the novel, where Sir Nathaniel cunningly remarked, "all's well that ends well."

Above, Vincent Price in the prototypical role of Verden Fell in *The Tomb of Ligeia*.

CHAPTER TWO

Colonial Horror

I. Edgar Allan Poe (1809-1849): Descent into the Maelstrom

> From childhood's hour I have not been
> As others were—I have not seen
> As others saw—I could not bring
> My passions from a common spring—
> From the same source I have not taken
> My sorrow—I could not awaken
> My heart to joy at the same tone—
> And all I lov'd—I lov'd alone."
>
> Edgar Allan Poe, "Alone"

The Obsessive Supernaturalist

Edgar Allan Poe is the apotheosis of what the French call the "auteur maudit." Frustration, misery, horror, madness, alcohol, drugs, and a obsessive fascination with the supernatural are the furies which tracked him all his relatively short life. He fulfilled in most aspects the ideal of the Romantic, Byronic poet. He was both a literary critic and a "prophetic" writer, who was unappreciated in his own country and only recognized by American critics after a rediscovery in France through Baudelaire's translation of his work. His personal life was a series of disastrous relationships which led to a deepening sense of alienation. His descents, via drugs, drink, and his writing, into the storm center of his own twisted unconscious became progressively deeper and more

41

difficult from which to return. Like a true Byronic figure, he was arrogant, sarcastic, especially in his criticism, and embittered. Even his appearance reflected the ideal—the dark, brooding mien, the sensitive eyes, the neat almost dandified dress, all to be adopted later by Baudelaire as emblematic of his great admiration for the master.

Poe's life, then, even as related by his more sympathetic biographers, reads like one of his own tales, for in many ways Poe *is* one of his own characters. He is a consummately solipsistic writer. His world, both exterior and interior, is a self-enclosed "maelstrom" whirling in on itself. Like the persons in his tale "A Descent into the Maelstrom" (1841) who stare into a huge and deadly eddy of water with "awe, horror, and admiration," Poe spent a good part of his life on that same edge looking into the depths of his own psyche—fearful of what he might find, yet irresistibly drawn to its center. From this center, this unconscious, Poe brought forth his most disturbing and disturbed characters: Roderick Usher, Ligeia, William Wilson, "the man of the crowd," Berenice, "the lost Lenore," and Arthur Gordon Pym.

There are several common threads in the tapestry of Poe's horror tales and poems. The preeminent theme is the obsessed supernaturalist. Poe's characters are trying, in psychoanalytic terms, "to work through" their neuroses; but, in doing so, they look to the world of the supernatural to solve their personal dilemmas, much as Poe did himself through his writing. Roderick Usher is guilt-ridden about his sister and his latent incestuous desire for her; and so she becomes a "walking dead" bringing doom and destruction to her brother and his house. In "The Tell-Tale Heart" (1843), the narrator cannot confront the fear and loathing he has for "the old man" and so fixates on the man's "evil eye," imbuing it with supernatural qualities. "He had the eye of a vulture —a pale blue eye, with a film over it. Whenever it fell upon me, my blood ran cold; and so by degrees—very gradually—I made up my mind to take the life of the old man, and thus rid myself of the eye forever." Unable to resolve his feelings for the old man, he murders him, burying him beneath the floor boards. Now that he has raised the human to the level of the supernatural by attributing those qualities to the man, his mind cannot cease weaving webs of terror. He begins to hear the beating of the dead man's heart, driving him slowly but inexorably insane.

Also running through Poe's work is his self-professed desire to achieve, as he states in "The Philosophy of Composition" (1846), one single "effect" and "a unity of impression": "If any literary work is too long to read at one sitting, we must be content to dispense with the immensely important effect derivable from unity of impression..." This self-imposed standard also lead Poe to follow, however erratically, the three classical unities of time, place, and action.

His next and most important objective in his work was "the rhythmical creation of beauty" ("The Poetic Principle," 1850). This explains why many of his tales read like poems, lyrical and filled with reiteration and rough meter. As examples: "Eleanora" (1842) with its refrain, "...brighter than all save the eyes of Eleonora...smoother than all save the cheeks of Eleanora...sweeter than all save the voice of Eleanora...more divine than all save the voice of Eleanora..."; "Ligeia" (1838), "It was blacker than the raven wings of midnight. And now slowly opened the eyes of the figure which stood before me. 'Here, then, at least,' I shrieked aloud, 'can I never — can I never be mistaken — these are the full, and the black, and the wild eyes — of my lost love — of the Lady — of the Lady Ligeia.'" Or "Eleanora" again:

> She had seen that the finger of Death was upon her bosom — that, like the ephemeron, she had been made perfect in loveliness only to die; but the terrors of the grave to her lay solely in a consideration which she revealed to me, one evening at twilight, by the banks of the River of Silence. She grieved to think that, having entombed her the Valley of the Many-Colored Grass, I would quit forever...

Lines like these are at their most expressive when read aloud like poetry. They are lines with staccato rhythm and rich images.

Below, a scene from *The Raven* (1935), which gives a literal rendering of Poe's sexual imagery: dark and veiled with a suggestion of pedophilia and incest.

What probably leaves the most indelible impression on the reader of Poe is the claustrophobic, morbid atmosphere pervading his tales. They are often set in decaying mansions ("I looked upon the scene before—upon the mere house, and the simple landscape features of the domain—upon the bleak walls—upon the vacant eye-like windows—upon a few rank sedges—and upon a few white trunks of decayed trees..." "The Fall of the House of Usher," 1839); or in "ancient, grey and gloomy castles" ("Ligeia" or "The Masque of the Red Death," 1842). They are all abodes where decay, decadence, and, ultimately, death reign.

This claustrophobic setting does not end with mansions or castles. Poe often situates his poems and tales in even more constricted area of action. A chamber or room usually associated with death becomes the focal point of the story. Obvious examples are cellars where victims are entombed ("The Black Cat," 1843, "The Cask of Amontillado," 1846), crypts ("The Premature Burial," 1840), or the pit in "The Pit and the Pendulum" (1843).

Examples rich in clues to the significance of this physical regression in Poe's work are found in "The Fall of the House of Usher." "Berenice" (1835), "Ligeia," and "Annabel Lee" (1849). Poe's characters, particularly Egaeus in "Berenice," Roderick Usher, and the narrators of "Ligeia" and "Annabel Lee," have literally and figuratively buried themselves alive. They share with Poe a dread of and fascination for images of entombment, images dark and unknown like death, redolent of horror, misery, and guilt, images which are also alluring, especially to a regressive psyche like Poe's, because they are womb-like, warm, protected, a refuge from the wretchedness of the world. "Misery is manifold. The wretchedness of earth is multiform." ("Berenice") Examples of this repulsion/fascination syndrome in Poe and his characters are also manifold:

> The recollections of my earliest years are connected with that chamber, and with its volumes—of which latter I will say no more. Here died my mother...In that chamber was I born. Thus awaking from the long night of what seemed, but was not, nonentity, at once into the very regions of fairy land—into a palace of imagination—into the wild dominions of monastic thought and erudition—it is not singular that I gazed around me with a startled and ardent eye—that I loitered away my boyhood in books...The realities of the world affected me as visions, and as visions only, while the wild ideas of the land of dreams became, in turn, not the material of my everyday existence, but in very deed that existence utterly and solely in itself. ("Berenice")

Is there a passage in Poe's work more evocative of the warmth, the care-less security, and the insulation of a womb-like existence?

> Let me speak only of that one chamber, ever accursed, whither, in a moment of mental alienation, I led from the altar as my bride—as the successor of the unforgotten Ligeia—the fair-haired Lady Rowena, of Tremaine. ("Ligeia")

In that particular chamber the scene is being set for the unhappy wedding night, for the death of the bride, and for the return of the dead Ligeia.

> And so, all the night-tide, I lie down by the side
> Of my darling, my darling, my life and my bride,
> In the sepulchre there by the sea—
> In her tomb by the sounding sea.

> "Annabel Lee"

Like the narrator of "Annabel Lee" Poe entombed himself in his work, a hypersensitive child in a lifelong retreat from the world, a retreat through supernatural horror and misery into the comforting arms of oblivion.

Of all of Poe's works the one that most consistently and emphatically echoes this theme of regression is **The Narrative of Arthur Gordon Pym** (1837). All of the classical elements of Poe's tales are there: the first person narrative; the atmosphere redolent of death and decay; the journey, physical as well as psychological in this case, through horror

Below, decay, decadence, and death: left, Roderick Usher (Vincent Price) struggles with his crazed sister in *House of Usher*; right, Rowena (Elizabeth Shepherd) before her shattered mirror in *The Tomb of Ligeia*.

to death and the peace of oblivion; the attribution of supernatural causes to obsessive, neurotic behavior. The major difference in this work is that Poe seems unable to let his "pure intellect," as he called it, reign over his imagination and consequently does not impose his usual limitations of place, time, and action on the story.

In a fictitious journal of an expedition southward by sea, Poe's ubiquitous narrator escapes horror after horror only to be preserved for a yet stranger fate. He is entombed alive in the hull of a ship, almost drowned, and finally stranded on an island with hostile natives. And through it all he is drawn irresistably south, towards the freezing embrace of the white Antarctic, towards a mysterious, godlike figure which overshadows the cool, white terrain:

> The darkness had materially increased, relieved only by the glare of the water thrown back from the white curtain before us. Many gigantic and pallidly white birds flew continuously now from beyond the veil, and their scream was the eternal 'Tekeli-li' as they retreated from our vision. Hereupon Nu-Nu stirred in the bottom of the boat; but upon touching him we found his spirit departed. And now we rushed into the embraces of the cataract, where a chasm threw itself open to receive us. But there arose in our pathway a shrouded human figure, very far larger in its proportions than any dweller among men. And the hue of the skin of the figure was of the perfect whiteness of snow.

As the figures float towards this cold oblivion, the regressive circle is closed.

Marie Bonaparte in her lengthy psychoanalytical interpretation, **The Life and Works of Edgar Allan Poe**, argues repeatedly for the theory

Below, a prototypical Poe heroine with dark hair and eyes, Barbara Steele shrinks from Vincent Price in *The Pit and the Pendulum.*

that most of Poe's female characters are direct transmogrifications of the mother he lost at an early age. She further asserts that most of the women in his life were "chosen" by Poe, consciously or unconsciously, with the archetype of his mother in mind. This would explain why many of the females in Poe's work are either dead or dying, and in their death, menacing. It is also significant that Poe's mother is described by friends as having black hair and dark, piercing eyes, physical characteristics Poe gave to most of his *femme fatales*. While this theory has the simplification common to Freudian literary analysis, it is nevertheless pertinent. Ligeia, Madeline Usher, Berenice are all women who often in life and most assuredly in death threaten Poe's various literary alter egos. In developing this creative obsession, Poe exploits the dark and light principles in order to illustrate the threat with appropriate archetypal imagery.

For example, when Ligeia comes back from the grave to take possession of the body of her husband's new wife, Poe describes the conflict in hues of black and white. Like the "shrouded human figure" overshadowing the white of the Antarctic in **Pym,** Ligeia, the dark lady ("the raven-black...tresses; the hue of [her] orbs was the most brilliant of black"), comes to dominate the personality of "the fair-haired and blue-eyed Lady Rowena"; and through her, Ligeia returns to her grieving husband who without her was "as a child groping benighted." Madeline Usher, who is entombed alive by her twin brother but returns to avenge herself on him, adds the taboo of incest to her dark allure. Poe again drew on his own life: he married a cousin, Virginia Clemm, whose death at a very young age undoubtedly inspired many of his female invalids. "Berenice" is also filled with implications of incest, differing from "Usher" in that the love-hate relationship ends with the male's revenge on the female. Obsessed with Berenice's teeth and, as Bonaparte has pointed out, in a stereotype of a *vagina dentata* Egaeus visits her tomb and extracts them.

It is one of his poems which most succinctly capsulizes Poe's attraction/repulsion for an entombed beloved, "Ulalume" (1847). The following lines appear as Psyche, the narrator's conscious principle, tries to lure him away from this tomb which fascinates him so:

> Thus I pacified Psyche and kissed her,
> And tempted her out of her gloom —
> And conquered her scruples and gloom,
> By the door of a legended tomb:
> And I said — 'What is written, sweet sister,
> On the door of this legended tomb?'
> She replied — 'Ulalume — Ulalume —
> 'Tis the vault of thy lost Ulalume.'

For all this literary decadence and dark Romanticism there is a classical precision to Poe's work. In his criticism, detective stories, and some of his more satirical tales he esteems the logical mind and exhibits a cutting wit and an admiration for balanced form. This is, of course, most obvious in his adherence to classical unities in many stories; but, in addition, his stress upon the importance of the intellect and his devotion to antiquity, especially in his poems which are filled with allusions to Greek and Roman myth, throws a classical light on an otherwise unrelentingly dark portrait.

There have been film adaptations of Poe's work almost continuously from the inception of the medium. This attests to his success in creating mythopoeic characters and situations as well as to the particularly cinematic quality of his imagery. Earlier commentators have pointed out how Poe's extensive use of the dash in writing is a verbal analog for the cinematic cut. Although most of the adaptations of Poe to the screen have not been faithful to the letter of the stories, most have at least attempted to capture the mood and spirit of the originals.

One of the earliest is D.W. Griffith's adaptation of "The Tell-Tale Heart" and "Annabel Lee," *The Avenging Conscience* (1914). The director, in keeping with his early sentimental-optimistic predilections, diluted the horror of the original by giving the film a frame of imagined events, which undercuts the reality of the supernatural: the protagonist falls asleep after reading the "The Tell-Tale Heart" and dreams of killing his tyrannical uncle. But within this nightmare of the protagonist, there are some images which evoke the mood of Poe's original. The mercilessness of nature is visually represented by the destructive cycle of life: a spider devouring a fly and a beetle being eaten by ants. For Griffith, these events precipitate the "birth of an evil thought"; and he maintains the motif of a malevolent nature with more close-ups of spiders and howling wolves. Even more effective is the montage when a detective interrogates the nephew about the uncle's death. Remarkably Griffith uses a series of images to convey sounds, as close shots move from the young man's thumbs twitching nervously, to a clock pendulum, owls hooting, footsteps, and a pencil tapping, all "like the beating of the dead man's heart." Finally an iris captures a single eye of the detective, as if, in the dream context, a godlike investigator were peering into the nephew's thoughts.

In 1919, Richard Oswald produced a silent anthology of five Poe tales that was part of the emerging tradition of horror films in post-World War I Germany. In 1928 French director Jean Epstein adapted Poe's "The Fall of the House of Usher." The result was an expressionistic hymn to Thanatos within the confines of the Poe narrative.

In 1934, an expatriate expressionist, Edgar G. Ulmer, directed a film ostensibly based on "The Black Cat." Although the only real link to the original is the presence of an actual black cat, the film approximates much of the sensation and structure of a Poe story. Most of the action takes place within twenty-four hours in the confines of a *moderne* mansion built by Hjalmar Poelzig, architect, satanist, and war criminal. He has, in fact, built this edifice over the bodies of those he betrayed during the war. To this marble mausoleum, seeking revenge, comes Vitus Verdegast, his former wartime compatriot.

Their subsequent duel of wits, betokened by the chess game over which they so patiently ponder, is set against Black Masses, occult visitations, and implied necrophilia. For not only has Poelzig committed outrages against his own nation, he has stolen Verdegast's wife and daughter and kept them "alive" in a zombie-like state, sleeping with the daughter as he worships the unconscious wife. Dressed in his black silk robe, his widow's peak carefully coiffed, Boris Karloff personifies Poelzig as a gaunt, towering figure who has given up on life to wallow in the dark pleasures of Satan. As he tells Verdegast, portrayed with unusual restraint by Bela Lugosi: "You say your soul was killed and that you have been dead all these years. And what of me—did we not both die here in Marmaros fifteen years ago? Are we any the less victims of the war than those whose bodies were torn asunder? Are we not both the living dead?" In the final scene Verdegast loses the game of chess but wins the life and death struggle. First he skins a screaming Poelzig alive, then he blows up the architect's art deco monument to death and the devil. In 1935 Karloff and Lugosi were teamed again in another ostensible adaptation of Poe called *The Raven.* Except for a torture cham-

Below, Boris Karloff as Poelzig convenes his acolytes for a black mass in *The Black Cat.*

ber outfitted with a swinging blade taken from "The Pit and the Pendulum," very little of either Poe's spirit or letter is present.

Undoubtedly the most familiar and popular adaptations of Poe's work
have been the series of films directed by Roger Corman in the 1960s.
Beginning with *House of Usher* (1960) and ending with *The Tomb of
Ligeia* (1964), in five years Corman, ably assisted by screenwriters
Richard Matheson and Charles Beaumont in many of his efforts,
produced eight films loosely drawn from Poe's collected works. All have
in common a zealous attention to detail and decor within the confines
of a B-budget film, ingeniously rearranging sets and props from one
film to the next and cutting corners where it would show least on the
screen. They also boast a saturated, almost lurid, color scheme, often
emphasizing an erotic and violent red created for most of the films by
veteran cinematographer Floyd Crosby.

The first adaptation, *House of Usher,* is also the most claustrophobic.
It adheres closely to the classical unities so dear to Poe, something the
other adaptations would not do. Like the story, it is a three-character
study taking place within a mansion during a limited period of time.
The only noticeable departure from the original occurs in the characterization of the visitor. He is given further dimension by making him
the putative lover of Madeline Usher, thus complicating the love-hate,
pseudo-incestuous relationship of the brother and sister.

The visual rendering of the character of Roderick is also particularly
striking. His delicate features and fine silver-grey hair subtly evoke the
hypersensitivity of the tale's character as do his silk clothes and soft
speech. "He suffered much from a morbid acuteness of the senses; the

Below, left, Roderick Usher (Vincent Price) is confronted by Winthrop (Mark Damon) in *House of Usher;*
right, Montressor (Peter Lorre) walls up Fortunato (Price) and Annabel (Joyce Jameson) in *Tales of Terror.*

Above, comic posturing and self parody: Boris Karloff and Vincent Price in *The Raven*.

most insipid food was alone endurable; he could wear only garments of certain texture; the odors of all flowers were oppressive; his eyes were tortured by even a faint light; and there were but peculiar sounds, and these from stringed instruments which did not inspire him with horror." As Poe describes him, Roderick is fragile, effete, the last of a decadent line whose portraits hang on the walls about him. On the other hand, Madeline, as interpreted in the film, is much darker and full-bodied than her model in the story, more akin to Poe's Ligeia.

It is the final confrontation between brother and sister in the film which crystallizes Poe's themes. Madeline, who has been entombed alive by her brother, probably out of jealousy, escapes from her crypt. Like a crazed beast, eyes red with blood, she attacks her brother. They grapple and their struggle evokes both physical violence and the tumult of repressed sexual passion. With its gradually cracking foundation and its solitary decay, the house has symbolized their inbred world throughout the film. Now it becomes a complete metaphor for their unconscious desire as it spontaneously bursts into flame, a fitting consummation to their tortured relationship. The rejected suitor flees the mansion as the fire consumes it in the background, evoking the story's conclusion: "...and the deep and dark tarn at my feet closed sullenly and silently over the fragments of the House of Usher."

The Raven (1962) is Corman's and writer Richard Matheson's parody of the series. Filled with puns, one-line gags and climaxed by a comic duel of wizards, *The Raven* is in the "tradition" of Corman's *Little Shop of Horrors*(1960). The "lost Lenore" becomes a "tramp" who throws over her heartbroken lover for a better sorcerer while "the raven" is transformed into a bumbling magician who has managed to imprison himself in the body of a bird. The duel at the end in which an entire set is destroyed—a set seen in several earlier Corman-Poe films—is a calculated display of visual special effects on a limited budget. The film as a whole is a pointed self-satire with Corman poking fun at most of the visual conventions he had recruited and embellished for the Poe films, from stock shots of storm-racked castles to the ever-present red candles and draperies. The prior year, Corman and Matheson had collaborated on *Tales of Terror* (1962), an anthology which included a comic rendering of "The Black Cat" and a serious adaptation of "Morella" (1835) which presages the later *The Tomb of Ligeia* in theme and style.

The Masque of the Red Death (1964) has sometimes been disparaged as being more a homage to Bergman's *The Seventh Seal* than to Poe. A walking, red-robed death does wander throughout the film, playing at Tarot cards rather than chess but with the same visual impact as in the Bergman classic. The similarity ends there, for Death's role in Corman's film is much more elaborate. His two-fold role is that of destroyer and liberator. To the tyrant and satanist Prince Prospero and his aristocratic guests, who have barricaded themselves in his castle to avoid the plaque and to "defy God's will," he is their own reflection, their own hell—an inferno they have created through self-indulgence, callousness, and arrogance. In the denouement the guests *gavotte* in a final *danse macabre* as Death moves among them. Prospero himself finally confronts the Spectre and learns to his dismay that Death's visage is his own.

Concurrently, Death is a liberating force for the innocent victims of Prospero's depredations, freeing the hero and heroine who have been captured and tortured by the Prince to satisfy his debauched desires.

Below, Prospero (Vincent Price) and his dead guests in *The Masque of the Red Death*.

Above, the scholar Verden Fell (Vincent Price) before the tomb of his first wife.

After fulfilling this dual purpose Death returns to his "brothers" in the final scene, and other hooded figures gather from the four corners of the earth to chant "sic transit gloria mundi" and move off like monks in a funeral procession.

The Tomb of Ligeia is the most delirious of the adaptations. In it Corman and screenwriter Robert Towne freely adapt Poe's original while making the main character, Verden Fell, truly their own. Corman's heroes are often seekers, almost seers, particularly in the outlandishly metaphysical science fiction *X — The Man with the X-Ray Eyes* (1963). While the symbolic use of the eyes may be quite different in a science fiction context then in *The Tomb of Ligeia*, it recalls Poe's words: "For eyes we have no models in the remotely antique. It might have been, too, that in these eyes of my beloved lay the secret to which Lord Verulam alludes. They were, I believe, far larger than the ordinary eyes of our own race. They were even fuller than the fullest of the gazelle eyes of the tribe of the valley of Nourjahad."

The film's Verden Fell, then, is a scholar and seeker who is inordinately sensitive to light as evidenced by his ever-present dark glasses. He collects Egyptian art and studies in dimly lit chambers, away from other men. His true obsession is much darker and more metaphysical: "The eyes they confound me...a mindless sort of malice in some Egyptian eyes." He tries to see into the soul of his possessions as he tried to penetrate the mysterious eyes of his dead wife, Ligeia; but in that endeavor he has never been successful.

In *The Tomb of Ligeia*, Corman and Towne elaborate on Poe's idea about the persistence of will, of a commanding, elemental soul, after death. This same concept figures prominently in "The Facts in the Case of M. Valdemar," (1845) which Corman had already adapted as one of the three *Tales of Terror. Ligeia* is Corman's most ambitious treatment of metaphysical considerations, of reality and illusion and the confutation of the two. As the dead Ligeia returns to possess Fell's new bride, Rowena, a series of incidents occur which upset both Rowena's and the viewer's sense of reality. Both women are played in the film by the same actress, thus complicating the distinction between the real and the imagined. As the two spirits struggle for possession of one body and Fell runs into the chamber to rescue Rowena, the style becomes increasingly hallucinatory as shots are repeated, leaving the audience with a sense of oneiric unease.

The Tomb of Ligeia is also Corman's most stylistically controlled picture. The color experiments of *X* and *The Masque of the Red Death* are abandoned for half-tones of red, ochre, and ultimately pure black with a suffusion of green in the exteriors. Corman also guides a performance from Vincent Price that is, along with *House of Usher*, his most subdued. Favorite Corman flourishes, such as the camera shooting from behind a fire in the grate, are present but not disruptive. Other visual usages, such as the long focal length lens in the close-ups during the first possession, have an appropriate distortive effect.

Below, Fell (Vincent Price) wrestles with the spirit of his dead, dark-haired wife Ligeia (Elizabeth Shepherd).

On the surface, the cyclical conclusion of *The Tomb of Ligeia* may seem complication for its own sake like the overtly symbolic epilogue of *The Masque of the Red Death*. There is a subtle distinction to the dream-like recurences of action in the costuming; but the effect itself seems inspired by a verse from the poem within Poe's story: "Through a circle that ever returneth in/To the selfsame spot."

Corman's other Poe adaptations are less memorable. *Premature Burial* (1961) takes up Poe's obsession with being buried alive but does little to develop that theme. There is a notable dream sequence which commences with a darkening of the screen and the sound of a beating heart. The cataleptic protagonist finds himself in the crypt he has out-fitted with mechanisms of escape, including, if all else fails, poison. To his dismay all the mechanisms malfunction, leaving him to experience his worst nightmare.

The Pit and the Pendulum (1961) like most filmic adaptations of this story attempts to expand the suspenseful tale of a man waiting for a swinging axe to cut his body in half. All the films have added other plot lines which have diluted the impact and distracted the viewer from the intensity of that horrific moment in which one faces certain death at the hand of an un-known force. Corman made numerous other films using the same actors, costumes, and/or sets in between the official entries in the Poe series, including such "faux Poe" as *The Tower of London* and *The Terror* (both 1962). The latter

Below, Guy Carrell (Ray Milland) smugly test drives his coffin, which comes equipped with a tool rack in *Premature Burial*.

features Jack Nicholson as an officer in the French army. His brash, uninflected performance is completely at odds with Boris Karloff's un-derstated menace. Ultimately *The Terror*'s only relationship to Poe is that it featured the same stars and the sets used in *The Raven*.

The 1968 *Histoires Extraordinaires (Spirits of the Dead)* features three tales adapted by different European directors. The first is "Met-zengerstein" (1836), directed by Roger Vadim and with his then-wife Jane Fonda and her brother Peter portraying siblings on screen. Of the three it relies too heavily, as is Vadim's wont, on sensationalist ele-ments. Gratuitous nude scenes and general kinkiness prevail as the

Below and right, the final episode of *Spirits of the Dead*. Toby Dammit drives his sports car through the night but cannot escape the vision of a young girl with a white ball.

Countess participates in a *menage à trois* with her maid and lusts after her brother. Suspension of disbelief is strained past its limits when she "accidentally" incinerates her brother and then is "raped" by his new incarnation, a stallion.

The second episode is a subdued and thoughtful piece adapted by Louis Malle from Poe's "William Wilson" (1839), the classic story of a *doppelgänger* who functions as a conscience to a arrogant, ruthless protagonist. As the double confronts the hero with the consequences of his deeds, the hero comes to despise him and plans his double's destruction. In so doing he destroys all that is good in himself, or as the double says in the story: "'You have conquered, and I yield. Yet, henceforward art thou also dead—dead to the World, to Heaven and to Hope.'"

The most imaginative episode is the Fellini adaptation of "Never Bet the Devil Your Head" (1841). Fellini constructs another of his fantasy worlds, although this one comes to resemble a nightmare. Toby Dammit is an English actor on his last legs. He is alienated, intoxicated, and obsessed with the vision of a young girl in white. As he arrives in Rome to film the first "Catholic western" ("a cross between Carl Dreyer and Pasolini with a touch of John Ford," says the priest-producer), Toby wanders drunkenly from an airport populated by talking-head video screens, an apocalyptic traffic jam, and a surreal awards ceremony. Shots of the pale Toby, looking more like an angst-ridden Christ than a movie star, alternate with POV tracking shots through this hallucinatory landscape.

Toby's only relief from this barrage of grasping agents, insincere filmmakers, fawning fans, and rude TV hosts is when a strange, exotic woman sits next to him at the ceremonies. As Ray Charles' version of "Ruby" plays in the background, she delivers a monologue which delineates his loneliness and alienation. She then offers herself to him as a companion and lover for life. Her tone is soft and lulling, so much so that he falls asleep like a child listening to his mother singing a lullaby. When he awakes she is gone.

Filled with self-loathing and despair, Toby takes the Ferrari waiting for him at the studio and drives off into a landscape of plastic sheep, barking dogs, highways to nowhere, and a broken bridge. After a seemingly endless series of point-of-view shots speeding down these highways with no destination, Toby spots his objective, the little girl in white. She beckons to him with her eyes. He stands at the edge of the bridge, looking into the chasm before him, much as Poe's character did in the original story. The abyss is tinted red with obviously hellish connotations. With suicidal verve, he revs the motor of his high-powered car and drives into oblivion. The final shots are of the little girl, now with two balls, one white, the other the head of Toby who has been decapitated by a wire stretched across the bridge. The camera tracks into the blood dripping from the wire. Toby has found his destination.

La Mansión de la Locura (1972) is another adaptation, like Fellini's "Never Bet the Devil Your Head," of one of Poe's more satirical writings. The source material is itself hardly supernatural, being the whimsical tale, "The System of Dr. Tarr and Professor Fether," (1845) of a dilettante who visits an insane asylum. While there he is taken under the wing of the director who has adopted the methods of a supposedly renown Dr. Tarr and Professor Fether. After being beaten in a brawl between the inmates and their keepers, he comes to learn that the director himself is a madman who had led a *coup d'état* of patients against the doctors and guards of the institution. Then, in keeping with the theories of his mentors, the director had these "guardians of sanity" both "Tarred" and "Feathered."

The adaptor of *La Mansión,* director Juan Lopez Moctezuma, who also made the disturbingly cannibalistic vampire film, *Mary, Mary, Bloody Mary* (1974), follows the general outline of Poe's story. There are some variations such as the additions of a love interest for the narrator in the person of Eugenie, but the overall effect is a transformation of Poe's bagatelle into a surrealistic canvas of horror and mordant satire reminiscent of the work of Luis Buñuel.

Throughout the film, the narrator, Gaston, encounters an array of living tableaux which alternately amuse and terrify him. From a priest exorcising the "devil" dressed in top hat and horns at the gates of the asylum; through the monumental "electronic sphinx" being constructed in the director's honor; to the emaciated man, appropriately named Dante, who while strapped to a torture table spouts classic poetry. Like so many of Poe's characters, Gaston soon becomes unable to distinguish between the natural and supernatural. Is this chicken-man real or a hoax? Is Eugenie a reincarnation of a Javanese goddess as the director claims or the sly daughter of the deposed director scheming to get her father reinstated? Does she appear to him at night, dressed in a diaphanous gown, or does he just wish it? Is the "horned man" at the gates really possessed or simply another deranged inmate on the loose?

In a climactic banquet scene the madness of the director reaches its apex as Gaston and Eugenie are put on trial in a mock re-creation of the citizen tribunals of the French Revolution. In a chaotic mix of gluttony, sex, and violence, the inmates carouse while the keepers revolt, escaping their cells and leading a counterrevolution against the director. The director himself is finally killed by one of his own who shouts out as she assassinates him, "Viva la revolución!" With the death of the impostor, the asylum and its inmates sink back into a stupor and the nightmare ends, at least for Gaston and Eugenie.

In 1983 Spanish director Jesus Franco made his own idiosyncratic entry in the Poe series with *El Hundimiento de la Casa Usher*. This unique film conflates the stories of Poe's Roderick Usher, Shakespeare's King Lear, and Franco's own character from his earlier films, Dr. Orloff, into a potpourri of lust, murder, incest, and psychic distintegration.

The film opens, like the story, with the narrator arriving at what Poe calls the "melancholy House of Usher" aloft a "foggy tarn." In this case the "melancholy mansion" is a mediterranean castle and the "foggy tarn," the snow-capped mountains of the Iberian Peninsula. A less ominous setting would be hard to imagine. But once Alan, the narrator and former student of Usher, is admitted to the castle, all that is sunny and exhilirating is replaced by claustrophobic interiors shot in low angle and illuminated in the Baroque style of Rembrandt and the Northern Italians, with a single source of light falling on the characters. With Alan's entry into this obscure milieu where, no matter the time of day outside, it is night within, the story of his mentor, Usher, begins.

In Franco's version, the character of Usher operates on three distinct levels. He does share many characeristics with Poe's Usher. He is hypersensitive, to the point of being on the edge of a nervous breakdown and possibly delusional. Three of the most important women in his life, his dead wife, his mistress, and his servant, torment him with children's games of ring-around-the-rosy and blindman's bluff; and he is incestuously obsessed with his catatonic daughter Melissa, who replaces Madeline from the story.

But Franco's Usher is also the re-creation of his own Dr. Orloff. Using extensive footage from his earlier Orloff films, Franco interweaves another tale with the Poe story, that of a scientist driven to preserve his love by means of blood transfusions. In order to be assured of a steady supply of fresh plasma, Orloff and his servant Morpho abduct prostitutes and drain them of their blood. In *Hundimiento* Orloff becomes Usher, as both characters are portrayed by the same actor, Howard Vernon; and his blood-starved love becomes his daughter Melissa.

On a final level, this Usher is a reincarnation of yet another figure, King Lear. As Vernon's theatrical flare emphasizes, Usher is an aged man, who claims to be "100 years old" and is distrustful of all the women in his life, except his daughter. As Melissa is the analog for Lear's faithful daughter Cordelia, so his wife and his mistress are his Goneril and Regan, the daughters who rebel against Lear and eventually destroy him. This analogy is reinforced in the final scenes of the

Below, Vincent Price as Julian Markham with the title object in *The Oblong Box*.

movie. As the castle crumbles about Usher, his wife and mistress, both of whom he may have killed, dance around him, driving Usher to the ground. As Alan flees from the decaying mansion, he does not look back, saying only, "Of what was real or what was unreal I cannot say."

In 1969 the short-lived career of British horror director Michael Reeves ended abruptly with his death while preparing *The Oblong Box*. As completed by producer Gordon Hessler and photographed by John Coquillon, the finished picture has much of the pictorialism of the Corman productions and restrained performances by the lynchpin of those films, Vincent Price, and by Christopher Lee. Without much plot added to Poe's short tale, the picture relies on atmosphere and produces scant fear or suspense.

In the last few years, there has been a new cycle of low-budget Poe adaptations. Roger Corman himself has produced several remakes such as *The Haunting of Morella* (1990) and *The Masque of the Red Death* (1989). The former combines the stories of "Morella," as adapted in *Tales of Terror*, with *The Tomb of Ligeia*, retaining the detail of a light sensitive protagonist who wears dark glasses. Corman did not direct either film, and the results are long on exploitation and short on style. Competing in the exploitation arena, producer Harry Alan Towers has also adapted some Poe stories with even more dubious results. Films like *The Masque of the Red Death* (1992) and *The House of Usher* (1989), despite featuring veteran performers such as Donald Pleasance and Oliver Reed, recall in their unconscious "campiness" the Corman/Matheson parodies. As with some of earlier Corman adaptations, films like *The Haunting Fear* (1990), ostensibly based on "The Premature Burial," take the cachet of Poe's name and very little else from his work.

Also in 1990 two veteran genre directors, George Romero and Dario Argento, each adapted a Poe story, "The Facts in the Case of M. Valdemar," (with Romero directing) and the oft-filmed "The Black Cat" (with Argento directing). The resulting film was called *Due Occhi Diabolici (Two Evil Eyes)*. Romero brings his documentary style to the first episode, while Argento directs with his characteristic melodramatic flourish. Although both directors might have complemented each other with their contrasting methods, both episodes are far too dependent on gore and other predictable shock effects to evoke any of the subtleties of Poe.

II. H.P. Lovecraft (1890-1937): The Lurking Fear

And yet I saw them in a limitless stream—flopping, hopping, croaking, beating—surging inhumanly through the spectral moonlight in a grotesque, malignant saraband of fantastic nightmare.

H. P. Lovecraft, "Shadow over Innsmouth"

Atavism and Regression

Howard Phillips Lovecraft's fame rests almost as heavily on his work as a scholar as that of a writer of fiction. In his now classic essay on "Supernatural Horror in Literature" (1936), Lovecraft's expansive analysis of supernatural horror and fantasy contrasted with the condescending tone of earlier essayists. Lovecraft used his sure knowledge of the works and authors discussed to trace the elements of supernatural horror back to Greek literature and then forward chronologically to the most prolific period for horror, the 19th and 20th Centuries. In that section he reintroduced, or in some cases introduced for the first time, to the reader the the names and works of authors such as Arthur Machen, Lord Dunsany, William Hope Hodgson, Robert Chambers, and M.R. James. If much of Lovecraft's generation had forgotten these masters of horror and fantasy, many subsequent scholars and/or fiction writers in the field today acknowledge their debt to Lovecraft's writings, and to him as researcher as well as creative inspiration.

Lovecraft was a scholar by both temperament and necessity. Sickly all his life, he spent most of it as a semi-recluse in the quiet of Providence, Rhode Island. There he immersed himself in the fantasy and horror writings of others, until he acquired the confidence to produce stories of his own. Lovecraft is probably the most imitative of the writers discussed in this book. Many of his stories can, if fact, be categorized according to the writers after whose style they are modeled. with the most obvious influences on his work being Dunsany, Machen, and Poe.

Many of Lovecraft's early stories bear the stamp of the writer whom he extolled in his essay: "Unexcelled in the sorcery of crystalline singing prose, and supreme in the creation of a gorgeous and languorous world of iridescently exotic vision, is Edward John Moreton Drax Plunkett, Eighteenth Baron Dunsany, whose tales and short plays form an almost unique element in our literature. Inventor of a new mythology and weaver of surprising folklore, Lord Dunsany stands dedicated to a strange world of fantastic beauty..."

One of Lovecraft's first stories, "The Doom That Came to Sarnath" (1919), bears a marked resemblance to Dunsany's "Bethmoora" in its Near Eastern setting and in its subject of a lost, mythical city in the desert. But the strongest tie to Dunsany is the lyrical, languorous prose, bejewelled with wondrously inventive names echoing Celtic and Near Eastern traditions. A side-by-side comparison of the two stories demonstrates this connection:

> Then close to the hour of midnight, all the bronze gates of Sarnath burst open and emptied forth a frenzied throng that blackened the plain, so that all the visiting princes and travelers fled away in fright. For on the faces of this throng was writ a madness born of horror unendurable... ("Sarnath")

> All day they came. And in the evening, just before lights come out and colours change, they appeared before Bethmoora's copper gates. They carried staves, such as messengers bear in those lands, and seemed somberly clad when the dancers all came round them with their green and lilac dresses. ("Bethmoora")

The tone, the classical language, the specific imagery, details such as the metal of the gate ("bronze" in Lovecraft's story; "copper" in Dunsany's), are more than coincidentally similar. Another story in which Lovecraft tries to recreate the mood of Dunsany is "The White Ship" (1919), this time borrowing from "Idle Days on the Yann." Both deal with an allegorical journey by ship into the unconscious, into a world of dreams, a world in which future and past are joined. In both there is an attempt by means of the prose to simulate the motion of the ship, floating effortlessly in time and space.

Lovecraft's longest work in the style of Dunsany is a novella entitled **The Dream-Quest of Unknown Kadath** (1926). That title alone and its direct evocation a fantasy world is lineally descended from Dunsany's "The Fortress Unvanquishable Save for Sacnoth" or "How Plash-Goo Came to the Land of None's Desire." In his novel Lovecraft introduces a character who will reappear in number of stories, Randolph Carter. Through him the readers journey into a milieu of phantasmagoric nightmares and fantasies.

Concurrently, Lovecraft was beginning to turn out stories with a more personal stamp. He made his prose harder-edged by adopting a more journalistic style and taking care to establish a believable context and an aura of *reportage*. But even as he endeavored to form his own identity as a writer, he still resembled another of his models, Arthur Machen.

Machen's vision of a universe in jeopardy, a universe under siege from atavistic, malevolent forces seeking to reconquer lost domains is very much in line with Lovecraft's cosmic view as developed in his later stories. But where Machen's evil was always ambiguous, Lovecraft used specific details in presenting his own vision. Ultimately he created a entire mythology, which has come to be known as the "Cthulhu Mythos." According to Lovecraft himself, this mythology was not formulated *a priori* to the composition of his stories but instead grew out of them organically, as he expanded and refined the particulars from tale to tale.

The pattern of these tales is fairly standardized or, one might even say, ritualized. They are usually set in contemporary time but in a locale with a long history and/or deep archaeological roots such as New England. Similar but fictional names stand in for real ones. For example "Salem" becomes "Arkham." The protagonist is typically a seeker, who is delving into forbidden lore such as the mythical **Necronomicon** of Abdul Alhazred. As a result of this quest the seeker comes face to face with an overpowering evil which antedates his own racial memory and can be fatally attractive.

This evil can be divided into two categories. The first is made up of the monsters and mutants whose power is more preternatural than supernatural. The inhabitants in "Shadow over Innsmouth" (1931), Wilbur Whateley in "The Dunwich Horror" (1928), or Dagon in "Dagon" (1917) are good examples of this first category. These creatures are also grouped by their similar appearance, leaving little doubt about their common origin: they are saurian in aspect, green in color, and give off a fetid odor. For instance from the "The Dunwich Horror": "Above the waist it was semi-anthropomorphic; though its chest, where the dog's rending paws still rested watchfully, had the leathery, reticulated hide of a crocodile or alligator...Below the waist, though, it was worst; for here all human resemblance left off and sheer phantasy began." In this description near the end of the story, Lovecraft invokes what is for him

Below, Lovecraft's "unimaginable" imagined: a monstrosity from *The Resurrected.*

the greatest terror, the regression of humanity to their primordial animalistic roots.

In portraying creatures of the second category of evil, the most power-ful and supernatural beings of his mythology such as "Cthulhu" and "Yog-Sothoth," Lovecraft uses a much subtler prose. He hints at their horror through imagery of sound, smell, and motion. Like many of his colleagues, Lovecraft uses subjectification in the final frantic, discon-nected journal entries kept by the seeker-hero of "The Haunter of the Dark" (1935):

> I can see everything with a monstrous sense that is not sight—light is dark and dark is light...those people on the hill...guard...candles and charms...their priests...I am Robert Blake, but see the tower in the dark. There is a monstrous odor...senses transfigured...board-ing   at   that   tower   window   cracking   and   giving away...Ia...ngai...ygg...I   see   it—coming   here—hell-wind—titan blue—black wings—Yog-Sothoth save me—the three-lobed burning eye...

The most typical of Lovecraft's New England tales of the "Cthulhu Mythos" is "The Dunwich Horror." It recounts the attempts of the Whateley family to call forth the "Old Ones," the ancient evil, from their refuge. All the Lovecraft iconography and conventions are present: the fabled **Necronomicon;** the researcher-seeker (here Dr. Armitage); the gradual revelation of the metaphysical dimensions of the horror; the rituals in deserted, ancient sites; and the saurian monsters. As the evil spreads throughout Dunwich, the villagers led by Dr. Armitage stand and fight the Whateleys' black magic with some of their own. On a hill in Dunwich they force the evil back to its source: "Trees, grass, and un-derbrush were whipped into a fury; and the frightened crowd at the mountain's base, weakened by the lethal foetor that seemed about to asphyxiate them, were almost hurled off their feet. Dogs howled from the distance..."

The third author from whom Lovecraft derives his style, structure and narrative content is Poe. While Lovecraft's fiction is generally free of Poe's obsessive, psychosexual content and, at the same time, is more concerned with establishing a realistic context, at least in the "Cthul-hu" tales, the overall influence is undeniably clear. Lovecraft is not alone in favoring a literary convention so often used by Poe, that of the first person narrator upon whom madness and horror are descending; but Lovecraft also models his rhyme and meter on Poe's. Lovecraft even punctuates like Poe, relying heavily on the dash and the ellipses to cre-ate a staccato rhythm.

The most explicit interweaving of Poe's style and themes with Lovecraft's is the novel **At the Mountains of Madness** (1931). Lovecraft drew his inspiration for this novella about explorations of the southern polar regions directly from Poe's **The Narrative of Arthur Gordon Pym.** Like Poe, Lovecraft created a journalistic posture for the story by asking that his warnings be heeded by scientists and explorers so as to discourage them from further exploration of that area. He further supports these "warnings" with precise, pseudo-scientific observations, giving the tale a scholarly veneer and coincidentally underpinning the reader's suspension of disbelief.

At this point, the two works diverge. While Poe's tale wanders from surface reality into a nightmare world of the psyche, Lovecraft manages to maintain his pose of scientific observation throughout, even when dealing with the most astounding phenomena. In the process, Lovecraft evidences an extensive knowledge of archaeology, geology, and paleontology. Lovecraft's narrator is a member of an expedition who recalls the horrors encountered in the icebound regions of the Antarctic. Building gradually from incident to incident, from horror to horror, each unsettling discovery is displaced by an even more devastating one, until the narrator reaches the most unsettling revelation of all direct from Lovecraft's mythos. The expedition stumbles upon the frozen, "star-headed Old Ones" whom they accidentally reanimate. With these creatures they discover their rebellious slaves called "Shoggoths" and a cyclopean city now in ruin which Lovecraft describes in fulsome architectural detail.

For decades there were no film adaptations of Lovecraft's work. Unlike Poe, Stoker, Shelley, and Stevenson, Lovecraft was virtually unknown outside of adherents of the genre. In addition, Lovecraft's stories were so dependent on the actuality of "unnameable" or "indescribable" creatures, on reptilian mutants and ancient evil ones, that any adaptation would likely require elaborate and expensive special effects. With the technological advances in mechanical and optical effects over the

Right, Vincent Price as Charles Dexter Ward stands before a portrait of his ancestor Joseph Curwen in *The Haunted Palace.*

last two decades, graphic depictions of Lovecraft's creatures have become more accessible to lower budget productions, the usual venue of the horror film.

In the 1960s American International, the mass marketers of Poe, first attempted to visualize Lovecraft's stories. Obviously hoping this was another literary mother lode which could be mined as profitably as the works of Poe, Roger Corman himself made the first, hybrid adaptation, which was released in 1964 as "Edgar Allan Poe's *The Haunted Palace*" and based both on a poem by Poe and Lovecraft's novel **The Case of Charles Dexter Ward** (1928). The story, which is one of Lovecraft's most meticulously crafted, records the grisly history of a man, Ward, who is possessed by his evil ancestor, Joseph Curwen. Curwen has sworn revenge on the town which burned him as a warlock in the 1700s. Returning to possess his descendant, he uses Ward's skills first to perform rituals from the **Necronomicon** and invoke the "Old Ones" and then to conduct experiments which include chemical reanimation and the consumption of human and animal flesh.

The horror mounts as Dr. Willett, who interviewed Ward when he was institutionalized, discovers the pieces of the puzzle. The climax of the novella comes when Dr. Willett explores the farmhouse cellar where Ward/Curwen has performed his experiments and destroys the laboratory. Lovecraft describes that scene:

> For racked though he was with horror, his sense of grim purpose was still uppermost, and he was freely determined to leave no stone unturned in his search for the hideous facts behind Charles Dexter Ward's bizarre madness. Failing to find a lantern, he chose the smallest of lamps to carry, also filling his pockets with candles and matches, and taking with him a gallon of oil, which he proposed to keep for reserve in whatever hidden laboratory he might uncover beyond the terrible space with its unclean altar and nameless covered walls. To traverse that space again would require his utmost fortitude, but he knew it must be done...So Willett went back to that great pillared hall of stench and anguished howling, turned down his lamp to avoid any distant glimpse of the hellish altar...

The novella also reveals Lovecraft's ambivalent attitude towards his Puritan roots. Like Hawthorne, Lovecraft obsessively revisits the physical, psychological, and supernatural terrain of Puritanism through his writings. While it may be partly an accident of birth, it is not an arbitrary decision when these stories are set in New England and the evil in his mythos is associated with the period of witch trials and Calvinist morality. In Joseph Curwen, Lovecraft expresses these contradictory feelings towards that past. On one hand, Curwen is a grave robber and a reckless conduit for the "old ones." On the other, he is a researcher and a recluse who abhors his small-minded contemporaries, much as Lovecraft and many of his other characters did.

By grafting Poe's poem, "The Haunted Palace," onto **Charles Dexter Ward,** Corman could again recycle the sets and costumes of his Poe series. Ward's New England farmhouse becomes a Gothic mansion replete with red candles and a sweeping staircase. The farmhouse laboratory is refitted from the earlier Corman adaptation of Poe's *The Pit and the Pendulum.*

What Corman does manage to transpose effectively from the original story is the character of Charles Dexter Ward. Vincent Price conveys the character's sense of growing madness as he resists the invasion of his body by his ancestor. His active persona alternates between the tortured Ward and the arrogant Curwen, much as the original character does. There is one significant difference, however. Although the laboratory and house are destroyed as in the original, Ward does not dissolve before the eyes of Dr. Willett. Instead he escapes the fire and regains his arrogant composure as he faces down the descendants of the villagers who immolated him centuries ago. A sneer slowly forming across Ward/Corwen's mouth, and evil is quietly triumphant.

Following *The Haunted Palace* Corman's regular art director, Daniel Haller, took over directing the Lovecraft series. The first, *Monster of Terror* (1965), was shot in England and is an adaptation of Lovecraft's story "The Colour Out of Space" (1927). The story itself is quasi-science fiction about a meteor which has landed in a rural farm, causing mutations among the inhabitants. The themes of regression and atavism are revisited, as humans return to a primordial state.

On film the style of the Poe series is again married to Lovecraft's themes with dubious results. The house more closely resembles the Gothic mansion of Usher than any rural abode. Despite these trappings and the presence of Boris Karloff, the plotting, effects, and overall result fall far short of the best of the Poe films.

Below, Curwen (Vincent Price) sneers at his captors in *The Haunted Palace.*

Haller's second film, from Lovecraft's story of the same name, was *The Dunwich Horror* (1969). With a style more appropriate to the source material and not just a revamping of old designs from the Poe films, Haller creates the first geographical and architecturally apt transliteration of Lovecraft. In this context, the story's extreme metaphysical horror, which posits a universe that is splitting in two, retains the contrast between cataclysmic events and innocuous locales that runs through all of Lovecraft. Dean Stockwell portrays Wilbur Whateley, a protagonist with Lovecraft's trademark attitudes of arrogance and reclusiveness. As he wanders through the town in an alienated, detached mood, he openly refers to the townspeople as "frightened, superstitious fools" who fear him for his secretive attempts to invoke the evil gods of Yog-Sothoth and Cthulhu.

There is a crucial difference between the film version of Wilbur and Lovecraft's original character. The screen Wilbur is sophisticated and sensual. He seduces the virginal Nancy, a character not in the short story, and incorporates her sacrifice on the altar at "the Devil's Hopyard" into the Lovecraftian ritual. The original Wilbur is described as "goatish" and ultimately revealed to be part-saurian.

Below, Dean Stockwell as Whateley invoking the gods of Yog-Sothoth in *The Dunwich Horror.*

The climax of the film at which time Wilbur invokes the "ancient ones" is a particularly effective montage, as Haller cuts from Wilbur at Devil's Hopyard and the sacrificial altar to the forces of nature displaying their elemental strength. A house bursts into flame; rivers overflow; the winds level terrain—all as Wilbur struggles to rend the universe and admit the ancient forces of evil to his plane of being.

In the last decade there have been a number of Lovecraft adaptations that prominently display blood-spattered violence and fantastically hideous creatures but transpose little if any of Lovecraft's detail of setting or characterization. A typical example is *The Curse* (1987), another adaptation of "The Colour out of Space" which relocates the action to rural Tennessee.

The Unnamable (1987) is adapted from the very spare 1923 story of the same name. In the original, Lovecraft uses the researcher/sleuth, Randolph Carter, as he does in "The Silver Key" (1926) and "The Statement of Randolph Carter" (1919), to express his distrust of scientific rationalism. In the story Carter, who is less skeptical, argues with a friend about the stories of an "unnameable" creature inhabiting a nearby Arkham house. The filmmakers recreate this dialogue, but nonetheless proceed to turn the plot into a stereotypical tale of brainless teens in a haunted house. Their confrontation with a technically impressive monster ends predictably.

The Case of Charles Dexter Ward was also adapted again in 1992 as *The Resurrected.* The film grafts a film noir style, complete with low key lighting, a private detective, and hard-bitten dialogue, onto Lovecraft's story of possession. By focusing primarily on the equivalent of Dr. Willett, the filmmakers reduce Ward's appearances to special effects set pieces. The result is as uneven and inappropriate as the worst of the AIP series and their mawkish Gothic trappings. Only the exploration of the farmhouse cellar with its hidden pits and "lurking horror" of reanimation captures some of the expressive anxiety of the original story.

The most imaginative of the recent Lovecraft adaptations is *Re-Animator*

Below, Chris Sarandon as Charles Dexter Ward in *The Resurrected.*

Above, Herbert West (Jeffrey Combs) speaks with Dr. Hill's talking head in *Re-Animator*.

(1985). Based on Lovecraft's novella **Herbert West—Reanimator** (1922), the story is constructed from an unusual perspective. Like many of Lovecraft's tales, the original is a first-person narrative which traces the history of the narrator's friend and eventual nemesis Herbert West in his single-minded attempts to reanimate the dead. The narration is not only extremely episodic but full of repeated phrases and incidents designed to convey to the reader that the narrator is not entirely lucid. The last few lines of the story confirm this: "They imply that I am either a madman or a murderer—probably I am mad. But I might not be mad if those accursed tomb-legions had not been so silent."

The character of West is equally odd. He is a monomaniac with an ironic sense of humor. For example, after failing in his attempt to reanimate the corpse of Dr. Halsey, whom West knows and admires, he discards the rotting carcass with the quirky observation, "Damn it, it wasn't quite fresh enough."

Re-Animator emphasizes these qualities of narrative incongruity and black irony. The filmmakers push the character of West "over the top" by emphasizing his arrogance and absolute disregard for human suffering. West exploits all those around him with great panache. He disruptes the life of his roommate, Daniel, first launching experiments in the basement and finally precipitating a rift between Daniel and his girlfriend. He injects his reanimation serum in a variety of subjects from house cats to human corpses with equal insouciance; and, as in the novella, he causes the innocent Dr. Halsey to become a mad zombie.

In the film, this ironic sense of the outlandish is further exploited through acting and special effects. After West decapitates the villain of the piece, Dr. Hill, who stands in for Major Clapham-Lee in the novella, he reanimates his head and torso separately. When Dr. Hill's head leads a revolt of the mutants which West has created, the reanimator answers Hill's threat to reveal his secrets with a mocking, "Who's going to believe a talking head?"

The graphic depiction in *Re-Animator* of scenes which Lovecraft so meticulously described, such as the decapitated head speaking or the revolt of the mutants, adds to the hallucinatory quality of the narration. The same is true in several other adaptations, where merely seeing Lovecraft's cosmic horrors graphically depicted has a visceral impact; but few of the visual devices or special effects retain their impact when reiterated. In examples such as *The Crimson Cult*, the suspension of disbelief which Lovecraft maintains with his deft prose is destroyed by the sheer outlandishness of images and events. As already noted Lovecraft's celebrated suspense relies on the use of detail and rhythms borrowed and refined from Machen and Poe, details and rhythms which can prove fragile if mistransposed. While *Re-Animator's* exposition begins slowly, once the central events have begun, the film moves forward briskly and seldom retraces its steps. Its sequel, *Bride of the Re-Animator* (1991), and most of the other Lovecraft adaptations fail to capture the unique and somewhat aberrant vision of the original literary works.

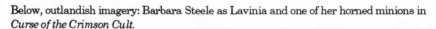

Below, outlandish imagery: Barbara Steele as Lavinia and one of her horned minions in *Curse of the Crimson Cult.*

Above, Fredric March as Hyde in the 1931 *Dr. Jekyll and Mr. Hyde.*

CHAPTER THREE

The Pre-Moderns

I. The Ambivalent Scientist:
Robert Louis Stevenson (1850-1894)

The Sea of Faith
Was once, too, at the full, and round earth's shore
Lay like the folds of a bright girdle furl'd.
But now I only hear
Its melancholy, long, withdrawing roar,
Retreating, to the breath
Of the night-wind, down the vast edges of drear
And naked shingles of the world.

Matthew Arnold, "Dover Beach"

Manicheanism

Robert Louis Stevenson's novella **The Strange Case of Dr. Jekyll and Mr. Hyde** (1886) is a true expression of the duality of the Victorian Age. When this classic supernatural tale was written the era had entered a time of social and and religious doubt. For fifty years the politically as- tute Queen Victoria had presided over a period marked by tremendous economic growth and industrial progress at home linked inextricably to colonial expansion and exploitation abroad. The mores promoted by Victoria and her ministers were part of an unwritten but strict code of gentility, enforcing concepts like the bourgeois family unit, the mother as "angel of the hearth," the repression of any hint of vulgarity or sexuality in public life, a euphemistic sentimentality in public discourse, and, above it all, a Manichean view of the supernatural. In this absolutist context, things were good or bad, black or white, acceptable or not, there was no in-between.

By 1886, the doubts expressed by the likes of Matthew Arnold in the opening epigraph were widespread. Smug, self-righteous Victorianism was being assailed in many arenas. Social philosophers as antithetical as Marx and Freud tore at the surface appearances to reveal the extremes of poverty, capitalist exploitation, and sexual repression in and out of England. Charles Darwin attacked the traditional religious view of the universe with his own revolutionary work that posited the development of the human species from primordial forms. "Decadent" authors like Charles Swinburne and Oscar Wilde were not only shocking through their prose and subject matter but through their personal life styles as well. The "naked shingles of the world," as Arnold called them, were indeed exposed for all to see.

In this climate Stevenson composed his overtly allegorical novella of supernatural horror. In telling the story of the tormented Dr. Jekyll, who believed so fervently that science could separate the "twins" of good and evil bound together in each man's soul, Stevenson reflected the social codes while giving voice to contemporary doubts about scientific progress and man's place in the universe.

Dr. Henry Jekyll epitomizes the ideal of the time, not just a doctor and scientist but a humanitarian. He is a man filled with dreams of progress, embracing a life of dedication to his profession with no distractions. Unlike the Jekyll character in most future film adaptations of the book, Stevenson's character is a true ascete, asexual and single-minded. His obsession is to isolate good and evil, "the separation of these elements. If each, I told myself, could but be housed in separate entities, life would be relieved of all that was unbearable; the unjust might go his way, delivered from the aspirations and remorse of his more upright twin; and the just could walk steadfastly and securely on his upward path."

Jekyll embraced a Victorian ideal of progress. Man could rid his soul of the evil that dragged him down, rid himself of all that he now had to repress. Science could find a way of relieving the unmentionable pressures built up behind the facade of Victorian morality. What result could be more ironic than the concoction of a potion which frees his evil self, whom he calls Hyde, to commit depredations? Many of these acts, from the trampling of a child to the murder of Sir Danvers Carew, were in fact too indelicate for a mainstream Victorian writer to describe. So Stevenson uses Hyde's appearance to persuade the reader that he is evil incarnate. As one character says, "God bless me, the man seems hardly human! Something troglodytic..." or "Evil was written broadly and plainly on the face..."

Like a dominant personality in schizophrenia, the evil Hyde gradually comes to control the idealistic Jekyll and is able to take over his body spontaneously, without the use of the potion. Jekyll's only recourse is suicide; and so he poisons himself. The fact that Jekyll must kill himself and end his experiments brings his contemporary readers face to face with the era's gnawing doubts not only about science but also about the progress of humanity on its quest for a more spiritual life. Is it possible that Darwin was right and that this "troglodytic" Hyde is the vestige of our simian ancestors? Is scientific progress worth all the suffering it creates? Will all this inquiry and experimentation but lead to man playing God, as in Mary Shelley's story, and only to end in suicidal madness? These are a few of the questions Stevenson raises in his novella, questions of immense relevance to his Victorian audience.

The structure of **The Strange Case of Dr. Jekyll and Mr. Hyde** is non-linear, with several characters telling bits and pieces of the story and ending with Jekyll's flashback narration of his history in the form of a journal found after his suicide. As already noted, such a structure was frequently used in 19th Century horror or Gothic fiction. In prose style the novella is typical of Stevenson's work, not psychological or poetic but rather journalistic. In his seminal essay, H.P. Lovecraft described it as one in a series of "horror tales [that] specialise in events rather than atmospheric details, address the intellect rather than a malign tensity or psychological verisimilitude and take a definite stand in sympathy with mankind and its welfare."

"Something troglodytic..." Barrymore as Hyde.

As with previous examples of classic supernatural literature, **The Strange Case of Dr. Jekyll and Mr. Hyde** was popular from the earliest days of silent filmmaking. From the first, visually rendering the transformation of Jekyll into Hyde was a primary challenge to those working in the new medium. A 1912 short starring and directed by James Cruze uses simple overlays of static medium shots in an effect that must have seemed sensational when it first appeared. In another sense, the sequence of Hyde's attack on the little girl was equally sensational. Two years later the first feature length version, *Ein Seltsamer Fall* (1914), appeared in Germany.

No less than three features were released in 1920, *Der Januskopf*, directed by F.W. Murnau and now lost, and two American productions. The less celebrated version, produced by Louis B. Mayer, starred Sheldon Lewis, a veteran of many stage performances. His Jekyll is effete and his Hyde, who delights in snatching purses, looks like a hobo. Under the influence of Sir George, a father figure who seems taken from Oscar Wilde and even suggests that "the only way to get rid of temptation is to yield to it," Jekyll visits a cabaret. This Jekyll is a much weaker person that in Stevenson's original. Accordingly his fall seems less than tragic.

The other American production in 1920 starred John Barrymore. Heavily drawn from Richard Mansfield's popular 1897 stage adaptation, this film was the first to emphasize the implicit sexual element in the atavistic Hyde. The filmmakers also underscored the virgin/whore dichotomy, so popular in that period, in the persons of the innocent Millicent and the decadent dancer Gina.

Millicent is Jekyll's love while Gina is the first carnal temptation of this "St. Anthony of London," as his friends call him. While Millicent appeals to his "good" side, Gina, when he first sees her dance, inflames his "evil" side. It is no coincidence that when the leering Hyde is first liberated he goes to Gina, not Millicent. This dark, Mediterranean woman is also representative of the "fatal woman" archetype adopted by the Anglo-Saxon Victorian. She is even tied to the Borgias by a flashback which tells the story of her poison ring. Millicent, on the other hand, is a blond "angel of the hearth," promising the comforts of home and family to Jekyll. Even when Jekyll, as Hyde, kills her father, she still forgives him, kneeling by his side after he has taken the fatal poison, touching his hand as his deformed face returns to its original, handsome aspect.

With the introduction of these two female characters, the sexual dimension of the story is defined. The overt link of Evil to sex is one which the prudish Stevenson was unable or unwilling to make. In the Barrymore verson, Hyde frequents opium dens looking for young prostitutes who resemble Millicent; he visits Gina, paws her with his elongated fingers, and bites her with his vampire-like teeth. There is no doubt that the drive which this Jekyll has unleashed is lust. His blasphemy against God's laws of creation becomes but an expression of his sexual desire. The sin is defined on his first visit to Gina in the variety club, when he tells Carew, who has taken him there, that "You made me long for evil." It is expiated with the religious pronouncement, after Jekyll's suicide: "He has taken his own life. It is his atonement."

John Barrymore is the first in a series of prestigious actors who would appear in the dual role of Jekyll and Hyde. The attraction for any actor is obvious. It permits, even requires, a range of emotions and characteristics as few other parts do. Barrymore, with his extensive stage background, brought a mannered acting style to the screen. His famed profile embodied the "saintly" aspect of Jekyll. Remarkably when he transformed himself into Hyde, Barrymore eschewed make-up or special effects, at least in the initial changeover. While the camera kept running in a sustained medium shot, Barrymore demonstrated his skill in altering his physical appearance unaided by prosthetics, falling back from the laboratory table and out of sight briefly but otherwise remaining in full view. After this initial transformation, close-ups of Barrymore as Hyde reveal an elongated skull, lengthened fingers, and capped teeth which create a fuller image of the "pure evil" which Stevenson described. His distorted features even anticipate Murnau's title character in *Nosferatu* which would not be released until the following year.

Barrymore uses his hands to suggest the insect-like quality of the character, a metaphor further reinforced by the vision of a giant tarantula entering Jekyll's body before one of his transformations. When Jekyll fondles the women of the film, whether Gina or the prostitutes in the opium den, he uses those hands like claws. This is particularly ef-

Below, Barrymore as Hyde with a tavern crony (Louis Wolheim). Note the elongated and deformed fingers.

fective when Hyde pushes a young, still unblemished prostitute in front of full length mirror next to a timeworn colleague, a diseased and wasted woman, Forcing the younger woman to look at her future not only dramatically underscores Hyde's cruelty but again typifies the underlying dualism of both novella and film.

In his 1931 adaptation of **Dr. Jekyll and Mr. Hyde** Rouben Mamoulian carries over many of the elements of the Barrymore version but appends a modern, Freudian interpretation. As portrayed by Fredric March, Jekyll is more liberated in his attitudes towards sex. He goes from a playful interlude with his fiancée, Muriel, to a flirtation with a prostitute, Ivy, whom he rescues from an assailant. He makes this transition without a second thought. He unabashedly recognizes the sexual drive in himself, "I'm dying of thirst," he says in relation to his desire for Muriel and as a way of justifying his visit to the half-naked Ivy in her room. Unfortunately for Jekyll, Muriel's father, Carew, considers Jekyll's haste to marry his daughter "indecent" and so forbids it. This drives Jekyll back to his laboratory and his solitary work.

The monster which is released from Jekyll's soul by the potion is a Darwinian throwback, simian in features and movement. With an exclamation that he is "free, free at last," Hyde revels in his own strength. In Freudian terms, Hyde is Jekyll's Id, free of any supervisorial control by the Superego. He is free to make Ivy a sexual prisoner of his sadistic lust and later to attack Jekyll's beloved "angel," Muriel.

The visual style of the film also is keyed to this Freudian subtext. There are several montages in the film. The first occurs when Jekyll drinks the potion and changes himself into Hyde. As the camera spins dizzyingly, superimposed are images of Carew calling him "indecent," of his angelic Muriel, and of Ivy's gartered thigh, swinging provocatively.

The second montage occurs after Carew has taken his daughter away from Jekyll on an extended vacation, frustrating Jekyll's desire yet another time. Trying to resist the temptation of releasing the libidinous Hyde, he paces the room, his foot tapping nervously, his teeth biting down forcefully on his phallic pipe, a pot boiling in the corner. When he finally caves in to his desire, the pot explodes in an orgasmic reaction.

The duality of the film is further reinforced by the use of the wipe. In transitions from one scene to the next, Mamoulian employs a slow wipe which at midpoint simulates a split image. Especially meaningful is the image of Muriel on one side of the screen and Ivy on the other.

In 1941 MGM bought the rights to the Mamoulian film and remade it themselves, starring Spencer Tracy. Reflecting the more bourgeois sensibilities of MGM, the film is a bowdlerized version of the 1931 classic.

Above, Fredric March in the 1931 version: Hyde suddenly emerges while Jekyll strolls in the park.

All the same elements are present: the dualistic view of the universe, the sexual repression, the battle of good and evil in the person of Jekyll. However this version has little of the visual flair of its predecessor. As a representative example, when Jekyll spontaneously turns into Hyde while walking through a park, Mamoulian's version incorporates a cat attacking a bird into the scene, a visual metaphor for Hyde devouring Jekyll. The scene reappears in the MGM version, but without the symbolic cat and bird.

The character of Ivy is also toned down. As played by Ingrid Bergman she is much less aggressive and lewd in her initial meeting with Jekyll. The effect of this subtle performance is to diminish the contrast between her and Jekyll's fiancee. Tracy's Jekyll also has little of the *joie de vivre* or ebullience which characterized March as both Jekyll and Hyde. Tracy is more brooding as Jekyll and more brutal as Hyde. In fact most of the lines of dialogue in the original dealing with his "thirst for life" have been deleted. This Jekyll is a prig.

The only unique sequences in the film are the Freudian montages during Jekyll's transformations to Hyde. The images are redolent with sadomasochism. In the first transition Jekyll sees himself whipping his two women, Ivy and his fiancée, who are harnessed to a carriage which he drives. In the second transformation the women's heads become corks in vials. With great relish, he twists their heads, popping them in and out of the tubes.

As with the Frankenstein series, after Hollywood lost interest Hammer took up the Jekyll and Hyde saga. With *The Two Faces of Dr. Jekyll* (1960), much as he did in the Frankenstein cycle, Terence Fisher reinterpreted established stereotypes to uncover again the arrogance and ruthlessness that he saw in the Victorian era. Like Dr. Frankenstein, Fisher's Jekyll sees himself as beyond ordinary ethical considerations ("I'm not concerned with the moral operation.") and has adopted an overtly Nietzschean philosophy: "I'm beyond good and evil" and "The higher man is free of all restraint." He ignores the sick children whom he is studying and who, in gratitude, offer him flowers. He even pushes one of them to the ground. His single-mindedness has also alienated his wife, forcing her into the arms of his rakish friend, Paul.

Unlike Frankenstein, Fisher and screenwriter Wolf Mankowitz imagine a Jekyll whose arrogance and inhumanity are meant to mask a deep existential anguish. After he has tasted the pleasures of life as Hyde, he writes in his journal: "Do I want to return to a life of frustrated isolation and loveless misery?" When he tries to reconcile with his now embittered wife, he asks her ingenuously, "Who are you really? Who am I?"

More to escape this sense of alienation than out of scientific curiosity, he injects himself with the transformational serum. The Hyde who emerges from Jekyll's existential crisis is his opposite in some ways but his double in others. He is handsome, lighthearted, and sociable, qualities for which the sober Jekyll can only yearn; but in his arrogance Hyde is Jekyll's equal. His inhumanity is also revealed in relation to several other the characters in the film. He casually exploits the exotic dancer with whom he has formed a liaison, even dressing her in his wife's negligée. He kills his "best friend," Paul, with a snake which he borrows from his paramour. His most heinous crime is the rape of Jekyll's wife. In a disturbing sequence, Jekyll's wife stumbles out from the bed in which she has been violated and stares down at the skylight of the nightclub below. As the tempo of the music and the pace of the cutting accelerate simultaneously, she leaps to her death, crashing through the

Below, dualism in ad art.

Above, *The Two Face of Dr. Jekyll*: Paul Massie as the bearded, professorial scientist and the rakish, dissolute Hyde

glass onto the dismayed dancers below.

Hyde/Jekyll's drive to assuage his alienation leads him from buying sex and the attempted seduction of a young girl to opium dens and gambling parlors. He finally awakens one morning, as Jekyll, to find himself literally in the gutter, beaten and robbed. Although he resolves to never become Hyde again, as with Fredric March's anguished portrayal, this Jekyll's alienation is too strong. Hyde takes over Jekyll's body and even stages a mock suicide, burning the corpse of a working man whom he has killed to establish the demise of his burdensome alter ego.

In contrast to Fisher's version, Jean Renoir's rendering of the Jekyll/Hyde myth, *Le Testament du Dr. Cordelier* (1959), is cold and precise, unexpectedly so from a director celebrated for his humanity. Renoir's Jekyll, called Dr. Cordelier, is haunted by past moral lapses, including the sexual exploitation of his patients. As he observes, "I had a great thirst for cruelty." This guilt over past indiscretions is how he justifies his fascination with releasing his evil side. Parts of Cordelier's story are told in flashback by means of a tape recording, which makes Renoir's narrative one of the few which directly adapts Stevenson's construction of literary flashbacks in the novella through Jekyll's journal.

In many ways *Le Testament* is as much a *tour de force* for Renoir's lead actor, the celebrated Jean-Louis Barrault, as the silent version was for Barrymore. His singular performance counterposes his "Jekyll," a cold, distinguished man with a full head of gray hair and imposing stature against Opale—Hyde's name here—who is a cruel, anthropoidal prankster. He is first seen loping down the street and assaulting a child, as in the opening of Stevenson's story. In another scene he kicks the crutches out from under a crippled man. And while he plays the tape for Jekyll's colleague, he lies on a table, writhing and moaning like a wounded animal.

Ten years after *The Two Faces of Dr. Jekyll*, Amicus, Hammer's short-lived competitor in English horror, produced *I, Monster* (1970). Despite the presence of Hammer regulars, Christopher Lee and Peter Cushing, the retrogression between these adaptations is analogous to that between the Fredric March and Spencer Tracy versions. It fell to Hammer's own sequel the following year, *Dr. Jekyll and Sister Hyde* (1971) to create perhaps the most outrageous reinterpretation of the Jekyll/Hyde myth. As one might surmise from its title, this Hammer film features a transsexual Dr. Jekyll. Sexist as it may be, this Dr. Jekyll discovers that female hormones can most easily unleash his evil side. So through his experimentation he is transformed into the ultimate Victorian fantasy of what Ronald Pearsall calls in **The Worm in the Bud**, "the predatory woman." With Martine Beswick in the role, Sister Hyde is dark, sexually aggressive, and sepulchral in features, erotic but still slightly androgynous. But her most overt threat to the orderly expectations of Victorian society is her sexual manipulation of weak men. Women like Sister Hyde were, as Pearsall writes, believed by Victorians "to strike at men who were psychologically ill-equipped for

Below, Christopher Lee as a bulbous-nosed Hyde in *I, Monster*.

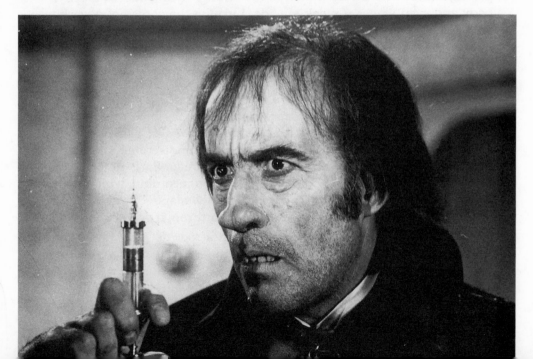

Above, two more faces of Jekyll: Ralph Bates (left) as the experimenter and Martine Beswick (right) as his transsexual alter ego in *Dr. Jekyll and Sister Hyde.*

the onslaught, at those who were uncertain of their sexual role...". "Awkward," "sensitive," and "effeminate"—all these adjectives used by Pearsall neatly describe Ralph Bates' lead performance as Dr. Jekyll.

By releasing the "demon woman" within himself, Jekyll precipitates a confusion of sexual roles that was entirely precluded by Victorian mores. When Sister Hyde forms a romantic liaison with the brother of Jekyll's "girlfriend," the web of conflicting emotions is further complicated. Is Sister Hyde as Jekyll still attracted to her/his male lover? Is Jekyll as Sister Hyde still flirting with his/her girlfriend? The homoerotic aspects of these confused identities and liaisons touch on sexual proclivities such as Lebianism that Victorians refused to admit even existed. In that sense Sister Hyde's seduction and murder of prostitutes in order to obtain their female hormones for Jekyll's experiments is remarkably deviant.

The phantasmagoric *Edge of Sanity* (1989) is in the immodest tradition of *Dr. Jekyll and Sister Hyde.* The film opens with a nightmarish flashback. In the midst of a thunderstorm, flashes of deep blue suffuse the screen as a young boy teeters on the edge of a loft. Below him is a young woman who taunts him with her laughter and sensual body. Presently the real object of her desire enters, an older, bearded man who proceeds to embrace her. As the flashes of lightning increase, the boy tumbles from the loft, his feet tangled in a nearby rope. The man sees him and whips him as the woman looks on.

This is the primal childhood memory of the illustrious Dr. Jekyll which reappears in variant forms throughout this surreal film. While experimenting with a new type of anaesthetic the melancholy and haunted Jekyll, portrayed by a lank Anthony Perkins, inhales the formula which releases Hyde. As Hyde, Jekyll searches the bordellos and streets of quasi-Victorian London in order to relive that childhood memory. In one encounter he orders the prostitute to masturbate in front of a young man, who is staring at her through a nearby window, while Hyde caresses her. When he finds a woman, Susannah, who most resembles the girl of his memory, he sets her up in a *menage à trois* with a local pimp so that Jekyll can watch them torture each other and "freebase" a narcotic formula which he has devised. By staging these events, Jekyll/Hyde clearly hopes to purge this memory; but this therapy only intensifies his malaise.

The visual style of this film is reminiscent of Ken Russell, not just in the supernatural piece *The Lair of the White Worm* but even more in his 1984 film *Crimes of Passion*, which dealt with psychological disturbance and also starred Perkins. The color scheme is saturated with blues and reds in the night scenes, as he searches for prostitutes, and in the bordello where his favorite whore, Susannah, resides. In contrast, the color scheme at Jekyll's residence and at the hospital is much more subdued and desaturated. Like Russell's films, *Edge of Sanity* uses its sexually charged material and conscious anachronism to sustain the mood of nightmare. The hyper-modern look of Jekyll's white, sterile laboratory contrasts blindingly with his warm Victorian mansion. Prostitutes who wear miniskirts and sport jeweled crosses but speak with Victorian inflections further unsettle the preconceptions of the audience.

Below, Anthony Perkins as Jekyll.

Television producers have also freely adapted Stevenson's novella, although not as frequently as Shelley's work. In 1968 Dan Curtis produced a television movie which reemphasized the array of metaphysical, moral and scientific concerns of the original without abandoning the Freudian imagery of previous versions. Using Stevenson's full title, *The Strange Case of Dr. Jekyll and Mr. Hyde* begins from the same basic moral premise as the original: good and evil are inborn and Jekyll's purpose is "to erase man's baser instinct" by freeing it. As in the 1931 film, in an early scene Jekyll proclaims this belief to a skeptical audience of fellow scientists and doctors. As they become openly hostile, Jekyll merely smiles because his colleagues' very behavior validates his theory that "All men are relatively primitive beings."

Curtis' version eliminates the character of Jekyll's fiancée, who is not present in the novella, removing one component of the sexual conflict common to the Barrymore, March, and Tracy vehicles. Curtis does keep the "temptress" figure, here named Gwynn, who, as in the former versions, triggers Jekyll's lust. When he first visits her as Jekyll, his fascination is complete. He even drops his aloof pose to linger shyly by her side.

Coincident with this readjustment of the sexual component of the story, the moral and scientific considerations return to the foreground. Jack Palance as Jekyll is far more reserved and serious than either March or Tracy and in that sense most strongly resembles Stevenson's character. Like his literary prototype, Palance's Jekyll is obsessed with his mission. His torment when Hyde comes to dominate his personality is as much over the loss of scientific detachment as it is over his alter ego's abhorrent behavior. Palance's Hyde also differs greatly from that of Barrymore, March, and Tracy. With prominent brows and cheekbones, he is far less simian in aspect and much more amiable. At the

Below, Jack Palance as Hyde.

club where Gwynn works, he is actually liked rather than feared. Even Gwynn is not immediately repulsed by him, as were her counterparts in the earlier versions. This Hyde is libidinous and forceful but also humorous and somewhat debonair. He is so engaging that even Jekyll finds him attractive which again conforms to Stevenson's work. When Jekyll of the novella releases Hyde for the first time, he describes the experience: "And yet when I looked upon that ugly idol in the glass, I was conscious of no repugnance, rather a leap of welcome...In my eyes it bore a livelier image of the spirit, it seemed more express and single than the imperfect and divine countenance I had been hitherto accustomed to call mine." Curtis parallels this description when his character returns from his night on the town as Hyde. He improvises a ditty: "Oh, Hyde, don't let me go. You're such a devil and I love you so."

Other television versions have been far less scrupulous about returning to the tone and substance of **The Strange Case of Dr. Jekyll and Mr. Hyde**. A 1973 production turned Jekyll/Hyde into a singing star (stars?). *Dr. Jekyll and Mr. Hyde* casts Kirk Douglas in three unlikely roles: Jekyll, Hyde, and musical performer. Using the plot of the various theatrical and film predecessors, the conflict of good and evil was reduced to the stuff of show tunes.

Showtime and Think Entertainment also produced a version as part of their "Nightmare Classics" series. Their *The Strange Case of Dr. Jekyll and Mr. Hyde* (1989) posits a Jekyll who seems to suffer from nothing more than a severe case of bashfulness, and Hyde is just the one to pull him out of it.

Just as Mel Brooks' *Young Frankenstein* mocked the conventions and icons of the Frankenstein films, Jerry Lewis' *The Nutty Professor* (1963) comically deconstructed the Jekyll/Hyde story. In Lewis' hands Jekyll becomes the fumbling, bumbling, buck-toothed Professor Julius Kelp, who alternates between blowing up labs and being shelved, literally, by hypertrophic football players. Like many of his serious antecedents, he is sexually repressed and desperately in love. The object of his desire is a classic blonde "bombshell" named Stella.

Lewis compresses the typical female dichotomy into Stella's single persona and creates a "modern woman" a la Marilyn Monroe who can be both virgin and whore. In a montage, Kelp drools over her curvaceous figure whether costumed in a virginal, white tennis outfit or a slinky red gown. As the strains of the classic tune, "Stella by Starlight," play in the background whenever she is present, Kelp's obsession with winning her is comically reinforced aurally as well as visually.

To achieve his objective, he turns first to body building and joins a gym where he is pummeled and stretched until he is weaker than when he entered. Returning to his class swathed in bandages but determined to build a better Jekyll worthy of his dream girl, he retreats to the world he knows best: his laboratory, a fantasy of multicolored liquids and oversized beakers, an overt cartoon of the labs in earlier films.

Professor Kelp's transformation into *The Nutty Professor*'s Hyde correlative, Buddy Love, is a complete send-up. In the darkened lab, the beat of a heart mixes with ominous crescendoes on the soundtrack.

Above, Stella Stevens as Stella (left) and Jerry Lewis as Kelp in *The Nutty Professor.*

After Kelp passes through a transition stage in which he begins to resemble March's simian Hyde, Lewis exploits the audience's expectations of the emergence of a monstrous figure by switching to a subjective camera. As he enters the local teen hangout, a shot from the as-yet-unnamed Buddy Love's perspective pans over the stunned faces of the patrons. When Lewis finally cuts, the comic irony is revealed. Kelp/Lewis has turned himself into a slick-haired, obnoxious, handsome, boozy, singing lounge lizard who bears an uncanny resemblance to Lewis' erstwhile partner, Dean Martin. As a fan later exclaims, "He's one of the truly great swingers of all time."

Buddy courts Stella who is both attracted and repulsed by this unctuous Lothario. For his part, Kelp keeps trying to repossess his body as evidenced when Kelp's squeaky tenor periodically inserts itself into the smooth, baritone song stylings of Buddy Love. As satire, this tale is permitted if not required to have a happy ending. Stella finally extricates the sincere and sensitive Kelp from the mass of inflated ego which is Buddy Love. In the end all this "Dr. Jekyll" really needed for redemption and sexual fulfillment was a set of braces for his buck teeth. What might Robert Louis Stevenson have thought?

Above, Hurd Harfield as Dorian Gray and the decayed portrait in the 1945 *The Picture of Dorian Gray*.

II. The Cynic: Oscar Wilde (1854-1900)

When they entered, they found hanging upon the wall a splendid portrait of their master as they had last seen him, in all the wonder of his exquisite youth and beauty. Lying on the floor was a dead man, in evening dress, with a knife in his heart, he was withered, wrinkled, and loathsome of visage. It was not till they had examined the rings that they recognized who it was.

Oscar Wilde, The Picture of Dorian Gray

The Unholy Grail

Albert Lewin's first experience as a writer and director was the adaptation of W. Somerset Maugham's fictionalized biography of painter Paul Gauguin, **The Moon and Sixpence**. Lewin's script for his *The Moon and Sixpence* considered the nature of the somewhat aberrant, artistic temperament in a naturalistic manner. His next project was Oscar Wilde's novella, **The Picture of Dorian Gray** (1881). In some ways, with its supernatural context and absence of historical figures, this was a radically different subject than Maugham's novel. And yet Gauguin the subject and Wilde the author were part of the same *fin de siécle* aesthetic and shared certain philosophical concepts on the state of European civilization. While Gauguin's monomania finally led him to physical flight from that civilization and its bourgeois values, Wilde's egocentricity led him to another type of flight. Wilde retreated inwardly and shielded himself behind a wall of unassailable cynicism. In his adaptations, Lewin derives much the same drama from the plight of both men, for both were fallen idealists, misanthropes unable to reconcile their innate romanticism with the repressive realities of Victorian society. The admixture of aesthetic appreciation and sensory pleasures, the aspects and preservation of beauty, these were equally important to the writer Wilde as to the painter Gauguin. As Wilde has Lord Henry Wotton remark shortly after meeting Dorian Gray: "A new Hedonism— that is what our century wants. You might be its visible symbol." How deliciously ironic Wilde might have found it that the MGM logo on the film of his novel bears the motto, "Ars gratia artis."

Lewin's *The Picture of Dorian Gray* is closer to its source material in narrative structure than many of the other adaptations considered in this study. This may be partly due to the fact that Wilde's novella, being

fiction of intermediate length, required less condensing or extrapolating
than the typical novel or short story would. Wilde also developed the
plot of his book with an episodic structure more akin to his own poetry
and plays than the prose of his contemporaries. While the narrative
divergences are few, there are certain key changes. Wilde makes Sibyl
Vane, Dorian's first love, an actress. Her ability, her "genius," as much
as her beauty are what actually enthrall Dorian. Lewin makes her a
music hall singer, whose voice has the same effect. This subtle shift
permits Lewin to introduce the concept of class distinctions. More importantly, the Dorian of Wilde's novella, breaks with Sibyl Vane because, distracted by her love for him, her acting has suddenly become
deficient. Wilde, whose concepts of art and love underscore all his writing, uses Wotton to attack Dorian's aesthetic heresy: "My dear boy, no
woman is a genius. Women are a decorative sex." In this value system,
it is entirely appropriate that she should be spurned for a wretched performance. For Lewin's Wotton, love of the uneducated and ill-bred Sibyl
represents social heresy. Whether an actress or a singer, for Wotton of
either novel or film, who "has loved so many of them," women of this
sort are meant only for carnal not emotional love. It is Lewin's Wotton,
however, that suggests to Dorian that he test Sibyl by making sexual
demands and who knows this strategy cannot fail.

In the film, the exposition of the main premise is not complicated.
While posing for a painting by his friend Basil Hallward, Dorian Gray is
introduced to the dissolute Lord Wotton. Dorian complains of being
depressed that the painting is almost finished and that, while his
visage on canvas will now remain perpetually youthful, the real person
he will see every day in the mirror will grow old. In a display of arcane
knowledge, Wotton notices that Dorian is posing with an Egyptian ar-
tifact of considerable antiquity, the golden statue of a cat which has the
legendary power to grant wishes. Jokingly, Dorian wishes to remain
young and to let the figure in the painting take on the all the corruption
and decay of advancing age.

Even for a viewer not familiar with Wilde's novella, the construction
and genre indicators in this opening are remarkably explicit. As easily
as Mephistopheles before Faust, the cat of "the seventy-three dynasties"
grants Dorian's wish. Unlike Faust or any other of the classic figures
who sell their souls, Dorian Gray does not do so purposefully. In fact,
he is at first completely unaware than any preternatural deal has been
struck.

For Lewin, whose few other films include the remarkable mixed myth
in modern dress, *Pandora and the Flying Dutchman*, and *The Living
Idol*, inspired by Aztec legends, it is the classical aspect of Wilde's

original which merits most attention. Lewin's Dorian is even slower to learn than Wilde's character of his unique condition. This both prolongs the audience's uncertainty and heightens the tension. Clearly all but the most obtuse viewer realizes that the dialogue about the cat's power and Dorian's half-serious wish are not idle chitchat. But the longer Lewin refuses to confirm what the audience expects, indeed what those who have read Wilde know, the longer he proceeds with the naturalistic development of the story line and the longer this tension continues to build.

Dorian does fall under the influence of Lord Wotton, but Lewin conceals the extent of his desire to mimic Wotton's decadent lifestyle. His romance with Sibyl Vane, the sexually innocent music hall singer, who dubs the handsome and kindly Dorian, "Sir Tristan," is an interplay of types. As the young and enthusiastic Sibyl and the jaded Wotton are emblematic of the contrasting emotional impulses within Dorian, the title figure himself, as played by Hurd Hatfield, never lowers his emotional mask. The restrained gestures and short range of facial expressions which Hatfield is permitted again frustrate any viewer who is trying to "read" the character on film. When Dorian plays a Chopin prelude for Sibyl, she remarks on how unhappy the music sounds. Dorian's explanation of the composer's forlorn love for George Sand is non-committal. On the one hand, such a love is the very thing which Wotton superciliously condemns. On the other, Dorian realizes that such pure emotion could be the cure for his abiding disaffection.

Below, Hurd Hatfield as Dorian and George Sanders as the jaded Lord Henry.

The wriest moment of the film, when Dorian reads Sibyl a passage from a book by a rising young author named Oscar Wilde, is also its fulcrum point. Soon thereafter, Wotton savagely mocks Dorian's infatuation with Sibyl; but when Dorian rejects his callous suggestion that he seduce her and have done with it, Wotton has an alternate proposal. Dorian should put her chastity to the test and see if her love for "Sir Tristan" is as pure as it seems. Dorian succumbs to the misogynistic logic of Wotton's argument. When a tearful Sibyl agrees to sleep with Dorian rather than lose him, she fails the test. The disillusioned Dorian writes a demeaning letter to Sibyl, who despairs and commits suicide.

In narrative terms, the effect of this tragic relationship with Sibyl is to convince Dorian that, having made the wish, he is fated to experience its consequences, to live corruptly and to watch the blemishes from that corruption slowly appear on the face of the portrait. When Dorian first notices a slight change in the expression of his painted likeness, he is still not sure whether the change is real or a product of his inflamed imagination. After Sibyl's death, the changes are still superficial; but there can no longer be any doubt that they are real. Dorian's removal of the painting from public view is the symbolic acceptance of his unwittingly made, Faustian contract.

In Wilde's piece, Dorian finds the transformation of the object a clear condemnation of his behavior, etched by the same unseen hand that predestined his fall from grace. Lewin translates Wilde's determinism into visual terms. When Dorian is alone in his drawing room, the camera repeatedly moves and reframes, each time forging a new visual link between the human figure, the picture, and the statue of the cat. The three principals in the metaphysical exchange are bound together within the graphic confines of the shot. In another sequence, Basil Hallward, disturbed by the changes in Dorian's behavior, comes to urge him to return to his former self. As the two men speak, the cat sits between them on the table. In the two dimensions of the film plane, the golden figure of the cat represents not merely the fate which grips Dorian and separates him psychologically from Basil. In Lewin's visual scheme, the objects are in some respect the center of the story and more significant that the human figures whom they control. The images are made to underscore this conception. So intent was Lewin on the visual impact of the object which is the title of the film that, in its initial release, *The Picture of Dorian Gray* had clips of the portrait shot in full Technicolor spliced into its otherwise black-and-white prints.

Because of or despite these elaborate visual metaphors, the Faustian context of *The Picture of Dorian Gray* permits classic supernatural

Left, Dorian (Hurd Hatfield) plays for Sibyl Vane (Angela Lansbury) in *The Picture of Dorian Gray.*

melodrama. Lewin's understated staging, the muted performances by the principal actors, create an almost sedate undertone. Angela Lansbury as Sibyl gives her consuming love for Dorian a hopelessness that seems borne from the lyrics of the music hall songs which are her livelihood. In a sense her lower-class costumes and ill-bred accent control her fate as forcefully as Dorian's wish determines his. Lansbury's portrayal evokes the same stereotype as Shaw's "Pygmalion" or Thomas Burke's Limehouse stories, which rely on a darkly comic bathos for dramatic impact. But the naturalistic touches, as when Sibyl first sees Dorian in the audience and becomes so flustered that she skips a line in her song, help to transcend the purely stereotypical. In contrast, George Sanders as Henry Wotton is type casting which exploits audience expectation based on Sanders' previous roles. For Lewin, Sanders had played Gauguin in *The Moon and Sixpence*, which was somewhat against type; but well before that role he had established a professional persona as an effete. sardonic, and vaguely threatening snob. Sanders' interpretation renders perfectly the bored decadence of Sir Henry; he is, in the early part of the film, the only actor decisive enough to attract and sustain viewer interest.

Hurd Hatfield's passive Dorian plays against both Sibyl's emotionalism and Wotton's contempt. His detachment reinforces the otherworldliness of his predicament. As it happens, this was Hatfield's first, and practically last, major role. He was cast after a highly publicized talent search for the beautiful youth of Wilde's invention. Lewin tailors the plot to his physical mien. The lighting scheme in most scenes, the broad, high-key that illuminates the detailed sets typical of

MGM means that Hatfield's face changes less in expression than in contour and depth. In dramatically charged moments, such as Dorian's murder of Basil Hallward, the lighting scheme changes radically. A hanging lamp, which the struggle between the two men has caused to swing wildly, becomes the source of illumination. With each oscillation the pivoting shadows and pulsing light play across Dorian's face like wild emotions. But Hatfield's chiseled features are never contorted from within. Like Dorian's dissolution, his emotions are reserved for the portrait. Even after Dorian has decided to regain control of his unnatural existence, even at the moment he plunges a knife in the picture's heart and sunders his diabolical pact only to destroy himself in the process, Hatfield's performance retains an underlying placidity.

Lewin's staging of Hallward's murder may take inspiration from Wilde's description of the ascent to Dorian's attic where a "lamp cast fantastic shadows on the wall and ceiling." Not only did Lewin reuse the effect of the swinging light to evoke a moment of terror in later films, but it reappears in *The Secret of Dorian Gray* (1972). This contemporary adaptation, which features a portrait of a bare-chested Dorian clad in hip-hugger bell bottoms and scarf, treats Dorian's depraved behavior like a tabloid exposé.

Secret actually opens with the murder of Hallward and uses an extended flashback to reveal past events. The flashback suggests that the film may take a subjective point of view, a possibility reinforced visually by the literal point-of-view shots that follow an unseen character's bloody hands as he walks to a sink to wash them. Neither the narrative nor the stylistic expectations are fulfilled in *The Secret of Dorian Gray*. The sex scenes, which should not be gratuitous, are. The matching zooms and cuts in and out of flames or red walls have more energy than the actors and only underscore the emptiness of the staging.

The earliest adaptation of Wilde's work is reputedly a Danish short from 1910. The first features, also from the silent era were produced between 1915 and 1917 in Great Britain, Hungary, and Germany; but until Lewin's version, there were no others. Nor has Dorian Gray proved as popular with contemporary filmmakers as Hyde or Frankenstein's monster. There are two U.S.-made television versions. The first from 1961 featured George C. Scott as a much less urbane but more energetic Wotton than George Sanders. Dan Curtis' lengthier production made twelve years later featured a cherubic Shane Briant as Dorian. As with other Curtis adaptations, the stated intention was a faithful rendering of the original plot. Much as with the adaptation of Bram Stoker's **Dracula**, **Frankenstein**, or **The Strange Case of Dr. Jekyll and Mr. Hyde** discussed earlier in this chapter, Curtis and his fellow filmmakers attempted a characterization that stressed the good intentions of the figure enmeshed by evil. Unlike Jack Palance as Dracula and Jekyll/Hyde, Briant's Dorian lacks the power, either in emotional resolve or sheer physical presence, to confront the trick of fate that Wilde posits. In a sense, this is faithful to Wilde's characterization, but it is also difficult to sustain viewer identification with such a portrayal particularly over more than two hours of running time.

As it happens, there is also a Dorian Gray equivalent of *Dr. Jekyll and Sister Hyde* in another television adaptation, *The Sins of Dorian Gray* (1983), which stars Belinda Bauer as a female Dorian and Anthony Perkins as a thoroughly dissolute Wotton figure named Henry Lord. While fashion had moved beyond hip huggers and bell bottoms, like the androgynous title character of *The Secret of Dorian Gray*, the "thoroughly modern Dorian" of this version is a far cry from Wilde's *naïf*.

Ultimately none of these film adaptations stress the one supernatural element any more than Wilde did. Wilde's prose style uses a slight dramatic emphasis at the end of each chapter for transitions and some of his descriptions may have seemed shocking at the time; but overall Wilde follows the preferences of Lord Henry: "I don't like scenes, except on the stage."

Below, two faces of Dorian Gray and their portraits: Shane Briant (left) in the Dan Curtis version and Helmut Berger (right) in *The Secret of Dorian Gray*.

III. The Mystic: Arthur Machen (1863-1947)

And yet, I said to myself, these two have partaken together of the great
mystery, of the great sacrament of nature, of the source of all that is
magical in the wide world. But have they discerned the mysteries? Do
they know that they have been in that place which is called Syon and
Jerusalem?

> Arthur Machen, introduction to **The House of Souls**

Pantheistic Evil

Of all the authors treated in this study Arthur Machen is probably the
least familiar to the general reading public, even to those who consider
themselves devotées of the supernatural genre. A simple, underlying
cause for this might well be that Machen's books have always been
rare, even in their first printings. For a brief period in the 1920s, many
of Machen's older works were republished along with a few newer
pieces by Martin Secker in London and Alfred A. Knopf in New York.
With writers as disparate in taste as James Branch Cabell and John
Dos Passos expressing their admiration for Machen, Secker and Knopf
might have hoped that his works would finally find an audience; if so,
they were overly optimistic.

At their best Machen's stories are extremely personal, mystical, and
lyrical pieces held together by their expressive qualities and a minimum
of plot. Even the more popular horror tales such as "The Great God
Pan" (1894) are driven by a sense of the arcane, of obscure, pantheistic
evil. This quality rather than any novelty in plot construction or any
knack for storytelling impels Machen's prose. In a literary market at-
tuned to the realism of a Fitzgerald or a Hemingway, the hard-boiled
genre work of Hammett and Chandler, and even the complex but explicitly horrific myths of Lovecraft, Machen found no toehold; and he
remains mostly out of print.

Machen spent most of his life with a minimal income, supplemented
in later years by a small government pension, and dabbled in almost
every style of writing and genre in order to eke out a living. When writing for himself he always returned to his first love: the legends of Wales
and the Celtic mysticism he had absorbed in his youth. That youth was
spent among the valleys and hills of Caerleon-on-Usk in Wales. There
he was nurtured on the local legends: of King Arthur, who in Welsh
tradition held court in Caerleon and rode by with his queen and en-

tourage; of the ancient woods where malevolent "little people" lurked, awaiting unsuspecting children; and of the **Mabinogion**, the Welsh saga of ancient heroes, including King Arthur. When worshipping in the parish church, Machen was also mindful of the hagiography and rituals of the ancient Celtic Church of Wales.

These legends left their mark on a young, solitary Welshman. They sustained Machen's imaginative efforts from his early years to his later life in London, where he remained the same shy and lonely individual. In **Far Off Things** (1922) Machen himself speaks of the importance of his heritage:

> I shall always esteem it as the greatest piece of fortune that has fallen to me, that I was born in the noble, fallen Caerleon-on-Usk, in the heart of Gwent. My greatest fortune, I mean, from that point of view which I now more especially have in mind, the career of letters. For the older I grow the more firmly am I convinced that anything which I may have accomplished in literature is due to the fact that when my eyes were first opened in earliest childhood they had before them the vision of an enchanted land.

Many of Machen's predilections as a youth and as a young man can be gleaned from his autobiographical and semi-autobiographical works: **The Secret Glory** (written in 1895; published 1922); **The Hill of Dreams** (1907); **Far Off Things** (1922); and **Things Near and Far** (1923). They are the stories of lonely protagonists, alienated by the vulgarity and tawdriness of life in a materialist society, often symbolized by the city of London, protagonists who gradually withdraw from the real world into their own mystical yet frightening world of myth.

The Hill of Dreams and **The Secret Glory** are the pinnacles in this series of autobiographical writings. Machen varied his style with an almost schizophrenic drive during his career, and these pieces are very much in the tradition of such Decadent, *fin-de-siécle* writers as Baudelaire, Gautier, Flaubert, Huysmans, Pater, *and* Wilde. The structure is loose, more a series of vignettes told in a Joyceian stream of consciousness from the viewpoints of sensitive artists, "Lucian Taylor" in the first and "Ambrose Meyrick" in the second. But Machen's characters go well beyond Stephen Dedalus in **A Portrait of the Artist as a Young Man** in that their interior mystical experiences become more intense as the outside world becomes more oppressive.

This alienation from the real world is not the only characteristic shared with the Decadents. Machen's literary tropes, his use of color images, and his lyrical prose often parallels that of Gautier or Pater. **The Hill of Dreams**. for example, opens with these lines: "There was a glow in the sky as if great furnace doors were opened. But all afternoon his eyes had looked on glamor; he had strayed in fairyland. The holidays were nearly done, and Lucian Taylor had gone out resolved to lose himself, to discover strange hills and prospects that he had never seen before."

Similarly the imagery at the end of the book, after Lucian's death, conveys much of the emotion of the story: "The man took up the blazing paraffin lamp, and set it on the desk, beside the scattered heap of that terrible manuscript. The flaring light shone through the dead eyes into the dying brain, and there was glow within, as if great furnace doors were opened."

The simile of the furnace and the use of red is particularly effective in conveying the intensity of Lucian's mystical experiences—experiences which finally lead to his physical dissolution, through drugs and sex, as well as a concomitant spiritual release. The same imagery plays a part in **The Secret Glory** as Ambrose finds his own spiritual release through martyrdom: "And after he had hung on the tree some hours, the infidels, enraged, as it was said, by the shining rapture of his face, killed him with their spears...It was in this manner that Ambrose Meyrick gained Red Martyrdom and achieved the most glorious Quest and Adventure of the Sangraal."

The image of the "Sangraal" or "Holy Grail" or "Holy Cup of Teilo Sant" is central to Machen's more introspective works. Of course, this quest for the Grail, the cup reputedly used by Christ at the Last Supper, runs throughout Celtic legend; but in Machen's symbology. it is more than a search for a relic. As a quest, it totally embodies man's intense need for ecstatic, mystical experience and ultimate spiritual transcendence.

This feeling of alienation from the mundane, materialistic world is even more keenly felt in **A Fragment of Life** (1906). In this novel, Machen describes a dull clerk and his wife who return to their roots in Wales in search of "the Great Mystery," which they hope can give their lives the meaning that they lack. In Wales they find "the Mystery," the spiritual experience which can sustain them; and, like Lucian Taylor and Ambrose Meyrick, they pierce the veil of Maya and discover the "ultimate reality."

What interest does exist in Machen's work today is centered largely on his horror tales rather than his more personal works. As in the more mystical pieces, the world of supernatural horror which Machen creates is a dramatic nexus where the spiritual is again the "ultimate reality" and the material world only a Platonic shadow game. In these tales, however, that resplendent spiritualism of Ambrose Meyrick and Lucian Taylor is transformed into a malevolent, destructive, pantheistic power. As it does when taken up by Lovecraft, this power lurks on the edge of that material world and seeks an opening, a fissure through which it can burst full force.

"The Great God Pan" is justifiably the most famous of these tales. It combines and distills many of the elements which are present in Machen's other horror pieces. There is the character of the sleuth/researcher, but one who is quite fallible and a far cry from Conan Doyle's contemporaneous Sherlock Holmes. There is also the evocation of crowded, urban centers, particularly London, counterposed against idyllic countrysides in Wales and Machen's birthplace Caerleon. Finally there is the sense of "other-worldliness," of Machen's "eternal mystery," which in these stories leads not to transcendence but to terror and death.

Like so many of his predecessors in 19th Century horror literature, Machen had a predilection for telling stories in retrospect, through journals, letters, and personal narrations. While this has a tendency to slow up the development of the narrative, Machen's concern was never, as we have pointed out, one of plot. In writing which relies so heavily on atmosphere and descriptive style, this indirection can actually prolong the suspense. Almost as a bridge between Poe and Lovecraft, the distinctive element in Machen's schematic of horror is the manner in which the sense of mystical evil is created. Because it emanates from a central source that is, in the pantheistic tradition, never clearly defined evil in Machen is never fully detailed. Given only hints and clues as to the power and source of this "great mystery," the reader is left all the more frightened by the lack of specificity.

In "The Great God Pan" the story is of a child, Helen Vaughan, born of a woman who, after surgery, has a vision of evil. This child's history is associated with horror and destruction. She leaves several victims in her path, victims who witnessed the organic growth of some horrible force around her. What is this force? There are allusions to the pagan god Pan, but it is never defined. Readers are left to fill in the details of the evil for themselves.

> Here too was all the work by which man had been made repeated before my eyes. I saw the form waver from sex to sex, dividing itself from itself, and then again reunited. Then I saw the body descend to the beasts whence it ascended, and that which was on the heights go down to the depths, even to the abyss of all being...I watched, and at last I saw nothing but a substance as jelly. The ladder was ascended again....for one I saw a form, shaped in dimness before, which I will not further describe. But the symbol of this form may be seen in ancient sculptures, and paintings which survived beneath the lava, too foul to be spoken of...as a horrible and

unspeakable shape, neither man nor beast, was changed into human form, there came finally death.

This understated yet terrifying evocation in the final dissolution and death of Helen is a near-parody of those of Lucian Taylor and Ambrose Meyrick in that Helen's fate leads like theirs to a release of the soul but unlike theirs through union with the principle of evil.

At times, Machen is quite specific in delineating this arcane evil which permeates his stories; and often the source is Celtic legend. Machen incorporates a purely Celtic imagery of evil into "The Novel of the Black Seal" which appeared in an anthology entitled **The Three Impostors** (1895), stories loosely strung together in the manner of Robert Louis Stevenson's **The New Arabian Nights**.

Machen's malefactors here are the Celtic "little people" and his interpretation of this myth through the person of Professor Gregg:

> More particularly I became convinced that much of the folklore of the world is but an exaggerated account of events that really happened, and I was especially drawn to consider the stories of the fairies, the good folk of the Celtic races...Just as our remote ancestors called the dreaded beings 'fair' and 'good' precisely because they dreaded them, so they had dressed them up in charming forms, knowing the truth to be the reverse...Then, again, there are myths darker still; the dread of witch and wizard, the lurid evil of the Sabbath, and the hint of demons who mingled with the daughters of men.

Below, in the tradition of the Great God Pan: at the base of a druidical oak, Oliver Haddo (Paul Wegerner) watches while a horned figure invites Margaret Dauncey (Alice Terry) to dance in *The Magician*.

Much as William Butler Yeats, Machen's brother in The Hermetic Order of the Golden Dawn, did in his **Celtic Twilight**, Machen dispels the mawkish, puerile aura which surrounded Celtic legend and restores it to its original moral and metaphysical dimensions.

In "The Novel of the Black Seal" Professor Gregg investigates strange occurrences in and around Caerleon, reports of disappearances, possessions, bizarre rituals. Piecing information together from what he has witnessed, the runes on the Black Seal itself, and his knowledge of ethnology, Gregg comes to the unsettling conclusion that the "little people," the "lost race," has regained a foothold in this isolated area. As in "The Great God Pan" the ramifications of this reinvasion are not explored in detail. When Gregg himself disappears mysteriously, the thrust of the horror is magnified now that the only one with knowledge of it is gone.

This final ambiguity appears again in two of Machen's longer works of supernatural horror: **The Terror** (1917) and **The Green Round** (1933). **The Terror** is Machen's most moralistic work, a precursor of Orwell's **Animal Farm**, in which a reign of terror over England begins as animals, particularly pets and domestic beasts, turn against their masters. There is a strong resemblance as well to Daphne du Maurier's later story "The Birds," as England is plagued by daily reports of humans being maimed or killed by dogs, sheep, horses, and cattle.

The most gripping scene in the novel is the siege of the occupied farmhouse by its former livestock. It is recounted in a discovered manuscript written by a guest who is witness to the event and is left alone to face the final horror. The style is appropriately apocalyptic in tone:

> Only a little while ago I heard a voice which sounded as if it were at my very ears, but rang and echoed and resounded as if it were rolling and reverberated from the vault of some cathedral, chanting in terrible modulations. I heard the words quite clearly...*Incipit liber irae Domini Dei nostri* (Here beginneth The Book of Wrath of the Lord Our God).

The terror continues unabated throughout the country while the government, in the midst of fighting World War I, tries desperately to hide the information from the general populace then, unsuccessful in this, shifts the blame to a more convenient and believable enemy, German saboteurs. But whatever the political implications of any subterfuge to obfuscate the real situation, Machen's theme is explicit enough. In fighting this savage war and in living a increasingly materialistic life, mankind has unleashed the evil forces in nature. This is borne out in the novel's final lines about man:

For long ages he has been putting off this royal robe, he has been wiping the balm of consecration from his own breast. He has declared, again and again, that he is not spiritual, but rational, that is, the equal of the beasts over whom he was once sovereign. He has vowed that he is not Orpheus but Caliban...If he were not king he was a sham, an impostor, a thing to be destroyed...Hence, I think, the terror. They have risen once—they may rise again.

The proportions of the menace in **The Green Round** are not as staggering as those in **The Terror** but unsettling nevertheless. This novel begins with some strange and occult incidents reported in a Welsh resort town. All of these center on a green round of land. As disappearances and mayhem directed against visitors increase, bizarre light and sounds are witnessed and, according to some, ancient pagan rituals are again taking place. Into this atmosphere comes the ostensible hero of the book, Lawrence Hillyer, who as he launches his own investigations finds himself haunted by a dwarfish individual and subjected to strange hallucinations. Driven half-mad by this, Hillyer is finally forced into seclusion to avoid his dwarfish nemesis. In the end he goes abroad, leaving his investigations of the green round to more detached specialists. In the epilogue Machen hints, in the manner Lovecraft would embellish, at an evil seeping through fissures in the universe and emerging in Wales.

Arthur Machen also had numerous works which do not fit into the categories of horror or autobiography. He translated **Casanova's Memoirs** into what is now the definitive English version. He wrote a series of tales set in the Medieval period, **The Chronicle of Clemendy** (1888), modeled after Rabelais and Boccaccio, both of whom he greatly admired. He wrote humorous and satirical pieces such as **The Anatomy of Tobacco** (1884), the title of which announces a parody of Robert Burton's **Anatomy of Melancholy,** and **Dog and Duck** (1924). He wrote a book of criticism called appropriately enough **Hieroglyphics** (1902), again demonstating his very aesthetic approach to literature. He even wrote, in stark contrast to the occult, the lyrical, or the spiritual, essays of dry, journalistic prose often debunking popular myths not that far removed from the Celtic lore that he cherished. Machen was an extraordinarily prolific writer, filled with contradictions and conflict. In his preface to the anthology, **Tales of Horror and the Supernatural** (1948) writer Robert Hillyer gives a succinct summary of Machen in his declining years: "An occultist, a mystic, and a devout Anglo-Catholic, Machen had more appetite, zest, bulk, and general enjoyment of the creature comforts of this world than any epicure."

None of Machen's stories have been adapted to the screen, although they contain many of the elements which filmmakers seek. They are visual, they feature palpable horror, and they use myth and legend for genre context. Not suprisingly Machen's thematic preoccupations coincide with certain films of supernatural horror. An early example is Rex Ingram's 1926 film, *The Magician*, adapted from a work by W. Somerset Maugham and starring the German actor Paul Wegener, best known for his work in *The Golem*. Wegener is the magician of the title, a hypnotist and would-be alchemist with a self-professed obsession akin to Victor Frankenstein's: "The scientific creation of life does indeed call for a magician." The conclusion of *The Magician* would seem, in fact, to have influenced James Whale, who transposed Ingram's images of the isolated, Gothic laboratory during a thunderstorm and the burning, hilltop tower into his Frankenstein films.

It is the presence of the great god Pan that is most suggestive of Machen. The opening sequence reveals Margaret Dauncey putting the finishing touches on a huge clay model of a planned statue of Pan. As she works, the clay ruptures under its own weight, and a close shot captures the smiling, horned face falling onto her. After her recovery she unwittingly comes under the hypnotic influence of Wegener's character. In a fantasy sequence, a dissolve takes Margaret while in a spell from the sculpted face of Pan to an animated figure playing the pipes and presiding over a pagan sabbath.

The pagan tradition of Celtic druidism figures prominently in a number of films, from *Night of the Demon* to *The Wicker Man* (1973), where the Machen-like world of druid ritual is reified in this graphic story of human sacrifice and the reemergence of ancient gods. In terms of its ominous pantheism, Alfred Hitchcock's *The Birds* (1963) also relates to Machen's world view. As already noted, the revolt of the birds against their masters is in theme, treatment, and plot quite similar to Machen's **The Terror**. The end of the film where the occupants of an isolated house barricade themselves against the onslaught unmistakeably echoes the apocalyptic conclusion of **The Terror**.

Right, the forces of
nature attack:
Melanie Daniels
(Tippi Hedren) and
The Birds.

Above, Deborah Kerr as Miss Giddens in *The Innocents*.

CHAPTER FOUR

The Two Jameses

Like one, that on a lonesome road
Doth Walk with fear and dread,
And having once turned round walks on
And turns no more his head;
Because he knows, a frightful fiend
Doth close behind him tread.

Samuel Taylor Coleridge, "The Rime
of the Ancient Mariner"

I. Demons: M.R. James (1862-1936)

Both Montague Rhodes James' short story, "Casting the Runes" (1911), and the Jacques Tourneur/Charles Bennett film adaptation, *Night of the Demon* (1957), begin in a naturalistic, almost documentary style. The introduction of James' story is "discovered" material: the text of three replies from the Secretary of an unnamed association to three letters which are not shared with the reader. The Secretary's letters are dated a few days apart in the month of April of an unspecified year near the turn of the century ("190-"). The mood of these missives changes rapidly from cordiality to coldness as they reject the insistent queries of a would-be author, whom the third note reveals is named Karswell, regarding an article entitled "The Truth in Alchemy."

Night of the Demon opens with several shots of Stonehenge, while an unidentified narrator's voice comments on the antiquity and unresolved

mystery of the ruins. Both the low contrast of the black-and-white images and the detached tone of the voiceover inject an immediate,
travelogue-like quality into the film. As with the short story from which
it derives, the first moments are dispassionate and anonymous. If they
are not strictly everyday in terms of their subject matter, they are certainly unmelodramatic in style, which are atypical beginnings for supernatural fiction.

By limiting from the first the amount of information which the reader
will receive, James broadly manipulates the expectations of his
audience. The reader, especially one who has a copy of the collection
More Ghost Stories, is probably aware of the genre of the tale before
taking it up. But the starting point, the fictional correspondence prof-
fered by James, does not project any sense of the horrific. The one-
sided exchange only indicates that a self-proclaimed expert named
Karswell is badgering—a reasonable assumption from the three days'
time which separates the replies—the Secretary over the society's rejection of his lecture proposal. The fact that this Secretary is otherwise
unidentified—the reader finally discovers his surname midway through
the story—severely limits the amount of initial reader identification.
This is appropriate enough, since this character is not the eventual
protagonist. The first words spoken in the present time of the narrative
come from the man's wife ("Mrs. Secretary"), who has ostensibly been
scanning the letters along with the reader and who now asks the question: "Who is this Mr. Karswell?"

James is slow in answering. In fact, the very casual interest with
which the early characters treat Karswell restrains the narrative and
keeps his significance from building up too quickly. The reader, however, having only tenuous connections with any of the active personages, has only the figure of Karswell on which to focus apprehension. As a result, Karswell acquires a portentous, even threatening aura
well before he physically appears.

By the end of what James labels the prologue, the reader has
learned, through a dinner conversation between the Secretary, his wife
and couple of their acquaintance, of Karswell's country home, of his
epithet, the "Abbot of Lufford," of his grisly slide show for the local
children, of his book called **History of Witchcraft**, and of the strange
death of the author of a scathing review of that work. The Secretary
ponders whether the expert who rejected Karswell's proposal to his
society, a man whose name he has refused to reveal to the petitioner,
might also be in peril but concludes that the chances of Karswell
making the connections are very slight. James closes this introductory

section with a chilling aside: "However, Mr. Karswell was an astute man."

The filmmakers take a considerably more direct approach to the introduction of Karswell and his unusual powers. In fact, there was a dispute and compromise over the appearance of the "fire demon" between the producers on one side and the writer, director, and star on the other. This has been much discussed and criticized by admirers of *Night of the Demon*'s otherwise subtle style. Indisputably, the appearance of the demon in the prologue, the chase through the woods, and the conclusion is hardly as ambiguous about the supernatural as other sequences of the film. But given the very title of the film, *Night of the Demon* (*Curse of the Demon* in the United States), not to mention

Below, the Fire Demon as it appears in the prologue.

the publicity materials which accompanied the initial release, what viewer could fail to expect that the subject of the film was Satanism and that a demon would appear. From the standpoint of genre expectations, putting the demon in the prologue immediately both fulfills the apprehension of the filmgoers and provides them with a palpable and frightening apparition that is, in the graphic context of the film, unmistakably real. Once this is accomplished, all the effects, from the pools of light in hotel corridors to the uncertain clicking sounds, acquire a menace that is equally palpable.

After the montage of Stonehenge and the title sequence, a night exterior of a wooded area and a road isolates some flashing lights approaching from the rear ground. Gradually these are revealed to be the headlamps of a car speeding down through the trees. The shot is held until the vehicle careens past in the foreground; then there are brief cuts to the driver intently clutching the steering wheel and a point of view shot up through the windscreen at the ghostly branches momentarily illuminated by the car's passage. The visual exposition is no longer detached, but, for a viewer familiar with the genre, already charged with connotations of peril. What else could impel the man be-

Below, Holden (Dana Andrews) compares the runes on Karswell's paper with those at Stonehenge.

hind the wheel to make such haste through so dark and alien a landscape?

What the driver, who is named Harrington, finds at his destination is a man, a round-faced, portly, goateed but basically average-looking man named Karswell. This Karswell, dressed in a lounging robe and preparing for bed, is introduced by the filmmakers in the middle of the night as an inconspicuous and unimposing figure. Although he rejects the pleas of the man who has hastened to rouse him, he does not do so harshly. In fact, he puts Harrington off in the same manner one might try to discourage any eccentric, firmly but politely. If there is any doubt engendered here about the nature of Karswell's power, it is soon dispelled.

When Harrington returns to his home after having failed in his entreaties, he is more overwrought than ever. Out of the woods near his garage come first a flurry of sparks, then a luminous cloud, and finally a smoking figure. As Harrington flees, the form materializes fully as a winged, horned monster sprung from the visions of classical demons recorded in medieval etchings and woodcuts. In a huge close-up this figure peers down at his puny human prey. A giant claw sweeps out to enclose the man then dashes him to the ground and rends his inert form with its talons until only a seared and shredded mass remains.

As it stands, and for purposes of this discussion, questions of what some of the filmmakers might have intended must be pre-empted by what is actually in the film. This prologue is explicit where James' is oblique, is steeped in visceral terror where James relies on subliminal dread. The graphic rendering of the invocation of the demon not only contrasts with the everyday, travelogue style of the opening at Stonehenge and the casual speculations of the narrator but immediately focuses the genre viewpoint. This is a film about real demons who kill people.

This focus necessitates a corresponding change in the narrative direction of the movie from that taken in "Casting the Runes." Both story and film continue with the introduction of the chief protagonist, a scientific authority on the supernatural, named Dunning by James and Holden (played by Dana Andrews) by the filmmakers. This man is responsible for the rejection of Karswell's treatise. In the story, the reader shares Dunning's nightmarish descent from the security of the ordinary world to the unrelenting dread of the unseen. He or she co-experiences events such as the mysterious advertisement on a train compartment window or the poisoning of Dunning's servants filtered through James' calculatedly understated and elusive prose:

The night he passed is not one on which he looks back with any satisfaction. He was in bed and the light was out. He was wondering if the charwoman would come early enough to get him hot water in the morning, when he heard the unmistakable sound of his study door opening. No step followed it on the passage floor, but the sound must mean mischief, for he knew that he had shut the door that evening after putting his papers away in the desk. It was rather shame than courage that induced him to slip out in the passage and lean over the bannister in his nightgown, listening. No light was visible; no further sound came; only a gust of warm, or even hot air played for an instant around his shins. He went back and decided to lock himself into his room. There was more unpleasantness, however. Either an economical suburban company had decided that their light would not be required in the small hours, and had stopped working, or else something was wrong with the meter; the effect was in any case that the electric light was off. The obvious course was to find a match; he might as well know how many hours of discomfort awaited him. So he put his hand into the well-known nook under the pillow; only it did not get so far. What he touched was according to his account, a mouth, with teeth, and with hair about it, and he declares, not the mouth of a human being. I do not think it is any use to guess what he said or did; but he was in a spare room with the door locked and his ear to it before he was clearly conscious again. And there he spent the rest of a most miserable night, looking every moment for some fumbling at the door: but nothing came.

James makes no attempt to intensify the events themselves. On the contrary, the lights nay be out but it is only a power company's economy or a faulty meter. As to the "mouth, with teeth," he merely records Dunning's terrified, fleeting impressions then withdraws with him behind the bolted door without elaboration. By the time these events have transpired in the story, Dunning is an unquestioning believer in Karswell's power. With characteristic economy, first through the Secretary and then through the brother of Karswell's earlier victim, James also gives Dunning the knowledge which he needs to fight back.

Still, James never produces a literal demon or anything more than that inhuman mouth, which could after all have been imagined by Dunning. His Karswell perishes not under the claws of a beast but is struck by a falling piece of mortise. As noted, for the film viewer there can be no question of imaginary demons. The scene of Harrington's death is clearly staged in a "third person" or objective format. Since it is not possible for the adaptors to maintain the story's ambiguity, the tone shifts also. When the inferences in James' prologue are transformed into the supernatural facts of the film's prologue, the audience is put in an ironic relationship to the character Holden. They know that his unrelenting cynicism about the supernatural is misguided. They also know that his need to trust only in what he calls "the reality of the seeable and the touchable, certainly not intuition or funny feelings" is so misguided as to imperil his life. This irony alone might be sufficient for a viewer to remain somewhat distanced from Holden as a character. The filmmakers restrict normal identification even further.

Holden is introduced in a scene on an airplane where a fellow passenger interrupts his nap and receives a rebuke. Andrews plays the scene straightforwardly but, at the same time, the sarcastic tone clearly types Holden as someone caught up in his own importance. A brief sequence at the airport establishes that Holden does have a high standing in his field; but a cutaway to the young woman who awakened him as she completes a telephone call asks the viewer to continue to empathize with her. At his hotel, Holden is apprised of the strange circumstances of Harrington's death by a Scottish colleague. When their discussion turns to parapsychology, the Scotsman produces a sketch done by an asylum inmate which closely resembles a centuries-old engraving. As he explains that it purports to be "a fire demon invoked by witchcraft," another man, an Indian, enters. Holden asks offhandedly what he thinks of demons, and the Indian gentleman replies ingenuously, "Oh, I believe in them absolutely."

Even without the events of the prologue, Holden's posture, that of the smug, rational American reluctantly putting up with the "funny feelings" of others, is not one which encourages audience identification. It is not until after his first encounter with Karswell, that Holden again meets Joanna, the young woman from the plane, and learns that she is Harrington's niece. By this time the viewer is prepared to shift a certain amount of identification usually reserved for the protagonist onto her. While Holden is being supercilious ("all scientists don't wear thick glasses") and condescending about his position as a recognized authority compared to hers as a schoolteacher, she is being simple and serious: "You can learn a lot from children. They believe in things in the dark until we tell them it's not so. Maybe we've been fooling them." Despite all the warnings from his associates, despite otherwise inexplicable events, Holden, of course, goes on doubting the reality of those "things in the dark." As he tells Joanna Harrington later in a police station, his childhood was spent "walking under ladders and chasing black cats."

This lifelong skepticism keeps pulling Holden back from acceptance of Karswell's power even after repeated demonstrations and drives him from the police station exclaiming in self defense that "I'm not a superstitious sucker like ninety percent of humanity, allowing myself to be stampeded like this into a state of hysteria." This skepticism is also what situates the film alternately in the subjective and ironic modes.

Purely on the level of plot, the audience sees many critical occurences about which Holden merely hears. Unlike a reader experiencing Dunning's story, from its perspective the film audience cannot reserve any doubt. From this perspective, they are also endistanced from Holden's doubts, they know that no matter how long and how firmly he has held them, he must discard them or perish.

On the one hand, the viewer vacillates between sharing Holden's mounting sense of peril and, in a scene such as the flight through the woods around Karswell's manor, direct apprehension over his physical safety. On the other hand, the audience may well be exasperated by Holden's insistent attempts to find rational answers. As a result, the underlying tension of the movie's plot line is intensified in a way not possible in James' story. The reader of the story may justifiably infer Dunning's survival from the fact that the record of his experiences, while not a literal "first person" narrative, is implicitly so because events are "as told to" the Secretary. In the film nothing guarantees that Holden will not be killed, not the viewer's genre expectations nor a first-person or flashback framework. In fact, at some level, a viewer might even want Holden to meet the fire demon and be convinced once and for all that such things do exist, even though it could mean his death.

Since *Night of the Demon* shifts modes narratively, the filmmakers have the option of also alternating visually between subjective and ironic points of view. When Holden returns to his hotel after encountering Karswell at the British Museum, there are inter-cuts of medium close shots travelling with Holden as he glances uneasily over his shoulder and subjective shots of what he sees: an empty corridor. The audience knows that the sounds and the sparks which begin to materialize in the vacant space mean the demon is coming; but because the point of view is restricted by the shot selection the greatest shock comes not from these manifestations but the sudden appearance of the Scotsman as he opens the door of Holden's room.

Obviously the filmmakers had at their disposal a variety of special effects which could reinforce either subjective or objective scenes in a manner unavailable to James. The film manifestations, from the demon itself to the metamorphosis of Karswell's house cat into a jaguar, the flutterings of the runes under their own power towards the flames, or the simple disappearing ink on Karswell's business card, all create an aura of the supernatural which is more tangible that the inexplicable lettering on the train window or the mouth under the pillow in "Casting the Runes."

At the same time, the way in which such images are constructed can either broaden or restrict their narrative impact. Even as the viewer watches the smouldering footsteps and the cloud of light chasing Holden from Karswell's grounds, the sidelight on his face, which creates one illuminated portion and one still in obscurity, acts like a metaphor of his lingering uncertainty. Shortly after this sequence, as Holden and Joanna sit in the police station, their conversation is staged so that the camera slowly pulls back from a medium close shot and holds them in a rim-lit, semi-silhouette, an uneasy composition that seems to express their emotional condition. The long take without a cutaway makes the viewer subconsciously anxious in anticipation of the cut and helps to underscore the tenseness of their situation.

Throughout *Night of the Demon*, director Tourneur's staging complements the action. The flickering shadows and general "instability" of the light in the prologue and pursuit outside Karswell's enhance the narrative suspense. The characters' frayed nerves are repeatedly externalized, as just described or in the single cut from Joanna in her car to a clanging ambulance bringing the patient for the hypnotic demonstration. Perhaps the most subtle visualization centers not on either protagonist but on the figure of Karswell. At the first "chance" meeting with Holden in the British Museum Karswell strikes the same, osten-

Below, at the conclusion, Karswell (Niall MacGinnis) cringes on the train tracks before the demon he has summoned.

sibly normal pose as in the prologue. Yet as Holden watches him leave, a long lens is used to distort his shape, and he is outlined by the sunlight refracted off the walls of a corridor, so that he seems to lurch eerily away. This shot is held for some seconds before a cut back to Holden reveals his disturbed expression, as if he had perceived something sinister in the odd play of light.

A more complex sequence is Holden and Joanna's first visit to Karswell's estate. Karswell is in clown make-up entertaining the village children. His demeanor is much less threatening that in James' description, for Karswell in the film seems genuinely kind to the children and is a multi-faceted character not merely an ill-defined perpetrator of evil. The film's Karswell goes so far as to offer Holden a demonstration of his magic to persuade him that it is hard to tell "where imagination ends and reality begins. How we can differentiate between the powers of darkness and the powers of the mind." At that point, a boy in a skull mask pops up from behind a tree startling both Holden and the viewer. Karswell placidly seizes on this opportunity to conjure up a small storm for his already slightly unnerved guest. From the tight two shot which had followed both men as they walked along, a

Below, Karswell's clown makeup lulls Holden into a false sense of security.

framing that suggested a visual balance through their equal
prominence in the shot, the images shift towards instability. A pan
down from a gust shaking a tree branch reveals Holden standing below
it and gazing apprehensively skyward. As dark clouds roll in, a low
angle medium shot captures Karswell standing with his hands folded in
front of his body, his satisfied smile exaggerated by the clown make-up.
Karswell is content in his display of preternatural ability and im-
placable in his warning to Holden: "Your time allowed is just three
days." Even comic relief becomes sinister, when a long shot shows that
Karswell has miscalculated the force of the wind, that even as Holden
staggers towards the house struggling to stay on his feet, Karswell
must strut mechanically after him holding onto his hat lest it blow
away.

In a sense the development of the personal relationship between Holden and Karswell in *Night of the Demon* alters the thrust of the narrative line which is adapted from "Casting the Runes." The understated
description of events which totally disrupt Dunning's life in the story
are linked to Karswell only by a slip of paper. The short story's Karswell
neither speaks to Dunning about these events nor seems interested in
any eventuality other than his
opponent's destruction. In the film,
Karswell personally offers to lift the
curse in return for Holden's endorse-
ment of the authenticity of witchcraft.
When Holden breaks into his home,
he is not overtly angry but almost
solicitous as he warns Holden not to
go back through the woods. The
vague unstated terror which
threatens Dunning in the story is not
the core of the film. Once that terror
is visualized in the opening, it is sub-
sumed into the conflict of wills that is
more accurately the dramatic nexus.
Dunning has no sense of triumph in
turning the curse back onto Karswell
in "Casting the Runes." Holden es-
chews it in *Night of the Demon*, as if
preferring to preserve a thread of his
shattered scientific beliefs by con-
cluding that "it is better not to know."

II. Ghosts: Henry James (1843-1916)

...the written statement took up the tale at a point after it had, in a manner, begun. The fact to be in possession of was therefore that his old friend, the youngest of several daughters of a poor country parson, had, at the age of twenty, on taking service for the first time in a schoolroom, come up to London, in trepidation, to answer in person an advertisement...

Henry James, **The Turn of the Screw**

Country parsonage! Healthy mental atmosphere, not!

Fritz Leiber, **Conjure Wife**

The best-known if apocryphal anecdote attached to **The Turn of the Screw** (1898) is that Henry James purposely set out to write a ghost story purely as an exercise in terrifying his readers. In his Preface to the New York Edition, James asserted that he had gotten the idea for the tale during a gathering at a country house, when a friend could not recall a ghost story that he had heard as a child. Obviously, James' prologue which contains a narrator based on himself is inspired by these actual events. The conflict between his protagonist, the unnamed governess, and his evil, spellbinding ghosts inspired by the "the old trials for witchcraft," is the core of what James curiously called an "irresponsible little fiction."

James admits that by instilling the notion of maleficent beings forcefully enough in the readers minds, he knew they would conjure up terrors much more frightening than any which he could describe. Perhaps this is what makes his fiction "irresponsible" in James' own mind. Having accomplished his purpose of evoking horror, he underscored his success both in choosing his title and in the prologue. There James creates a competition not unlike the one at Geneva during the Haunted Summer in which guests at a country home compete with each other for the best ghost story. How well James succeeded is still a matter of literary debate. The premise of the tale is simple enough: a new governess is sent to Bly House and discovers that her two young charges, Miles and Flora, are enthralled by the spirits of the former governess, Miss Jessel, and her lover Peter Quint, who was the estate's stable master. Still there are some who would argue that **The Turn of the Screw** should win not only James' fictional contest but the unspoken

Above, Miss Giddens (Deborah Kerr) restrains Miles (Martin Stephens) in the final confrontation with Quint in *The Innocents*.

competition between all authors of supernatural fiction, that it is the scariest ghost story every written.

It may be ironic, particularly for the proponents of supernatural fiction as serious literature, that a "dabbler" in the genre such as Henry James should have created one of its most highly regarded examples. Obviously much of the interest in **The Turn of the Screw** is because James is one of the most celebrated authors in the English language with a body of work that is justly classic. Whether or not one agrees wholeheartedly with James' narrator that the tale is "beyond everything. Nothing that I know touches it," the novella is incontestably suspenseful and unnerving. **The Turn of the Screw** remains nearly a century after its publication one of the most widely read works in the supernatural genre.

Almost as well known to students of literature as the novella itself is Edmund Wilson's psychological interpretation, "The Ambiguity of Henry James," an essay which appeared in 1934. This Freudian reading of James' story asserts that the ghosts which plague his central character were not at all unworldly but merely symbols of the libidinous desires springing from a repressed *id*. Wilson's phallic reading of Quint on the tower and Flora's poking one stick into another became part of a standard reading which continues to influence adaptations of James' work. This is despite the fact that subsequent commentators have substantially refuted Wilson by citing James' own assertions about the reality of the ghost and key moments in the narrative, such as the governess being able to describe Quint to the housekeeper, Mrs. Grose, before she has ever heard anyone speak of him.

James employed the conceit of the "discovered manuscript," so the actual narrative of the young, unnamed governess is in the first person. While this conceit is itself quite common, not just in the supernatural genre but fiction in general, James' use of it in **The Turn of the Screw** is remarkable. Although technically, this first person format prevents the reader from receiving any information or from perceiving situations except through the heroine's eyes, James used his elaborate and enigmatic prose to make the narrative less subjective. Whether or not one accepts Wilson's reading of James' ambiguities, the presence of uncertainty is unquestionable. As the governess herself asks at the beginning of chapter four: "Was there a 'secret' at Bly—a mystery of Udolpho or an insane, an unmentionable relative kept in unsuspected confinement?" James' uses the governess to invoke the archetype of Ann Radcliffe's Gothic novel, **The Mysteries of Udolpho**. Does this mean that she comes to Bly full of youthful fancies, predisposed to a find a mystery, even before she learns how her predecessor and Quint died? Perhaps the most compelling conundrum of **The Turn of the Screw** are Miles' final words, when he shouts, "Peter Quint—you devil!" Is the tormentor at whom he hurls the epithet Quint himself or the governess?

Both the reputation of the story and the uniquely literary, stylistic manipulation imposed by James posed significant challenges to the filmmakers who adapted it. As always, dealing with a "classic" means fulfilling very particular expectations on the part of many viewers. But whereas Shelley's **Frankenstein** had a central, mythic premise that could survive transpositions and amendments without destroying the sub-text of "The Modern Prometheus," the impact of James' chilling prose is more evanescent. Moreover, filmmakers were also confronted with two popular but somewhat antithetical interpretations: one which accepts the ghosts as literally real and another which treats them as the hallucinations of a disturbed psyche. If the adaptors chose an enigmatic treatment, what devices would be used to translate James' writing style to the screen? Even if the supernatural aura could be approximated by restricting the audience's perspective to an analog of the heroine's, how precisely is the image of a ghost, which must have a graphic and tangible presence to be seen on a screen, to be kept enigmatic?

Most of the adaptations of James' novella have been influenced by the Edmund Wilson explications. One of the most recent, the 1989 adaptation starring Amy Irving which is otherwise flaccid and full of uneven performances, contains one of the most graphic visualizations of a scene singled out by Wilson, in which Flora pokes a spar into a ship model. The filmmakers go so far as to add another phallic symbol by having Miles, who is not even present at this point in the novella, simultaneously pushing a primer rod into a toy cannon. Whatever uncertainty may be generated in such scenes, however, is undercut by scenes such as the governess finding the ghost couple embracing on her bed. As might be expected the graphic reality of the ghosts suggests to the viewer that they are real apparitions, not imagined spectres. Most of the other sexual aspects of the narrative are omitted or distorted. Quint's first appearance in the novella is on a tower, an extremely suggestive location for Wilson. Here he springs up at a roof's edge standing on a terrace, in all likelihood because the shooting location chosen by the filmmakers did not have a tower.

Another aspect of the original, Miles' precocious sexuality, is effectively removed by casting an adolescent actor and making Miles not ten but fourteen, an age at which any carnal behavior would not be called precocious. Finally, the governess' infatuation with the worldly uncle is effectively undercut by casting a dissolute-looking David Hemmings as

"Mr. Harley" (an irony outside the work is that, as a child, Hemmings portrayed Miles in Benjamin Britten's opera, *The Turn of the Screw*). The ending, from which no adaptors have strayed entirely, is the most reworked portion of this version. After the uncle has appeared at Bly and sacked the governess, he goes riding. Flora goes into the woods; and both she and the uncle's body, his neck broken when his head wedged in the fork of a tree limb, are discovered by Miles, Mrs. Grose, and the governess. When the governess confronts Miles, who has proclaimed himself the new master of the manor, he starts to break down. What is normally James' ending is interrupted by Flora's cries. The two ghosts are threatening to fling her from the terrace. Miles pushes Peter Quint over the railing but dies in the fall as Quint dematerializes. When Miss Jessel follows suit, the governess is left clutching Flora protectively as they look down on Miles' body.

Whether or not the reader/viewer subscribes to Wilson's interpretation, the psychosexual undertone of **The Turn of the Screw** is unmistakable. The 1989 adaptation represents an extreme in its restructuring and obfuscation of James. Most of the others have focused on the theme which James himself deemed central to his "sinister romance": the conflict of innocence and evil. It is the perception of a threat to children who epitomize innocence that both unnerves and galvanizes

Below, Lynn Redgrave as "Jane Cubberly" and Jasper Jacobs as "Miles" in the 1974 *The Turn of the Screw*.

James' governess. It is this perception and reaction that makes the governess both narrator and protagonist and that guides all the dramatizations of the novella.

Ingrid Bergman starred in an early (1959) television adaptation directed by John Frankenheimer. This live telecast and Jack Clayton's 1961 film, *The Innocents*, with Deborah Kerr, are still the versions which retain the most of James's ambiguity; and they achieve this through the actor's performance. Bergman, in particular, brought an air of repressed emotion to James' governess that could easily give way to fantasy and hallucination. The intensity of her anguish in the final scene, where she wrestles with Quint for Miles and wins back his soul only to lose his body, is the kind of behavior that could connote either literal madness or sexual frenzy. A more recent television version was produced and directed by the ubiquitous Dan Curtis in 1974. Lynn Redgrave's portrayal of the governess (given the curious name of "Jane Cubberly") lacked the focus of the earlier work of Bergman or Kerr. The fact that Megs Jenkins reprised her role of 13 years earlier as Mrs. Grose permits even further dramatic comparisons. Unlike his work with *Dracula* and *The Strange Case of Dr. Jekyll and Mr. Hyde*, Curtis emphasized shock value in the manner of *Dark Shadows* that ran somewhat counter to the thrust of James' prose.

Between the U.S. television versions, **The Turn of the Screw** became a moderately successful Broadway play adapted by William Archibald as "The Innocents." The narrative line of director Clayton's *The Innocents*, was drawn from James' original and Archibald's play by the dramatist and Truman Capote. The opening scenes are not superficially complex. The governess, here called Miss Giddens, seems a cultivated woman of modest means who is hired by a wealthy gentleman as tutor for his wards, an orphaned niece and nephew. Despite the fact that Giddens has not held such a position before, the unnamed Uncle is more concerned with whether she has "imagination" than he is about her background and references. Although uneasy over the amount of responsibility which she will assume, Giddens accepts the employment. From this first sequence, the filmmakers attack the paradoxes of James' novella and rely heavily on the performances of Kerr as Giddens and Michael Redgrave as the Uncle to establish a naturalistic undertone. The visual style in the wide screen black and white frames lit without heavy shadows by Freddie Francis reinforces this.

Two brief cuts actually open the *The Innocents*: a shot of a pair of hands being wrung followed by Miss Giddens crying in distress. This informal prologue creates the first person context, as the film dissolves from this melodramatic start back to a close-up of Kerr, smiling and controlled at her job interview. In fact, Kerr's mien immediately suggests that despite her age, Giddens has lived a sheltered life and that her lack of worldly experience may make her slightly uncomfortable in the presence of someone like her prospective employer. In that role, Redgrave is the stereotypical, self-possessed and manipulative "gentleman." As he paces the room before Giddens and speaks of his discomfiture and need for a reliable replacement after the sudden death of his last governess, he never interrogates Giddens but merely assumes that she is qualified. While the woman may be concerned about being entrusted with two children, she cannot resist the Uncle's charm. When he takes her hand and asks for her decision, she is, in effect, seduced into acquiescence.

The staging of this introductory sequence, juxtaposed as it is with the disconnected impact of the first two shots, implies that Giddens' apprehension may prove to be well founded. Even a viewer not familiar with the supernatural overtones of the original and bringing no particular expectations to the film must appreciate that Giddens' frame of mind as she embarks on a new career is more than slightly naive and quite susceptible to outside influences. As in the novella, Giddens arrives at the country house where she is to work still unaware of all the reasons for her employer's concern over his wards. The housekeeper, Mrs. Grose, gives her no indication that there is anything extraordinary about the children whom she is to supervise. Giddens is charmed by Flora, her younger charge, and her older brother, Miles. Although she is worried about Miles' discharge from his boarding school for being a bad influence on his fellows, Giddens quickly reassures herself that Miles' intelligence and inquisitiveness must have been misunderstood by his schoolmasters.

The chain of occurrences which follow Miles' return to the house are not conveyed through a literal exposition but filtered through Giddens outlook. The children's behavior and the manner in which the film presents Giddens' perception of events sustains the ambivalent quality at the heart of James' narrative. As Giddens is gradually convinced that the children are being possessed by the ghosts of Miss Jessel and Peter Quint, she herself sees apparitions of both of them and believes that they are somehow conspiring to harm her charges. After several inconclusive attempts to compel the children to admit that they see and have a relationship with the ghosts, Giddens sends Flora away with Mrs. Grose and girds for a final confrontation with Miles and the spectral Peter Quint.

The Innocents, like **The Turn of the Screw**, never resolves the issues of Peter Quint's actions in the final scene nor the nature of the ghostly

Above, Quint (Peter Wyngarde) appears behind Miss Giddens (Deborah Kerr) in *The Innocents*.

presences, whether they are real or imagined and, if so, by whom. Clearly there is some preternatural link between Miles and Flora. Giddens is struck by it even before Miles has returned home, when an excited Flora knows that he is coming even before the letter announcing his expulsion arrives at the house. The truth of the school's accusations against Miles is never explored. Miles subsequently vacillates between acting more childish than his age and surprisingly adult. This behavior that makes Giddens uneasy. Her own emotional immaturity, implicit from the first scene, is again a factor. Just as the worldly and self-assured Uncle charmed her, so does the handsome, adolescent Miles. The adult *persona* which Miles consciously projects both disturbs her and attracts Giddens sexually. Miles' awareness of his effect on Giddens is graphically underscored in the scene when he asks her for a good night kiss. As she bends towards his cheek, he suddenly covers her mouth with his and she recoils in horror.

Giddens' horror of the ghosts is closely tied to her fears for Miles and Flora's safety, but it is also related to this possible threat presented by Miles' sexual precocity. In fact, she is as shocked by what she considers his carnal behavior as she is by Mrs. Grose's tale of the perverse liaison between Jessel and Quint. These circumstances add credibility to the view that Quint is merely a product of Giddens' confusions and inexperience in dealing with either responsibility or sensuality. The staging of the final sequence also supports this perspective. Giddens peers out into the darkness surrounding the house but sees only the silent statues on the lawn. She turns, shakes Miles violently, and screams at him to confess that Quint is out there. Low angle lighting alters her expression, makes her appear frantic, almost crazed. When she looks out again, a point-of-view shot pans across the lawn and stops on the figure of Quint which now stands where a statue had been.

When Quint enters the house, Miles and Giddens always share the frame with him, as if he could not be physically present without one or both of them being aware of him. Even in the chaos of this climactic moment, the visual style undercuts the reality of Quint's spectre. Is he merely a statue animated by Giddens' terror? Is he actually in the room or only a manifestation of the emotional conflict between Giddens and Miles? Even after Miles has died and Giddens bends to kiss him and cry, "You're safe," the two shot is not held to confirm or deny what has happened. As the film abruptly ends, the only facts confirmed are the simultaneous destruction of Miles' life and Giddens' obsession.

While the Clayton/Capote collaboration remains the best-known adaptation of the novella, there have been several subsequent to it. The most unusual is *The Nightcomers* (1971), which stars Marlon Brando as Quint in a "prequel" to the events of **The Turn of the Screw**. The central premise of *The Nightcomers* is that Miles and Flora are anything but "innocents" when the new governess arrives. To prevent them from leaving, they have, in fact, murdered both Quint and Miss Jessel, inspired by Quint's assertion that "if you really love someone, sometimes you really want to kill them."

Much of *The Nightcomers* is a sensationalized treatment of the contrast in mores which was, for James, an ancillary concern at best. Quint is less sinister than vulgar, less evil than antisocial. To a certain extent, Brando does Quint as Stanley Kowalski but with more native intelligence. When Quint tells Miles and Flora of their parents' deaths, he reveals a sense of irony: "They travelled to India and the tip of Africa. Well, they had an accident. They were driving a gas-powered motorcar in France."

The early scenes of *The Nightcomers* set a tone of eroticism and decay. The worm which migrates from a head of lettuce to Mrs. Grose's hair and the butterfly which Flora recounts "lives to love" for only forty-eight hours are part of the natural process, as is Quint. When the

Above, Stephanie Beacham as Miss Jessel and Marlon Brando as Quint in *The Nightcomers*.

children watch him catching frogs or in a tryst with Miss Jessel, they accept his behavior as natural. While Quint is the one who makes faces at the children while Miss Jessel leads them in prayer, both he and Jessel dissuade their acceptance of heaven and hell, which Jessel calls "absolute piffle" and Quint dismisses saying that "the dead go nowhere."

In a real sense, the supernatural does not figure directly in *The Nightcomers* but is reserved until after the film's conclusion. Quint's "lessons" whether sticking pins in a doll resembling Mrs. Grose or showing Miles how to practice archery "Chinese-style," i.e. blindfolded, are preternatural affectations, not real belief. It is in their "innocent" imitation of the behavior of adults, whether it is "doing sex" or shooting arrows into Quint's body, that the children may "appear dark and cold, as if you're about to be evil." When the new governess, James' narrator, does arrive at this film's conclusion, her avowal that "you could not hope in all your life to meet more exquisite angels than Miles and Flora" adds a new irony to the events of the novel.

A motion picture of Britten's 1954 opera, *The Turn of the Screw*, which combined a British recording of the score with a Czech/German film production, was released in 1982. Britten's work is a chamber opera in two acts, in which he and his librettist, Myfawny Piper, introduce Quint and Jessel as full-fledged characters. This opera, like others among Britten's dramatic works, is also "notorious" for its overtones of homosexuality. While the relationship between Quint and Miles is not as obsessive or erotic as that in Britten's adaptation of Thomas Mann's **Death in Venice**, Quint's ghostly call of Miles' name with its tremulous colorations, which have often been compared with a siren's song, are just that: rife with lascivious and occult overtones.

The opera itself must address these issues through its dramatic mechanisms and its tonalities. Like other adaptors, Britten and Piper focus on the conflict of innocence and evil. Britten uses standard devices to create an ominous undertone. A typical example is the melodic quartet of higher register voices of women and children when the governess arrives and meets Miles, Flora, and Mrs. Grose. This cedes at the end to woodwinds in a much lower timbre. Britten's musical ironies include the style of Miles' Latin lesson song, where he produces a series of hymn-like, melodic variations on the word "malo," or "evil." There is a similar admixture of the guileless and sinister in the children's duet outside the church. One of the most subtle effects is the use of high pitched bells as a transition to the vocal introduction of Quint and Miss Jessel. Long before they sing that "the ceremony of innocence is drowned," the dying bells are like a music box winding down and an aural metaphor for childhood's end.

For the filmmakers the overall structure of scenes separated by orchestral variations meant that there would be ample opportunity for narrative invention; and director Petr Weigl visually elaborates on the themes of both Britten and James. Before the opera's prologue sung by an unseen narrator, the film begins with a prologue of its own, a long, almost silent sequence at the estate. Shots of the Uncle playing chess while Quint stands nearby and the children frolicking with Quint and Miss Jessel visually foreshadow the underlying eroticism of the relationships in the opera. The Uncle, whom the narrator will shortly describe as "innocent and gay," is a silent stereotype of unrequited homoerotic desire. While Quint may have rejected the Uncle's advances, the scenes of him playing with Miles, both of them bare-chested and only wearing towels after swimming, have a different implication; and Quint's concern when Miles stumbles upon him and Jessel embracing seems to confirm it. The counterpose in the Uncle's departure is telling: this older "innocent," dressed in white, leaves the keys on a table and sadly walks out. Standing before him on the stairs as if in a tableaux are the children, also in white, Quint in black, Jessel in red, and Mrs. Grose in gray. In these two shots, Weigl summarizes the entire "back story" of novel and opera: with the Uncle gone and Mrs. Grose a neutral gray, Quint and Jessel will impose the emotions symbolized by their somber and erotic colors on the white-clad children. If there is any doubt the last scene of the film's prologue clarifies it with another metaphor for the loss of innocence. Up to this point, the only sounds have been birdsong and human laughter, as if to anticipate the musical interplay of strings and woodwinds of the first act. As Quint swings onto a tree branch and plucks off some fruit, Jessel and the children approach. As they collapse in laughter on the lawn, Quint throws down an apple. The sound effect of Jessel biting into an apple before passing it to the children is an echo of an analogous moment in Eden.

One thing is clear in both the opera and this film, which James leaves unsettled. As already noted, any appearance of the ghosts in a film has an innate, objective reality not in James' prose. Here where the ghosts not only appear but are full-fledged characters, who sing a duet outside the context of any dream or fantasy by Miles or the governess, the reality is incontestable. The final trio in which Quint and the governess struggle for Miles' love and soul is between three real entities. With the ambiguity of whether or not the ghosts are actually there effectively removed by Britten, Weigl is free to explore other aspects of the drama in his staging.

The overall visual scheme often recalls—not inappropriately in light of Britten's other work and personal proclivities—the style of Luchino Visconti's *Death in Venice* (1971). The shifting images, which are embodied in pans, dollies, and mostly zooms in and out, are like an orchestration, a visual equivalent to the aural shifts in instrumentation, tempo, and volume by the composer. The opera's first scene as the governess travels to Bly is transposed from a coach compartment to a train by Weigl but the staging is keyed to the dramatic aria. The entire sequence is photographed in one take, which sets up a tension in the viewer based on the expectation of a cut, a tension which makes the viewer coexperience the character's nervous apprehension. As she sings and her emotions vacillate between eagerness to begin her new job and concern about fulfilling her trust, the camera pans with her as she moves about the compartment and the lens zooms in and out three times, holding her relentlessly within the limits of the frame and even tightening that hold. The zooms out are keyed to her words and actions, as when she loosens and removes her bonnet. The last zoom inward captures her against the window, still and contemplative while the countryside outside rushes past in a blur. That image externalizes the anxious rush of feeling within her.

The same devices are used in the duet when the governess describes a man whom Gross recognizes as Quint. The scene begins with intercut medium close shots; but after Grose has realized to her horror who the man is, a sustained take is used again. As Grose and the governess move excitedly around the room, pans and zooms are elaborately choreographed and constantly reframe to link and hold them within the confines of the shot. Since neither the governess nor (in theory, at least) the viewer knows that Quint is dead, the tension of the long take is anticipatory of that discovery. The cut and release of tension come just before Grose tells what happened to Quint. A close-up suddenly frames her face tightly as she sings, "He died, too"; then a fast zoom out recoils from the governess to a medium close shot that catches her stumbling back from Mrs. Grose.

The overall pictorialism of this film of *The Turn of the Screw* is very different from the work of Jack Clayton and Freddie Francis in *The Innocents*. Obviously, the use of color is in itself a major change. Instead of the somber grays of *The Innocents*, Weigl and his cinematographer, Jiri Kadanka, capture the costumed characters on the sunlit lawns of the estate in the manner of cameraman Pasquale de Santis in *Death in Venice* or the even more archetypal work of Jorgen Persson in *Elvira Madigan* (1967). But whereas those are naturalistic melodramas, Britten's work is not, so that pictorialism and color values can be either realistic or not. The shot of the governess getting off the train, a long shot of her figure dressed in white climbing into the black coach that waits in front of the otherwise deserted station is an appropriate visual coda to the emotion of her aria on the train, a silent and slightly foreboding restatement.

Equally realistic is the quartet and variation following her arrival at the estate. The setting is in a kind of solarium filled with potted plants ranging from ferns and wisteria to more tropical palms and spider plants. While this may not be entirely "realistic" in the context of an English country estate, Bly itself is a detached and separate world, where the structures and plants work as natural background in much the same way as Britten's initial use of only natural keys for the music. At the end of the singing, a zoom pulls back to reveal a vignette of the four humans enclosed by a green iris formed from the encircling plants. It is when the children lead the governess upstairs, where she is momentarily embarrassed to see a nude figure in a painting, that the ominous woodwinds intrude in the music and an electric blue wall paper adds an unnatural tone to the room.

The unrealistic effects are reserved for the ghosts. Quint with his, loose fitting shirts and flowing cape seems real enough if somewhat ominous. But the pale Jessel is a wraith-like figure. As she calls to Flora at night, heavy mist seems to drip from the edges of her rhinestoned, black crepe dress and cling to the ground. With the memory of Britten's bells still fresh, the viewer might well take her for a demented, music box ballerina. Both she and Quint appear to walk in pools of this mist as they begin their duet. After Miles sings of evil, the governess' costume also becomes unreal. Her white dress is suddenly fringed in black, entirely representative of the evil aura which now clings to her. Before Quint's siren song, the governess removes her black night shawl as if it were a cobweb. Most unreal of all, after the governess' duet with Jessel, where she admonishes the spirit repeatedly to "Begone," a black patch suddenly appears on her white bodice.

As with several other adaptations, the most overstated symbolic usages in this film are the sexual ones. Some are fairly subtle, such as the agitated governess walking down a corridor lined with antlers, uncomplicated emblems of male animalism or the children riding double on a hobby-horse, which is directly from the opera's stage directions. In light of the erotic link between Miles and Quint in both opera and film, the attraction between Miles and the governess is also understated by comparison. Nonetheless, her sudden caress of his cheek after his Latin song, which he uses as an opportunity to kiss her hand, are clearly sensual. While this Miles looks older than the ten years of the novel and *The Innocents*, he is no adolescent as in the 1989 *The Turn of the Screw*. In their constant white garb, both he and Flora are literally and symbolically pre-pubescent.

What, then, could be more pointedly wry than to have the tower, the most pervasive sexual symbol of this adaptation, first seen in a shot from the children's point of view. The first glimpse is, in fact, a distorted one of the tower reflected in the water of a pool rippled by a stone which Miles has thrown. Edmund Wilson entirely aside, as the camera pans up to the edifice itself, the revelation and the structure itself are palpably phallic. The building is almost an exaggerated emblem of male arousal. Like a lubricious Taj Mahal, its tapered sections end in Moorish roof topped with crescent moon. This tower, which is next seen when the governess, as in the novel, spots Quint behind the parapet of its highest level, becomes a primary visual motif. It is from here that Quint calls to Miles. It is framed behind Quint and Jessel on the lawn when they sing of the "ceremony of innocence." It is repeatedly used in the montages that accompany Britten's musical variations, often with a slow zoom into the top or a pan up that echoes the first scene.

This is not to say that the use of the tower as an obvious symbol is inappropriate, no matter what reading one has of the novel and the governess' possibly repressed libido. As noted, these operatic ghosts and their erotic singing and behavior are real, not sights and sounds from the governess' id; but Weigl does use her Victorian gentility for added irony. She sees the tower while singing about her happiness at Bly and "only one thing I wish, that I could see him and that he could see how well I do his bidding." It is as if her asexual infatuation with the Uncle becomes the stridently licentious figure of Quint. Before she sees him, she lifts a brass telescope to one eye, turns, and closes the other, so that she is posed in silhouette like a cameo. A panning shot, using a long focal length lens to render her POV through the telescope, follows a flight of ducks and gives a brief, blurred glimpse of the tower as the birds fly past it. Even a viewer unfamiliar with the novel may well sense from genre expectation what is to come; and Weigl withholds the shot to extend the tension. After she has seen and been startled by Quint, phallic symbols are suddenly everywhere. The telescope becomes one, as she notices it and drops it as if the metal were burning her hands. Even the long shot as she flees places three thick tree trunks in the foreground. Even Edmund Wilson might have been found this amount of symbolism overwhelming.

For all this, the ending of this adaptation evokes icons of the supernatural. After the inconclusive struggle for Miles' soul, Quint fades into

Above, Miss Jessel (Clytie Jessop) appears in the schoolroom in *The Innocents*.

the mist; and in the last shot walking away from Bly House the governess disappears into it also.

The Turn of the Screw (1992) uses a black-and-white sequence of a
kind of group therapy session set in the present day to recreate the
prologue of James' novel. The person that introduces the story "about
children who were visited by visitors of a most unusual kind" is a
woman. In a unique twist, and although she appears considerably older
than the thirty years she should be, this woman turns out to be the
grown Flora. The period of the governess' experiences is in the mid-
1960s and her interview with the uncle is a pastiche of 60s fashion and
icons. As she sits in a wire chair shaped like a skeleton, Cooper, the
opium smoking guardian, tells her that the children live in the country
estate "to protect them from the influences of modern society." The
script conforms to the events of the novel in all major respects. In fact,
one could assert that placing the film in the present day is also being
faithful to James' work which began contemporaneously and "flashed
back" via the governess' manuscript an indeterminate number of years;
but the uncle's explicitly dissolute lifestyle sets a far different tone. In
this modern context the governess' physical attraction to the uncle
which James obliquely expressed becomes a groupie-like infatuation
with a rock star.

Once at the estate the governess, here named Jane Gooding, alters
her own attire and exchanges the miniskirt and hat worn to the interview for a kind of "granny" dress that is almost antique. This and her
hair style make her physically resemble all the prim portrayals of the
past. Miles, however, is no innocent. When chastised about his behavior, his proclamation that he does not want to go to heaven suggests
the influence of a Quint like that of *The Nightcomers*. Given that the
events at the estate are colored both by the genre expectation of viewers
familiar with James' narrative and/or past adaptations and the spatial
and temporal detachment of the place itself, the filmmakers freely add
overt symbolism. In the classroom, Miles spills red ink which suggests
the color of blood and evil. Later, the governess spills holy water.
Another fashion statement is made, this time along sadomasochistic
lines, when she finds the key to the armoire in her bedroom and inside
of it is a black *bustier*, which Miles says he had seen Miss Jessel wear.

As the governess' dreams become a confusion of sexual images involving Cooper and Quint and animated statues, the visual treatment
reinforces her own naivete. The casting of an actress (Patsy Kensit) who
is not only young but blonde and thin suggests as did James from the
first scene with the uncle, someone barely past adolescence. High angle
shots as she crosses the parquet inside the house or outdoors in the

garden make her appear small, childlike, and innocent herself. The later low angle of her in an oversized chair as she writes to Cooper has the same visual effect. The staging of Quint's appearance on the tower, quite unlike the 1989 version, is, as James wrote it and Wilson interpreted it, both a supernatural and sexual event. In this context that intimates her sexual inexperience, the appearance of Quint on the tower or as a bare-chested vision in her bedroom bespeaks a psychological disturbance that is more akin to the period of James' original than the "modern society" of which Cooper spoke. In this context, also, the insistent symbolism of the filmmakers can be overdone. That Jessel appears by the pond shore after Miles does a magic show in the garden is a new metaphor but entirely appropriate and consistent with James. The white owls, the devil masks, and the other odd bits and pieces are needless distractions.

Also consistent with James, and contrary to Wilson, the ghosts are objectified. The scene from the novel in which the governess describes a man unknown to her whom Mrs. Grose recognizes as Quint is staged as James wrote it. As with past adaptations Jessel appears to be more Quint's victim than a co-conspirator, particularly when her ghostly hand writes a plea to "save them," which could refer either to the children or the ghosts. Jessel's appearance during the thunderstorm is staged using reverse printing and a cacophony of sounds consistent with an objective reality, i.e. a haunting whose supernaturalism can only be depicted with special visual and aural effects.

All of the psychosexual and religious overtones of past versions are bound up in the final confrontation for Miles' soul. Since an actress so young cannot be expected to have the physical presence of more mature performers like Ingrid Bergman or Deborah Kerr, it is as if filmmakers are compensating by having her cut her hair. This act has its own ritual overtones of purification but also makes her look like Joan of Arc, invoking a different kind of preternatural power to assist her struggle with the purely malevolent Quint. This adaptation may throw the whole issue of the supernatural into question when it cuts back to the narrator who reveals that she is Flora and blames the governess for killing her brother; but there is one aspect of James' story which remains inviolate when the governess wrestles with Quint:

> [Miles] uttered the cry of a creature hurled over an abyss, and the grasp with which I recovered him might have been that of catching him in his fall. I caught him, yes, I held him—it may be imagined with what a passion; but at the end of a minute I began to feel what it truly was that I held. We were alone with the quiet day, and his little heart, dispossessed, had stopped.

Tansy (Janet Blair) prepares to destroy her charms at the insistence of her husband, Norman (Peter Wyngarde) in *Night of The Eagle*.

CHAPTER FIVE

Modern Classics

I. Witches

He was thinking: "Businessmen buy stocks on the advice of fortune tellers, numerologists rule the careers of movie stars, half the world governs its actions by astrology, advertisements bleat constantly of magic and miracles, and most modern and all surrealist art is nothing but attempted witchcraft borrowing its forms from the primitive witch doctor..."

Conjure Wife

Just a Woman's Eccentricity: Fritz Leiber (b. 1910), **Conjure Wife**

Although it is written in the third person, **Conjure Wife** (1943) is effectively a first person novel. None of its narrative events are revealed outside the presence of its protagonist, Norman Saylor. Because Saylor's thoughts are frequently quoted in the narrative, as in the excerpt cited above, the reader fully participates from the beginning in his point of view. Not until the final three of the novel's twenty-one chapters are there events which involve Saylor that are not immediately revealed to the reader. Leiber only breaks his own convention here to trick the reader and create surprise and suspense.

There are two key narrative lines in **Conjure Wife**. Scientific skepticism in the face of magic and witchcraft is the first context. This resonates back to earlier characters in supernatural fiction, such as M.R. James' Dunning or, even more strongly, his analog in *Night of the*

135

Demon, Holden. Leiber's Norman Saylor makes a living from debunking magic and witchcraft. As a "distinguished ethnologist" and professor of sociology at a small liberal arts college, he lectures and writes articles about the practices which he and the rational world deem superstitions. While his attitude in the novel may not be as sarcastic as Holden's, his reaction in the first two chapters, when he discovers that his wife, Tansy, has been using charms and conjuring formulas, is every bit as rigid. He makes her burn them all.

The opening of *Night of the Eagle* (1961; *Burn, Witch, Burn* in the U.S.) is even closer to *Night of the Demon*. Peter Wyngarde who portrays Saylor is lecturing to his class. As he speaks, he writes on a chalk board: "I DO NOT BELIEVE." Not only are the words all capitalized but he underlines "NOT" and then circles "BELIEVE." Saylor's scorn for the magical processes which he studies is even more vigorous than Holden's in *Night of the Demon*. Having driven this home the filmmakers proceed to Leiber's narrative and the destruction of Tansy's protections. In both novel and film, the genre expectations are clear. As Flora Carr will remark in *Night of the Eagle*, Norman Saylor doth protest too much; and both viewer and reader expect that, like the cynical Holden, those forces which he disdains will soon give him an unnerving comeuppance.

As Saylor begins to suffer from the loss of Tansy's charms, as he dis-

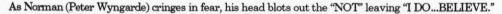

As Norman (Peter Wyngarde) cringes in fear, his head blots out the "NOT" leaving "I DO...BELIEVE."

covers that the timing of negative events belies the likelihood that they are mere coincidences, he begins to experience that vague sense of dread which Karswell visited upon Dunning/Holden. **Conjure Wife** shares many allusions with M.R. James' story from the mention of "time allowed" to references to James Frasier's **The Golden Bough**; but what seems the clearest echo is the intangible figure that stalks first Saylor and then Tansy, the figure which she calls "He Who Walks Behind" and which Saylor glimpses momentarily and describes as "a shaggy black form twice her height, with hulking shoulders, outstretched massive hands, and dully glowing eyes."

The second key event of the novel is Tansy's loss of her soul. The mindless shell of a woman which Tansy becomes, the animated corpse that frightens and upsets the normal people whom she encounters, anticipates such later creations as the revived beings in Stephen King's *Pet Sematary*. Leiber treats this event with the same detached prose as the first part of the narrative. Never does he allow anything remotely resembling a Gothic mood to creep in.

Saylor, whose personal belief system has explained away the effects of magic as neuroses, psychoses, and/or mass hallucinations, must deal with the emotionless shell that was his wife, first, and probe the reality of events second. On the train ride back, Saylor looks for an answer in an elaborate analogy between science and magic. Both are systems, he concludes, each with rules and methods governing them. Systems are, in fact, the cornerstone of belief for Saylor and his educated associates. Even the bridge game is a metaphor for mixed belief when the pontificating Professor Carr explains how experts can defy "the laws of chance" and laments that he would like to use a more modern convention for bidding during their bridge games. This is the context in which Saylor first wonders to himself, "Suppose you applied this principle outside bridge? Suppose that coincidences and other chance happenings weren't really as chancy as they looked? Suppose there were individuals with a special aptitude for calling the turns, making the breaks?" The equation of the diverse rituals of a card game, science, and magic is completed when Saylor translates the diverse formulas that might help him restore Tansy's soul into symbolic logic. At that point, he can ask Carr, the mathematician, to help him reduce them and isolate the common element, which, by implication, should be the most effective for magical purposes.

By interconnecting magic and science through his protagonist, Leiber leaves all possibilities open. At the book's end Tansy asks Saylor, "...do you honestly believe all this, or are you once more just pretending to believe for my sake?" His terse reply is "I don't know." This may not be complete acceptance of the reality of witchcraft, but it is far removed from his position at the narrative's beginning. There is a wry paraphrase of the line which gives this book its title directed at the rational protagonist in *Dracula's Daughter* (1935): "There are more things in heaven and earth than are dreamt of in your psychiatry." For Leiber the witticism is the same: there are more things in heaven and earth than are dreamt of in Saylor's ethnology. But because the nature of those things is reducible to formulas, a portion of their supernaturalism is suspect to those like Saylor. In that sense, Leiber's book may be a modernist reaction to the outlook of the 20s and 30s, where many "natural" behaviors and rituals were debunked through Freudianism and other scientific reductions.

Certainly this psychological viewpoint is active in the first adaptation of Leiber's novel, an entry in Universal's B-budget "Inner Sanctum" series entitled *Weird Woman* (1944). For whatever reason (rumored to be star Lon Chaney's inability to memorize lines), this version transposes Leiber's rendering of his protagonist's inner thoughts into whispered voiceovers. As the Saylor character, here called Norman Reed, ponders the "struggle of man against superstition," his wife, Paula, returns home late at night. Flashbacks reveal that Reed met his wife while on an anthropological trip to the South Seas, where she was a white woman raised by islanders who learned the traditions of totem and taboo. The direction of Leiber's narrative is entirely rerouted by a script which changes Ilona Carr into Reed's former fiancée and an ongoing rival for his affections with Paula. This also means that the purely academic rivalries of the novel become a more traditional romantic con-

Below, in *Weird Woman*, Reed (Lon Chaney, center) breaks a taboo as his future wife Paula (Anne Gwynne, right) looks on.

flict. While Ilona's actions are clearly malevolent, as she embroils Reed with a love-struck secretary and her jealous boyfriend and drives his colleague, Sawtelle, to suicide, nothing in her behavior is clearly tied to the supernatural.

Despite Evelyn Sawtelle's assertion to her that "you're a witch...you killed my husband," Ilona Carr is not like her counterparts in Leiber's work or *Night of the Eagle.* Her actions, such as plaguing Paula with telephone calls of the "death chant" music, are psychological rather than preternatural ploys. Ilona Carr perishes when the Reeds and Mrs. Sawtelle use the same tactics on her. While their technique for extracting a confession, which includes the prophesy that "13 days are allowed," drives Ilona to nightmares and a flight which ends in her death, the resolution is less ambiguous than Leiber's and, except for the question of why Ilona dies as she foresaw in her dream, entirely naturalistic.

Night of the Eagle also reduces much of Leiber's novel to the same three-way conflict between Saylor, Tansy, and Flora Carr; but the script, drafted by Corman writers Richard Matheson and Charles Beaumont, retains the central irony of Saylor's disbelief and plays against it from the earliest scenes of him lecturing his students and hosting a bridge night for his colleagues. As with most successful adaptations, *Night of the Eagle* assumes that the viewer has expectations about the film as a genre piece. Just as Saylor protests too much while lecturing his class, Flora Carr's ingenuous question about Saylor's professional accomplishments at the bridge gathering—"What's the answer? Have you sold your soul to the devil?"—has an obvious double meaning. The event is part of Leiber's sub-text of systems. Card playing itself is a ritual that combines aspects of the magical in the cards' historial association with fortune telling and the scientific in the methods of bidding and play. By including the bridge game early in the narrative, the filmmakers carry over those connotations to the film. They are even reinforced in the next sequence, after the others have gone and while Tansy is searching the parlor for something, Saylor sits nearby playing solitaire. This ritual behavior of his is often visible in the background of the close-ups which capture Tansy's anxious expression.

There is more added meaning in Saylor's reply—"Heart and soul. Here she is [indicating Tansy]: my good luck charm." For the viewer already aware of Saylor's passionate skepticism, the words with which he chooses to answer Carr's apparently innocent question are telling. Assuming that he is aware of the politics of academia and the jealousies of his female colleagues and faculty wives, Saylor is to some extent being consciously ironic. "Heart and soul" is a common phrase, but it immediately links the material and spiritual worlds by invoking the emblems of their vitality. Taken with his offhanded use of another cliché in the characterization of his wife as his "good luck charm," a more profound and literal irony is created. Tansy has, indeed, been a provider of good luck and Saylor will painfully come to discover just how true his statement is. If the dialogue were not clear enough, the reaction shots confirm the dynamic of the situation. When Flora concludes that Saylor "certainly leads a charmed life," Tansy fumbles; and Flora smirks knowingly.

Throughout *Night of the Eagle* the filmmakers use abridged narrative and visual style to enhance the ironies in Leiber's original. Unlike Tansy of the novel, the film character leaves no clue to her destination for Norman when she goes off to "die in his place." In the film, Saylor's pursuit is by car not train, and only an accident as he tries to flag down Tansy's bus prevents him from overtaking her. Saylor's improvised ritual takes place in a seaside graveyard not a hotel room. When Tansy is called back from the ocean without her soul, she comes to Saylor in that graveyard. The use of moving shots of the gravestones from her viewpoint, being carried in his arms, and her monotone request to "take me home" create a play of meaning not in the novel: the graveyard should be home to the soulless Tansy.

The stone eagle which is substituted for Leiber's dragon figure is, as the title suggests, a central visual motif of the film. Repeatedly a single shot frames Saylor and the figure, often so that the mass of carved stone in the foreground restricts the space and adds a deterministic value as well. The frequent use of high and low angle and staging in depth invoke the conventions of the genre and refine the specific relationships. The background/foreground staging between Saylor and Tansy as she searches for an evil charm after the party is a metaphor of her concern for his safety not hers. The two shot of Saylor and Flora Carr in her office both indicates her influence over his career and portends her malevolence towards him and Tansy.

Leiber's last three chapters are a complex of migrating personalities, which has Saylor capturing Mrs. Gunnison's soul and then discovering that the "libidinous old bitch Mrs. Carr," as Tansy called her early on, has planned on taking over his wife's body. In light of these unabashedly supernatural exchanges, one wonders how Saylor can close the novel by saying, "I don't really know."

Despite discarding most of the elaborate "chess game" from Leiber's novel between Saylor and the three faculty wives/witches, the script and the staging of the final sequence capture and sustain the core conflict of **Conjure Wife**. Flora Carr's attack on Tansy is intercut with a confrontation with Saylor in her office. At first Saylor tries to hold on to his rationalism, accusing Carr of hypnotizing Tansy and asking, "Why did you try to drive my wife out of her mind?" Before answering Flora stands and leans forward across her desk so that a lamp harshly illuminates her features from below as if invoking a stereotype of demonic lighting. She proves Saylor's belief to him by igniting a house of tarot cards. When he screams for her to stop, she taunts him: "But why? You don't really believe in this, Norman. You couldn't be concerned with a few bits of burning paper. Just a woman's eccentricity."

Leiber introduces the concept of "perfidious music" in **Conjure Wife** through Alexander Scriabin's Ninth Sonata. Saylor listens to it when he readies a charm to save Tansy, a phonograph needle that has played the second movement of the piece. The filmmakers use a more modern technical icon: a tape of one of Saylor's lectures is a key prop in the conclusion of *Night of the Eagle*. Knowing that the tape has an undertone which alarmed Tansy, that she was clutching it when she tried to kill herself and that he was plagued by discordant sounds played back to him over the telephone, Saylor brings the tape when he confronts Carr. After he leaves her office upset by the burning cards, it is the sound of this tape played over the school's public address system by Carr which seems to animate the stone eagle that attacks Saylor.

"Just a woman's eccentricity." Below, Flora Carr (Margaret Johnston) burns the house of tarot cards as Norman (Peter Wyngarde) watches in *Night of the Eagle*.

The sound of the tape works in concert with the visuals. Its rumbling undertone enmeshes Saylor as firmly as the shots which constantly frame the stone eagle in the foreground. These culminate with a long shot of his tiny figure seeming to run from the statue's open beak. Carr remains secure in her office as the Saylor house burns and the stone eagle is transmogrified into a giant raptor swooping out of the sky with deadly talons poised. It pursues Saylor into the anthropology building by crashing through the front doors and corners him in his office. As he cringes in terror in front of the blackboard on which his declaration of disbelief is still written, Carr's husband reaches her office. Believing she has inadvertently been playing the tape over the public address, he switches it back to being heard in the office, which forces her to turn it off. Not only is Saylor spared, but the smashed doors and his torn coat are restored. His home has burned but Tansy has escaped the flames. Has it been hypnosis after all? Was the cat knocking over the heater and starting the fire at the same time Carr set a match to the cards just a coincidence? As Flora and Lindsay Carr leave the campus, the stone eagle falls from its perch and crushes her. The final shot, which pans down from her lifeless body to the reel of audio tape fallen from her hand and lying on the cobblestones, asks the question posed by Tansy at the end of the novel, which the filmmakers superimpose instead of an end title: "DO YOU BELIEVE."

II. Spirits

...[A] house arrogant and hating, never off guard, can only be evil. This house, which seemed somehow to have formed itself, flying together into its own powerful pattern under the hands if its builders, fitting itself into its own construction of lines and angles, reared its great head back against the sky without concession to humanity. It was a house without kindness, never meant to be lived in, not a fit place for people or for love or for hope. Exorcism cannot alter the countenance of a house; Hill House would stay as it was until it was destroyed.

The Haunting of Hill House

The Spiral Staircase: Shirley Jackson (1919-1965), **The Haunting of Hill House**

Shirley Jackson's understated 1959 novel is not really a ghost story, any more than **Conjure Wife** is merely about witchcraft. Like **Conjure Wife**, **The Haunting of Hill House** is a third-person novel with a lot of interior monologues and other first person aspects. Also, like Leiber's

Above, the designer's conception of "a house arrogant and hating."

Norman Saylor, one of Jackson's protagonists, Dr. John Montague, is an anthropologist; but the resemblances end there.

To begin with Montague is not a debunking anthropologist but pursuing "his true vocation, the analysis of supernatural manifestations." More significantly the key character in Jackson's ensemble, Eleanor Vance, is neither a para-psychologist nor a believer, but a disheartened spinster yearning for escape and adventure; or as Jackson puts it, "During the whole underside of her life, ever since her first memory, Eleanor had been waiting for something..." After brief, objective introductions of Montague, the sophisticated Theodora, and the heir to the house, Luke Sanderson, it is alongside Eleanor in the car which she has taken without her sister's permission that the reader travels to HIll House. It is from Eleanor's perspective that the reader first "sees" the building: "The house was vile. She shivered and thought, the words coming freely into her mind, Hill House is vile, it is diseased; get away from here at once."

In Jackson's occult vision, Hill House is ultimately the cause of Eleanor's deliverance *and* destruction. Eleanor's plaintive homily, which Jackson uses as an ironic motif by having it constantly return to the character's thoughts, is that "journeys end in lovers meeting." And

Eleanor's relationship with the object of the title, with Hill House, is clearly one of love as well as hate.

The house's expression of love, its writing "Help Eleanor come home" on its own walls, both horrifies and excites her; but she cannot admit to these feelings: "You think *I* like the idea that I'm the center of attention?" Hill House with its dark secrets represents the intimacy which Eleanor has never had with any other being and which none of her new companions, each preoccupied with his or her own problems, can offer in the house's stead. Given this context, the ending of the novel is inevitable: "Silence lay steadily against the wood and stone of Hill House, and whatever walked there, walked alone." Like the first and last paragraphs of Jackson's prose which mirror each other with repeated sentences, Eleanor embraces Hill House and, with her car and her body smashed against a tree, her journey does end in lovers meeting.

As a genre work, Jackson's novel relies as much on psychological construction as it does on the supernatural. For Montague, no Norman Saylor but still a scientist, the house is a chance to prove himself. "They *cannot* explain this," he exclaims exultantly about the "cold spot." Then he proceeds to compare it to others on record in terms of coldness, size, and intensity, other cold spots which, one might assume, are equally unexplained. In a sense Montague's method follows from Norman Saylor's deduction that witchcraft, however supernatural it might be, is also a system with its own set of rules analogous to those of natural science. Montague's allusions to the Winchester house and other "haunted" places, to the number of fires set by poltergeists in a Scottish manor, to the record of inexplicable events, are allusions to a jumble of data in search of organizing principles. Montague has, in fact, already extracted certain rules, such as his glib reassurance that "No ghost in the long history of ghosts has ever hurt anyone physically. The only damage done is by the victim to himself. One cannot even say that the ghost attacks the mind, because the mind, the conscious, thinking mind, is invulnerable; in all our conscious minds as we sit here talking, there is not one iota of belief in ghosts."

If there is a shortcoming in Jackson's novel, it is in this reliance on the observations of others, whether spoken aloud or secretly thought. The reader comes to Hill House expecting ghosts and finds none. Bumps in the night, cold spots, general spookiness, yes; but couldn't these all be the kind of mass hallucinations which Norman Saylor suspects in **Conjure Wife**? Or perhaps Eleanor, who is recruited by Montague in the first place because of a shower of stones that fell on her house as child, possesses the psychokinetic ability to make her nightmares materialize. "Suppose," as Eleanor asks directly in the film, "the haunting is all in my mind."

If Jackson never fully reveals what really happened at Hill House, the filmmakers create a different and often more compelling version of the same incidents in *The Haunting* (1963). Rather than invent new occurrences or characters screenwriter Nelson Gidding and director Robert Wise subtly reinterpret them with significant results. A prologue begins with a shot of the house as the actor who is to portray Dr. Markway (Montague) reads Jackson's stark description in voiceover then continues with a montage of the past events which Jackson rendered piecemeal. The viewer watches the carriage accident which kills the first Mrs. Hugh Crain which ends with a kind of visual synecdoche, as her lifeless hand falls into the shot. Then an obscure figure moves down a hallway, its dark, Victorian recesses framed and lit like the house in *The Magnificent Ambersons*, which Wise edited twenty years earlier. But whereas these trappings were part of the irony of *Ambersons*, they are the root terror of *The Haunting*. The audience is thrown into the point of view of "the second Mrs. Crain" as she tumbles down the stairs and blurred, twisting shots approximate the last things she saw in life. Finally a grim but striking deep focus wide angle captures her sprawled at the foot of the main stairs, eyes wide in fright and her corpse in the lower foreground of the frame and behind her shadowy killer, the house itself.

Below, the visitors to Hill House, Dr. Markway (Richard Johnson), Theo (Claire Bloom), Eleanor (Julie Harris), and Luke (Russ Tamblyn) discover the oversized statue of Hugh Crain.

After an establishing sequence such as this, Mrs. Sanderson's casual remark as she negotiates the rental of Hill House with Dr. Markway has a sardonic and foreboding impact: "The dead are not quiet in Hill House." As more events from the novel are transposed to *The Haunting*, the filmmakers continue to exploit genre expectation and the plastic reality of their medium. Long before the Doctor's remarks about her ability at dinner, Theodora's ESP is dramatically established in her meeting with Eleanor. While the housekeeper, Mrs. Dudley, repeats her litany of doom in the background, Theodora probes Eleanor. "You wear your thoughts on your sleeve," is her wry reply when Eleanor asks how she knew what was in her mind. The residual, paternalistic presence of Hill House's builder, Hugh Crain, is graphically emphasized in the staging of the visitors' discovery of his oversized statue where a wide shot reveals them arrayed before him like his new children.

The same kind of understatement is applied to the doors which close by themselves. After Markway has explained, as in the novel, that Hill House is built at odd angles and doors hung to swing shut on their own, he tries to demonstrate but the house won't cooperate. After the distraction of more dialogue, they turn to go, and the door is suddenly shut. The cold spot outside the nursery acquires an even more graphic dimension when Luke takes its measure by exhaling and watching his moist breath frosting into long, white plumes.

The most unusual visual manipulations are reserved for Eleanor. As in the novel, the viewer is drawn into her POV by riding along with her. Parts of Hill House have, of course, already been seen in the main titles. But now when Eleanor assesses it, the audience not only hears her thoughts on the soundtrack rather than reading them on the page but hears them in a telling whisper: "It's staring at me. Vile, vile..." On the veranda outside the library, Jackson spends a page on Eleanor's musings as she looks up at the tower before noticing that "she was gripping the veranda rail tightly and leaning far backward." In the film, a reverse angle of Eleanor from high in the tower actually shows her standing against the rail from an omniscient perspective that could only be that of the house itself. Abruptly the camera swoops down, like the malignant press of the house's soul, and forces her backward. Jackson's description in which "the lawn seemed somehow tilted sideways and the sky turned and swung" becomes another shot from Eleanor's point of view.

It is the Doctor who grabs Eleanor on the railing; and this is part of the most telling narrative extrapolation of Jackson by the makers of *The Haunting*. Consistent with the psychological profile of Eleanor which Jackson only suggests is her infatuation with Dr. Markway, the man who has taken her away from her drab existence. The filmmakers go even further and suggest that Markway reciprocates some of her feeling. The house itself interrupts a moment when they seem about to embrace in a music room, by striking a low note on a nearby harp with its unseen hand.

The harp, the knockings, the writing on the wall—all these have a visual and aural presence in film which contradicts any inclination of the viewer to believe that Eleanor is doing this herself; and yet the word on Markway's questionnaire which Luke doesn't understand, "psychokinesis," makes it possible that she is. Even the interruption of her most flirtatious moment with Markway permits two readings. The house, her possessive, predestined lover, strikes at the harp strings out of jealousy and the need to control her. Or, like Henry James' repressed governess in Edmund Wilson's reading, Eleanor does it herself out of fear of sex. Both are possible.

As in the novel, the Doctor's wife eventually arrives at the house. But whereas this was for Jackson a planned event, and Mrs. Montague and her admirer, Arthur, are almost caricatures, who believe in and pursue psychic experiences like players at a ouija board, Mrs. Markway is a sceptic come to warn her husband that journalists know of his presence and that their reports could besmirch his academic reputa-tion. Most importantly in novel and film, the Doctor's wife is the catalyst which brings the narrative to its chaotic climax and resolu-tion. Again even as the filmmakers combine and condense certain parts of Jackson's plot, they also add a layer of complexity.

Below, Eleanor (Julie Harris) flees down the corridor.

While Luke tries to prevent the Doctor from opening the parlor door which has bulged but not broken under attack from some force, Eleanor goes out the back to finish her dance with Hugh Crain. The visuals all externalize Eleanor's emotions for the audience. First she runs

down the corridor in her nightdress and yelps in alarm at a carved figure. A cut to a low angle permits the camera to move directly below, as
she covers her ears against the noise. The distortion as she hurries
down another hallway is revealed to be caused by a mirror when she
runs into her own reflection. A longer focal length lens pans with her
past another figure. As she struggles to open a door, a zoom back
catches the features of an amorphous carving on a banister in the
foreground. The noise becomes a creaking, like a ship at sea; and the
frame tilts off the horizontal, first down at the right, then at the left,
like the rolling of a vessel in time to the sound. The door gives way and
inside the room, Eleanor is caught in a curtain. A wider angle reveals
her twisting around, the white cloth draped around her like a parody of
a restless ghost. As she looks up at a swinging chandelier, a reciprocal
high angle shows the entire room from the house's omniscient perspective. Like the images, her mind is confused, hemmed in by obscure
forms, imbalanced. When she reaches the nursery and finds Mrs.

Markway (Richard Johnson) brings Eleanor (Julie Harris) down from the spiral staircase.

Markway is gone, she believes that this intruder has stolen both her lovers. She hurries to the library, to die, to couple with the house psychically if not physically.

The close-up of Eleanor as she sneaks off fades out then cuts to a matching close-up of the statue of Hugh Crain, waiting for Eleanor to finish the dance. Crain's marble eyes anticipate the last close shots of Eleanor driving off, where her tears and the reflections of several lights make her eyes seem metallic and inhuman. As Eleanor climbs the spiral staircase and tells herself, "I'm home," the shots of her painted toes on the steel steps begin a silent parody of human vanity and courtship. She is, in fact, transfigured. Under the influence of the house, her hair flows freely, loosed from its prim French bun. It curls down over her forehead softening her features; and the lighting reinforces the effect making her appear almost glamorous. In the novel, Luke brings her down; in the film, of course, it is the Doctor.

In the novel, it is the doctor who sends Eleanor away alone because she "has to go back the way she came"; in the film, Luke is to accompany her but she slips away. In the novel, Eleanor surrenders to the power of the house; in the film, the sight of the frightened Mrs. Markway in the drive may have caused her to veer into the tree. The film permits Markway to pontificate about Eleanor's death: "It wanted her to stay, and her poor, bedeviled mind wasn't strong enough to fight it." But Eleanor has the last word. It is she, not the Doctor, who rereads Jackson's repeated sentence with one telling change: "...and we who walk here, walk alone."

III. Demons

Faustus is gone; regard his hellish fall,
Whose fiendful fortune may exhort the wise
Only to wonder at unlawful things,
Whose deepness doth entice such forward wits
To practise more than heavenly power permits.

Christopher Marlowe. **Doctor Faustus**

The Faustian Pact: Stephen Vincent Benet (1898-1943), "The Devil and Daniel Webster"

The story of Faust who sells his soul to the devil for power and riches was elevated to the status of popular myth beginning with Marlowe and followed by Goethe, Gounod and scores of others. In this century the

American, Stephen Vincent Benet, retold the Faust story for a new generation in his "The Devil and Daniel Webster" (1937) and reworked the elements into a New England setting in the 1830s. Although both Faust and the Devil resurfaced in the forms of the luckless Jabez Stone and the crafty Scratch respectively, Benet gave the story a more American flavor by adding the historical figure of Daniel Webster, famed New England orator and politician. It is this wily lawyer who defends Stone when the devil comes to collect Jabez's soul for services rendered.

The Daniel Webster of Benet's story, while based on an historical person, also acquires truly mythological proportions when described early in the story: "They said, when he stood up to speak, stars and stripes came right out of the sky, and once he spoke against a river and made it sink into the ground. They said, when he walked the woods with his fishing rod, Killall, the trout would jump out of the streams right into his pockets...and when he argued a case, he could turn on the harps of the blessed and the shaking of the earth underground." Not just an advocate of the poor farmer against predatory bankers and exploitive land grabbers, Webster is the an idealized politician who always had time for a New Hampshireman with a problem. Like any fabled defender of the everyman, when Jabez Stone asks for his help he drops everything in order to defend him.

The mythological dimension of the story is integral to the film version as well. *The Devil and Daniel Webster* or *All That Money Can Buy* (1941) contains most of the components of the original story. This is partly because the co-writer of the screenplay was Benet himself, but also because the director was a man whose background made him a sympathetic adaptor. William Dieterle, who was both producer and director, was trained as an actor and director in the Germany of the 1920s where the style of expressionism as applied to the supernatural tale was pioneered. Working on stage with Max Reinhardt and at UFA studios, Dieterle was part of the tradition established with *The Cabinet of Dr. Caligari* (1919), *Nosferatu* (1922), and *The Golem* (1920), part of the German film industry which set the earliest standards for supernatural horror.

From its opening shot of Daniel Webster laboring over a speech, as the shadow of Scratch on the wall behind him whispers promises and warnings, to its final image of Scratch in close-up surveying the scene for another victim and then staring straight into the camera and pointing to the viewer, *The Devil and Daniel Webster* deftly combines Americana with German expressionism. The first appearances of Scratch and later those of his sensual familiar, Belle, for instance, are heavily backlit so that they seem to enter from pure light. In genre terms the staging economically signifies their supernatural status even before the audience is aware of who they are.

Similar techniques are applied in the film's two party scenes. The first is after the birth of Stone's son and the culmination of a year of good luck and riches resulting from his pact with the devil. It is a traditional New England barn dance but with a supernatural touch as the dancers' own shadows, moving frantically to the tempo of Scratch's fiddle, tower menacingly behind them. The staging of the second dance, after the once kindly Stone has alienated his family and friends by exploiting his neighbors and building a mansion for his mistress, Belle, is much different. With Stone no longer able to attract neighbors to his house, Belle calls upon the dead to dance and cavort at his party. In a *danse macabre* the ghostly figures with muted voices twirl and prance, while Belle takes the soul of Miser Stevens, whose contract with the devil has now come due.

The climax of the film, like the original, is the trial of Jabez Stone. Webster has agreed to defend him against the devil and his unbreakable contract. Tricked into accepting any jury as long as they are Americans, be they "the quick or the dead," Webster finds himself facing a convocation of murderers and traitors risen from the underworld to sit in judgment. In order to defend Jabez to this "jury of the damned," Webster must summon the full measure of his fabled oratorical skills. He avoids the issue of the legality of the contract, for it is signed and sealed. He appeals instead to the scoundrels' emotions, to their implied desire for a second chance, as the only hope that they will give Jabez the opportunity they never had, to repent his sins and start anew. As the foreman of the ghostly jury rises from his seat and tears up the contract, the barn, which heretofore had been bathed in a hellish, stifling mist, is suddenly filled with light and clear air. Webster has won, although the devil warns him, he will be back another day for yet another fight.

The politics of the film, like those of the story, are basically, populist, reflecting the New Deal view of the world. Like the United States of the 1930s, Benet's New Hampshire of a century earlier was facing a depression. Many farmers were losing their land while a few, like Miser Stevens and Jabez Stone after his deal with the devil, loaned them money at exorbitant rates and then mercilessly foreclosed on their notes. Daniel Webster is presented as the friend of these downtrodden farmers as is the socialistic "Grange," a farmers' coalition the others keep urging the luckless Stone to join. Part of his problem, on the political level, is that he refuses to unite with his neighbors and only comes to realize that there is strength in unity after his supernatural ordeal, when he does finally join the Grange.

This political undertone also affects the character of Scratch. Although he is presented as a supernatural being, whose goatee and crouching stance are as much Pan as a traditional Western devil, Dieterle and Benet have also dressed him like a country squire. This

Below, Walter Huston as Mr. Scratch in *The Devil and Daniel Webster.*

ties him by appearance to the elite of the town, the mayor, Miser Stevens, and the landed gentry with whom the wealthy Jabez Stone plays cards. His arrogance and craftiness also type him as an exploiter who is capable of taking advantage of struggling souls like Jabez Stone, preying upon their lack of knowledge as well as their poverty.

The Unwonted Power: Ira Levin (b. 1929), **Rosemary's Baby**

> ...even stripped of these supernatural surmisings, there was enough in the earthly make and incontestable character of the monster to strike the imagination with unwonted power.
>
> Herman Melville, Moby Dick

With its release in 1968, *Rosemary's Baby* began a new cycle of horror movies (culminating with *The Exorcist* in 1973) that were marketed not merely as supernatural tales but as frightening experiences in themselves. Because *Rosemary's Baby* neither relies upon nor exploits mechanical or visual effects for its impact, *The Exorcist* eventually displaced it on the moviegoer equivalent of a "fright meter." The elaborate dream sequence in which the "baby" is conceived is much more unusual in its use of ritual and religious archetypes and psychological symbolism than in its special effects.

It is all the more ironic that William Castle should have been the producer of *Rosemary's Baby.* Castle initiated the project and remained attached to it because he had optioned Ira Levin's novel prior to publication, and the book's popularity made it possible for him to acquire major studio backing. Castle had previously specialized in low-budget horror with advertising gimmicks ranging from life insurance policies in case anyone in the theater should have a heart attack to wired seats which gave unwary patrons a slight electric shock while watching *The Tingler.*

Despite his exploitation career, Castle understood that a detailed, atmospheric, and essentially realistic adaptation would be the most effective approach to bring Ira Levin's best selling novel to the screen. As director, he chose Roman Polanski, the Polish emigré, whose best known previous film was the Franco-British psychological thriller, *Repulsion* (1965). That film which dramatized the descent into psychosis by an alienated and sexually terrified young woman, contained several scenes of grisly violence, such as the woman slashing a man to death with a straight razor. There were also several stylized, hallucinatory sequences, most notably her fantasy of a sexual assault in which arms burst from the walls and grope at her body.

Polanski's script of Levin's novel subtly exploits both viewer expectation and the motifs of the genre. The long panning shot of New York
City which opens the movie is graphically realistic. The female voice
chanting a wordless, monotonous lullaby under the shot in a slightly
flat tone is subliminally unsettling. Then a sudden tilting downward
and a zoom back precipitate a visual disorientation, which leaves the
audience momentarily confused and apprehensive. Medium close shots
follow the young couple, Rosemary and Guy Woodhouse, as they search
for a new apartment. Then a cut to a rooftop angle peers down
ominously at their tiny figures. This contrapuntal cycle of visual and
aural effects is repeated several times as the film's milieu and narrative
direction are concurrently established.

By the time the couple's friend, Hutch, tells them about the unsavory
reputation of the building they are considering, the "Black" Branford,
most of those watching *Rosemary's Baby* know from either the novel or
the film's advertising campaign, what this film is about and where its
horrific events will now transpire. When Rosemary and Guy actually in-
spect the apartment, it appears perfectly ordinary and contains nothing
more unusual than the previous tenant's herb garden and an old
secretary positioned in front of a service closet. By using details of
decor and moments of everyday conversation, Polanski heightens
suspense in an already wary viewer and produces an introductory coda
more effective and evocative than any Gothic novel's florid descriptions
of haunted houses. Even a seemingly innocuous cutaway to a television
commercial can become unnerving when the camera tightens on the
small screen and fills the frame with a colorful and explosive wipe. As
in *Repulsion*, Polanski uses naturalistic detail for subtle shock effects
and to confuse the genre expectations.

In fact, nothing extraordinary, much less supernatural occurs in the
opening minutes of *Rosemary's Baby*. Polanski's staging creates the
mood of uncertainty. When, for instance, Rosemary makes her first trip
to the laundry room in the basement of the building, she encounters
the young woman who lives next door. For a few moments, they exchange pleasantries, discussing the fact that the neighbor resembles a
certain actress and that Rosemary's husband is an actor. Then the conversation turns to the basement itself with its dark corners and limited
escape routes; and the women shudder at the possibility of a concealed
assailant. This seems a natural enough fear; but when the neighbor
shows Rosemary a protective charm given to her by the older couple
with whom she lives, the tone of the scene begins to shift. The one
drawback to the charm, Rosemary is told, is that it smells bad. Instinc-
tively Rosemary bends forward and sniffs it. As she straightens up,

repulsed by the odor, the camera zooms into a tight two shot of the women. The angle is from the side, so that the background is a dark, indistinguishable mass. Abruptly, they are no longer in a laundry room, scaring themselves with the talk of real attackers but somewhere else, lost in the contemplation of less tangible, preternatural fears.

Again and again Polanski takes the novel's details and manipulates the staging to translate their impact into film terms. As in *Repulsion*, he modifies an ostensibly objective camera placement to underscore a character's perspective and/or to make the audience co-experience that point of view. When the conversation of Rosemary and her young neighbor shifts in tone, the angle is altered accordingly.

The gap separating the quasi-normal from the supernatural is closed with the introduction of the older couple who live next door to the Woodhouses. When Minnie Castevet pays her first visit, Rosemary literally opens the door to more than she could ever have imagined. The

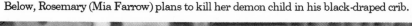

Below, Rosemary (Mia Farrow) plans to kill her demon child in his black-draped crib.

sight of actress Ruth Gordon as Minnie, with her hair and makeup done to suggest a grotesque caricature of 60s style, is already unappealing. When the camera assumes Rosemary's point of view and looks at Minnie through the distorting lens of a peephole, the pasty, deformed visage that peers back is more ludicrous than frightening. As Minnie tours the apartment, Gordon gives the character all the garrulous, inquisitive energy of an aged and disliked godmother. Although Minnie is the nosiest person that Rosemary has ever met and actually asks the price of things, Rosemary does not perceive her as the deadly gargoyle she is, because she seems so raucously pathetic. So Rosemary is badgered into accepting an invitation to dinner.

From this point forward, through a succession of new details—the charm filled with noxious tannis root; the young neighbor's suicide; the paintings missing from the Castevet's walls; and Minnie's "chocolate mousse"—Polanski builds to the inevitable demonic rape. It is inevitable because the viewer knows that it is coming. How can Rosemary's baby be born unless it is conceived? It is demonic not just because of the nature of the rapist but because Polanski uses the rituals and icons of Rosemary's lapsed Catholicism to create an elaborate, phantasmic Black Mass. The use of unusual but real images, such as a newscast of the Papal visit to New York and the scene aboard the presidential yacht, may initially deceive the audience into thinking that Rosemary's nightmare could be just that, a bad dream and nothing more. As the sequence progresses, other visions and sounds encroach on the oneiric ones, until Rosemary's "Sistine Chapel" is filled with black-robed figures and she sits up screaming, "This is no dream—this is real."

The conception of Rosemary's demon child is a *tour de force* of visual effects even in a genre where the audience expects such effects. The second half of the movie and Rosemary's gradual realization of what has happened to her are in some ways anticlimactic. Having so powerfully established the reality of the devil and the deadly menace of his worshippers, Polanski is content to carry the film with the usual devices of the straight thriller. The ending, while certainly sardonic, also has a touch of weird bathos. The baby is finally born but is transformed by Rosemary's maternal attentions to a semblance of humanness. With the child's enigmatic nature unpenetrated and the sound of its whimpers covered by Rosemary's lullaby, the horror of its birth quickly cedes to irony. The self-conscious parodies of Christianity are effaced by a final, wry moment; and the film ends as it began with a panorama of a city unaware of what horrors it harbors.

My Name is Legion: William Peter Blatty (b. 1928), **The Exorcist**

> Now when He [Jesus] landed, there met Him a certain man who for a
> long time was possessed by a devil, and wore no clothes, and lived in
> the tombs, not in a house. And when he saw Jesus, he fell down before
> him, and crying out with a loud voice said, "What have I to do with
> Thee, Jesus, Son of the most high God? I pray thee, do not torment
> me." For He was charging the unclean spirit to go forth from the man.
> For many times it laid hold of him; and he was bound with chains and
> fetters, and kept under guard, but he would break the bonds asunder,
> and be driven by the devil into the deserts. And Jesus asked him,
> saying, "What is thy name?" And he said, "Legion," because many
> devils had entered into him. And they entreated him not to command
> them to depart into the abyss... And the devils came out from the man
> and entered into the swine; and the herd rushed down the cliff into the
> lake and were drowned.
>
> **The Gospel of Luke**

The Exorcist (1973) is, by its own assertion, one of the most controver-
sial horror films ever made. From pre-production through release, the
producers used the terrifying aspects of their product at every turn as
the basis for their advertising and publicity campaigns. Tales of "unex-
plainable" occurrences while shooting, such as sets burning down
mysteriously and actors encountering unusual obstacles to their performance, were leaked to the press, which eagerly repeated these suggestions of demonic intervention. Even the death of actor Jack Mac-
Gowran, who played Burke, was sensationalized by media emphasis on
possible occult implications. From the press releases, it might have
seemed that Satan himself, or at least an evil minion of his, was doing
all in its power to stop the distribution of the film. A larger aura of
melodrama surrounded the actual shooting. Sets were closed, material
was tightly guarded, and actors could not be interviewed without
publicists hovering protectively nearby.

What is most remarkable about all this self-aggrandizement and
promotion is that it worked. Within a year and a half of its release *The
Exorcist* had become, according to *Variety*, number five on their list of
top-grossing American films of all time, an astonishing accomplishment
for a horror film. With newspapers full of stories of wayward souls
returning to the Church after watching the movie, of audiences
frightened into bouts of nausea, of frantic calls in the night to be-
wildered Catholic priests asking for advice about possession, the movie

was a national phenomenon. Few priests could escape the inevitable question, "Have your seen *The Exorcist*, Father?"

For all this, *The Exorcist* was never a critical success. Many were offended by its crass publicity campaign and so attacked the film on that basis. Many considered the exploitation within the film itself even more distressing; critic Pauline Kael went so far as to call it pornographic. None of this is so unusual if one remembers that no matter what its pretensions, *The Exorcist,* is first and foremost a horror film. Horror films, being basically sensationalist, have always been denigrated by the artistic establishment. Many of the same objections voiced about *The Exorcist* in 1973 were echoes of those in the early 1930s when *Frankenstein* and *Dracula* were released.

What distinguishes *The Exorcist* from most of its predecessors in the genre is its sophisticated manipulation of viewer expectations for maximum shock value. Audiences came to be frightened, came to feel a profound *frisson* and to share a terrifying, medieval view of the universe. There was a psychological reverberation between the audience and the film projected before them more sustained and acute than the apocryphal moment in Tod Browning's *Freaks* which sent a crazed spectator screaming up the aisle towards the exit in 1932. Forty years later, watching *The Exorcist* with an audience in its initial release, was like attending a Black Mass with a congregation of believers; one could not help but be caught up in the hysteria.

The opening sequence in Iraq is a classic example of visual and aural manipulation in a genre context. Fast tracking and panning shots across diggers in an archaeological site are complemented by the amplified sounds of their tools striking hard earth mixed with their excited speech. Everyday noises were amplified beyond normal levels. Telephones RANG, clocks TICKED, shovels and picks DUG. In fact, throughout most of the scenes in Iraq there is a constant din, enhanced by the atonal music and combined with a nervous visual energy: dogs fighting, merchants peddling wares, speeding vehicles emerging from darkened alleys. It is as if this place in its "primordialness" evoked the kind of Lovecraftian evil which lurks in another dimension.

Much of this same energy is carried over into the scenes in Georgetown but with a slightly different orchestration. Here the filmmakers create an ambience of security and normalcy that the audience comes to understand as just a calm before the storm. Appropriately, there are the homespun scenes of surburban Georgetown life, wind blowing the multicolored leaves, nuns strolling through picturesque streets, children at play. Only sporadically do adumbrations of what is to come appear: the sound of rats in a cellar where there are no rats; a statue defiled in a church; Regan, the possessed girl, urinating on the carpet at a cocktail party; Burke, the film director, attacking a servant he believes to be an ex-Nazi. All foreshadow the assault on the senses which is to follow, as Regan is possessed and exorcized.

As the climax of the film approaches, the moments of calm, the pauses between the scenes of horror become shorter and shorter. By the time Father Merrin, the exorcist, arrives, the bedroom of the little girl has become a literal *and* figurative battlefield for the forces of good and evil. While the fray is quite graphic and technologically "real," as the filmmakers utilize a variety of make-up and special effects to actualize this supernatural encounter, the context remains that of religious ritual. Objects levitate, humans are thrown across the room, furniture flies through the air, the girl's head spins on her torso—all help maintain the suspension of the audience's natural instinct to disbelieve. But underlying all this, the turmoil within the characters that struggle for a child's soul provide the real drama and the real horror.

Before the film, the novel, **The Exorcist** (1971), used the tradition of supernatural horror as both context and counterpoint. The original by

Below, as the body of Regan (Linda Blair) levitates, Fathers Merrin (Max Von Sydow) and Karras (Jason Miller, right) struggle for her soul in *The Exorcist* .

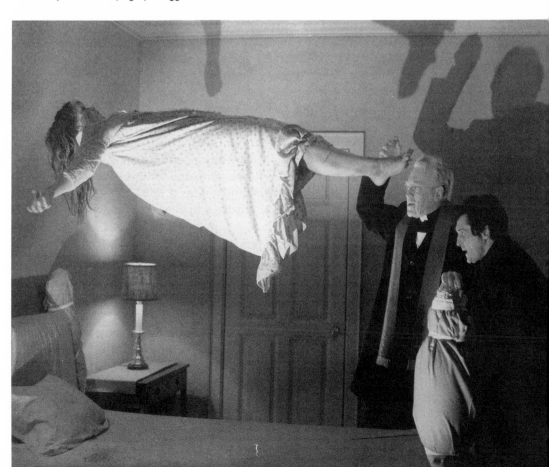

William Peter Blatty is a minimalistic and sketchy piece, full of shifting perpectives and shocking descriptions that leave the impression of being written with the screen adaptation in mind. More than any other literary works in this study, even the other contemporary "best-selling" fiction, the prose original seems designed simultaneously to fulfill the requirements of both novel and screen treatment.

The Exorcist does share the thematic obsession of two of the earlier writers of supernatural horror, Machen and Lovecraft. The real and omnipresent threat of evil forces which lurk just outside the natural world, waiting for a fissure in the time-space continuum to reemerge and claim their their luckless, predestined victims, is a central part of Blatty's view. The central encounter in **The Exorcist** is not unlike that in Machen's "The Great God Pan" or in Lovecraft's "The Dunwich Horror."

With Blatty, the moral dimensions of the encounter with evil are much more dogmatic and therefore less ambiguous. Blatty's theology is basically dualistic with the universe as a Manichean battlefield on which the opposing forces of good and evil are aligned. Regan's bedroom is, of course, a nexus of this contest. Although it may appear to be a struggle contained within a single person, it is also a combat between the supernatural forces of God and Satan, his fallen prince.

It is significant that in the first draft of the screenplay for *The Exorcist* Blatty juxtaposed, in a very non-linear fashion, scenes of Christ's crucifixion, a conversation about a brutal gangland killing, and other moments of violence related thematically but not temporally or narratively to the story. These scenes served to reinforce his concept that all evil is interrelated in a complex web. The manifestations are varied: the wanton fury of a Mafia killing; Burke's murder; the callousness rooted in fear typified by Father Karras' rejection of the bum and his attitude towards the patients in the hospital; the simple, emotional instability of Regan's broken home. All of these are man-made fissures through which the devil may enter this world and claim a soul. They are, like the window in Regan's room, open invitations to the entry of evil.

The battle which inevitably ensues is a ritualistic repetition of the archetypal one between the archangel Michael and the fallen seraph, Satan. The variants in Blatty's story are embodied by Father Merrin and the Assyrian demon Pazuzu. Their confrontation begins as merely symbolic: Merrin, after finding an image of the demon buried with a holy medal, confronts the statue of Pazuzu in a deserted ruin. He is framed on the right with Pazuzu on the left, alluding to the right and left hands of God. A large red sun occupies mid-frame. The epic conflict ends in Regan's bedroom with Pazuzu defeated not by Merrin but by

Above, Father Merrin faces the statue of Pazuzu in *The Exorcist.*

the self-sacrifice of the fear-ridden Father Karras as he takes the demon upon himself and leaps out the window to his death. The image of the empty, shattered window neatly symbolizes the resolution: the devil has returned to his world while the agnostic Karras has burst through his veil of despair to emerge "on the other side."

Below, the figurative doorway, the shattered open window of Regan's room.

IV. Visionaries

As he was a bachelor, and in nobody's debt, nobody troubled his head anymore about him. The school was removed to another quarter of the hollow, and another pedagogue reigned in his stead.

Washington Irving, "The Legend of Sleepy Hollow"

The Wheel of Fortune: Stephen King (b. 1947), **The Dead Zone**

In many ways, *The Dead Zone* epitomizes the adaptation of the current supernatural best seller. To begin with, it is adapted from a novel by Stephen King, whose work over the last twenty years has brought new marketability if not respectability to the genre. Unlike the more critically accalimed writings of Anne Rice, there have been many film versions of King's work, all of which have profited from the pre-existing interest from the readers of the novels.

Many of those films such as *Firestarter*, *Stephen King's Graveyard Shift*, or *Pet Sematary* emphasize the sensationalist and exploitive elements of King's fiction with predictable results. King's prodigious output has, at times, worked against his literary reputation. Again unlike Anne Rice who produces erotica and romances under pen names, King's use of a pseudonym earlier in his career was under pressure from publisher who did not want his works to compete directly with each other. Also unlike Rice, whose serial works of fantastic fiction are in the "classic" tradition, King's characters discover the horrific and supernatural under every rock and behind every tree. Ironically, the work of Rice, whose elegant tales of vampires and Egyptian mummies seem to have been inspired by the Universal horror films of the 30s, has resisted adaptation whereas filmed versions of King's more "plebeian" narratives show up constantly both in theaters and on television.

By the time of **The Dead Zone**'s writing, King was already concerned about self-imitation and burnout. King's narratives are always tied to certain stylistic preferences. The prose is straightforward and realistic. The horrors which his characters encounter are varied; but the descriptions are never embellished with grisly adjectives. Geography and brand names are used to evoke a sense of the everyday, the world next door. If there is a method behind King's reputation as the contemporary author of horror fiction who can most thoroughly frighten his readers, it is that evil is everywhere waiting to be found. In **The Dead Zone** with the Castle Rock killer and the bible-salesman-turned-politician, Greg

Stillson, King creates his usual, simplistic archetypes of this evil. King's antagonists are merely that, the narrative irritants which impel his protagonists to action.

With his preference for italicized asides and flash "cuts" to other times and places, King also has a reputation as a "cinematic" novelist. Almost of all of King's novels contain parallel stories, a device which can sustain narrative suspense over a lengthy work by constantly bringing the reader to the brink of a climactic moment only to abruptly begin a new chapter and/or shift to another venue entirely.

King's fertile plot ground poses the greatest challenge to would-be adaptors who have two hours or less of screen time. All must combine characters and merge events. Some exploit the genre expectations and even the viewer's likely familiarity with the antecedent novel. The usual result is a film full of abnormal happenings and one-dimensional characters. For whatever reason, it is King's earliest novels, **Carrie**, **The Shining**, and most notably **The Dead Zone**, which have been most successfully turned into movies.

King summarizes his thematic focus in **The Dead Zone** with his subtitles: "The Wheel of Fortune" and "The Laughing Tiger". The wheel of fortune is what turns first for and then against King's protagonist, as it brings him some winnings at carnival roulette then sends him hurtling head on into a five-year coma. The laughing tiger epitomizes not just Stillson, the psychotic politician hiding behind a smile and a glad hand, but the menace behind every innocent facade.

Perhaps the most significant development in terms of King's work in **The Dead Zone** is the central character, Johnny Smith. The name itself is both wry and symbolic, not just an everyman but one who ultimately must struggle for anonymity despite having a true name which is the stereotype of a false one. Like Carrie White, John Smith has a mother unhinged by religious fervor, but that is tangential here to an otherwise normal man whom God or fate or the wheel of chance has touched without reason. John's experience is actually closer to the father and son, Jack and Danny, of **The Shining**; but where they are plagued by the past, it is the future which torments John Smith.

At one point in the novel, when his prediction of a fire and great loss of life at a roadhouse comes true, Smith is accused by another character of being responsible: "He made it happen! He set it on fire by his mind, just like that book *Carrie*." King also makes two separate allusions to Ray Bradbury's **Something Wicked This Way Comes.** This tactic is like that of a filmmaker who invokes an awareness of the genre to create irony and/or play with expectations.

For the adaptors, the position of John Smith suggested a course in turning novel into film. Screenwriter Jeffrey Boam and director David Cronenberg use Smith as a filter. While is it not entirely a "subjective" film, only a few, short scenes take place outside of Smith's awareness. In contrast, King has over three chapters, nearly one-eighth of the novel's length, while Smith is in a coma, and numerous third person scenes paralleling those which Smith experiences.

In finding substitute icons, much of King's symbolic structure is discarded. The winning streak at the Wheel of Fortune becomes a single, disquieting roller coaster ride; but two medium close reaction shots of Johnny and a single objective view of the roller coaster streaking by from below have the same dramatic portent as pages of King's prose. Of course, the filmmakers also use genre expectation. The title sequence, which uses the same graphic treatment of the words "The Dead Zone" as the cover of the novel with letters that slowly form and recede over shots of rural New England to create a sense of foreboding from the first. In contrast to King's metaphorical introduction of the adult John Smith as he frightens his girlfriend, Sarah Bracknell, with a "Jekyll-and-Hyde mask," the film introduces Johnny Smith in his classroom. He reads from memory, without any ominous undertone, a section from Poe's "The Raven." "Pretty good, huh?" he asks his class, as he closes the book and assigns them a reading of "The Legend of Sleepy Hollow" for the next time: "You'll like it. It's about a schoolteacher who gets chased by a headless demon." Rather than Bradbury, the filmmakers invoke Poe a second time, by equating the lost love of Sarah Bracknell with "the lost Lenore"; they even include a passing allusion to Sleeping Beauty.

Although, at some level, any invocation of Poe's raven or Washington Irving's demons, is ominous, the filmmakers play against that. Talking birds and headless horsemen are fiction, fodder for English classes, not objects that need really be feared. It is on the roller coaster, where many people are actually frightened, that Johnny is first disturbed. But, as the expression on actor Christopher Walken's face clearly conveys, it is not by the ride. The car accident that shortly sends John Smith into a coma is also changed subtly but significantly by the filmmakers. King has Johnny's cab hurtle into one of two drag racers. The adaptors use a sleeping driver and a capsized milk truck. The images of the "Cloverfield Milk" tanker slowly gliding down the highway on its side throwing sparks and of John Smith's inability to react in time behind the rain-streaked windshield of his Volkswagen bug capture the chilling irony of King's penchant for brand names and common objects.

For King, John Smith's fate remains mostly ironic. Various characters besides Smith mouth or think the obvious "if only." For Cronenberg, Smith is a tragic figure. Where King's parallel structure might tend to distance or even depersonalize, Cronenberg's focus is uninterrupted. Before he adapted **The Dead Zone,** King praised Cronenberg in his survey of supernatural fiction, **Danse Macabre,** as "The only director I can think who has explored this gray land between art and porno-exhibitionism successfully—even brilliantly—again and again with never a misstep..." This assessment of King's is based on *The Brood, They Came from Within,* and *Rabid;* but it is Cronenberg's subsequent remake of *The Fly* which confirms his dramatic predilections. Both there and in *The Dead Zone* he takes pre-existing narratives and charts alternate courses toward final scenes that are closer to grand opera in their tragic dimensions than the science fiction or horror genres from which they respectively spring. In both *The Fly* and *The Dead Zone,* it is Cronenberg's characters who believe that they have the fate of the world in their hands and Cronenberg who emphasizes the sense of *hubris* in both stories.

All the elements in Cronenberg's visualization underscore this course. There is obvious visual impact and figurative values in the scene where Smith stands in a drainage tunnel with the Castle Rock sheriff and the deputy who is actually the killer. Leaning against the stones with the light from beyond reflected off the wet surfaces, it is as if Smith stands inside the barrel of a giant gun about to be blown to pieces. As dramatic as this imagery may be, it is no more effective than the subtler staging when the Sheriff first comes to ask Smith's help. When this emblem of law and order suggests that God has given Smith psychic abilities for a reason, Smith dismisses him with a bitter retort:

Below, Johnny Smith (Christopher Walken) "sees" himself inside the burning house from his hospital bed.

"God's been a real sport to me." After the Sheriff leaves, Smith stands alone, shot from a slight low angle. There is a lamp at the left foreground and a patterned tin roof above him which, in the two dimensions of the frame, perfectly betoken his enclosed situation, where he is hemmed in, stripped of his free will, and poised as if to fall.

The power of *The Dead Zone*'s visual style is inherent in the unique way which a motion picture has of capturing and rendering tangible Smith's precognitive visions. The prologue of events before John's accident in *The Dead Zone* is brief. At the end of the fifth scene Sarah stands at the foot of Johnny's bed praying that he will survive. A fade out from her POV of his battered face and a fade in to the brass sign of a clinic condenses the five years to a few seconds. It is the psychic experiences which become spare but stunning moments inside Johnny's mind. When the hospital nurse touches him, he sees her house catching fire and then he is inside it. From his mental POV of her daughter cringing in terror from the flames, there is a cut to John lying helplessly in the hospital with his bed covers ablaze. The roadhouse fire in the novel becomes an accident on thin ice, probably inspired by King's own prologue. The shots of the uniformed youngsters dropping into the freezing water as John holds one of his special pupil's hands have a spare, visceral reality quite unlike the original.

Stillson, the novel's personification of evil, appears in only five scenes in the film; and one of those is Johnny's vision. In the novel, John Smith sees both Stillson's past and an obscurely menacing future through a prose montage of disconnected sights and sounds. The film has a shuddering clarity: Stillson launching a nuclear assault. In the novel, John Smith does not move against Stillson until he learns of his fatal brain tumor. In the film, it is the sense of what must be done that impels him. "I'm scared, Sam. What's happening to me?" he confides to his doctor. He shows him stacks of mail in his closet from those seeking help. In the end, Johnny Smith both personifies everyman and saves everyman by attacking Stillson. As he rides a bus, a "common carrier," to his fateful rendezvous the setting sun is behind him, visually connecting the everyday bus with a mythic pose.

Both the film and the novel's characters fail to kill Stillson directly. In the novel, a dying John manages to grasp Stillson's ankle for an instant and learns that "*Everything had changed*." King's epilogue intersperses letters from John to Sarah and his father with a Senate investigation of Stillson, who is discredited for shielding himself from John's bullets by holding a baby. Coming after John's death, all this information is necessarily outside of his living consciousness and again in the ironic mode.

For Cronenberg, a tragic treatment requires that John, Stillson, and Sarah all participate in the final events. It is her baby which Stillson grabs. Cronenberg's version of John's last vision is much clearer. Again using King's "brand name" technique, a *Newsweek* cover shows Stillson and the baby. A cut back reveals a gun in Stillson's hand which he plans to use on himself. Johnny whispers, "Goodbye," as a distraught Sarah reiterates her love for him. The tragic vision is complete. No further statement is needed. Cronenberg holds it for a moment and then fades out.

Below, while Sarah (Brooke Adams) looks on, Stillson (Martin Sheen) uses her baby to shield himself from Johnny Smith's bullets in *The Dead Zone*.

Above, in a publicity pose for *The Raven*, Boris Karloff, Vincent Price, Peter Lorre, and a stuffed bird.

Filmography

This Filmography is organized into subsections which conform to the main text. Each subsection contains all the feature films based on the literary work(s) of a particular Author which are discussed in the main text. These also appear in the same order as in the text from Mary Shelley to Stephen King. Besides listing only feature films, we have omitted films in which cameo appearances or token allusions are the only relative contents. To avoid redundancy in the credits, where appropriate the name of the Author may appear only once at the head of subsection.

Within the subsections, a film is listed alphabetically in bold italics by the title of its first release in its country of origin. This is followed by all known alternate titles under which it may also have been released, if any, in normal italics. Some of these alternate titles are for video releases. Films with the same title are listed chronologically. The year is based on the Academy of Motion Picture Arts and Sciences method, that is, the year of the initial public showing in the country of origin. This may lead to occasional discrepancies with other sources, particularly those published in Europe, which may use the year of production. We then list the main technical credits and principal cast with character names *or* as much as we have been able to obtain, which in a few instances may be little more than the year and country of origin. Square brackets ([]) are used to note real names following pseudonyms. Running times and their reliability vary greatly depending on the source. Wherever possible timings are from the original release. Otherwise or whenever disparities exist, we have either used a consensus or what we believe to be the most reliable source, for example the American trade periodicals, *Variety* or *The Hollywood Reporter*. While every attempt has been made to avoid errors and omissions, the authors invite comments and information from readers in this regard.

Below, the Creature imprisoned in *The Bride of Frankenstein*.

Mary Wollstonecraft Shelley

NOTE: All the scripts in this section are based on Mary Shelley's novel, **Frankenstein,** or the characters contained therein. Other stories, novels, or plays noted below are similarly based.

Abbott and Costello Meet Frankenstein. (Universal, 1948). USA. Directed by Charles T. Barton. Script by Robert Lees, Frederic Rinaldo, and John Grant. Director of Photography, Charles Van Enger. Production Designers, Bernard Herzbrun, Hilyard Brown. Music, Frank Skinner. Editor, Frank Gross. Starring Bud Abbott, Lou Costello, Lon Chaney, Jr. (Lawrence Talbot), Béla Lugosi (Dracula), Glenn Strange (the Monster). 83 minutes.

Blackenstein. (Exclusive International/Stewart Productions, 1972). USA. Produced by Frank R. Saletri. Directed by William A. Levy. Script by Saletri. Director of Photography, Bob Caramico (Color). Music, Walco Productions Editor, Levy. Starring John Hart (Dr. Stein), Joe De Sue (Blackenstein/Eddie Walker), Ivory Stone (Winnifred Walker), Roosevelt Jackson (Malcolm), Andrea King (Eleanor). 87 minutes.

The Bride. (Columbia/Delphi III, 1985). USA. Produced by Victor Drai. Directed by Franc Roddam. Script by Lloyd Fonvielle. Director of Photography, Stephen H. Burum (Color). Production Designer, Michael Seymour. Music, Maurice Jarre. Editor, Michael Ellis. Starring Sting (Frankenstein), Jennifer Beals (Eva), Clancy Brown (Viktor), David Rappaport (Rinaldo), Geraldine Page (Mrs. Baumann), Anthony Higgins

(Clerval), Alexei Sayle (Magar). 118 minutes.

The Bride of Frankenstein. (Universal, 1935). USA. Produced by Carl Laemmle, Jr. Directed by James Whale. Script by John L. Balderston and William Hurlbut, from their story "Frankenstein Lives Again." Director of Photography, John J. Mescall. Production Designer, Charles Hall. Music, Franz Waxman. Editor, Ted Kent. Starring Boris Karloff (the Monster), Colin Clive (Henry Frankenstein), Elsa Lanchester (the Bride/Mary Shelley), Ernest Thesiger (Dr. Pretorius), Valerie Hobson (Elizabeth), Una O'Connor (Minnie), Dwight Frye (Karl), O.P. Heggie (Hermit). 80 minutes.

Carne per Frankenstein *(Flesh for Frankenstein; Andy Warhol's Frankenstein; Il Mostro è in Tavola...Barone Frankenstein; Frankenstein 1973).* (Compagnia Cinematografica Champion/Jean Yanne/Jean-Pierre Rasam, 1973). Italy/France. Produced by Andrew Braunsberg. Directed by Paul Morrissey and [uncredited] Antonio Margheriti. Script by Morrissey. Director of Photography, Luigi Kuveiller (3-D and Color). Production Designer, Gianni Giovagnoni. Music, Claudio Gizzi. Editor, Frana Silvi, Jed Johnson. Starring Joe Dallesandro (Nicholas), Monique Van Vooren (Katrin Frankenstein), Arno Jerging (Otto), Udo Kier (Baron Frankenstein), Carla Mancini (Girl Monster), Srdjan Zelenovie (Man Monster). 95 minutes.

Il Castello della Paura *(Frankenstein's Castle of Freaks).* (Classic Films, 1973). Italy. Produced by Dick Randall. Directed by Robert

H. Oliver. Script by Oliver. Color. Starring Rossano Brazzi, Michael Dunn, Edmund Purdom, Christiane Royce, Boris Lugosi, Gordon Mitchell, Xiro Papas. 89 minutes.

The Curse of Frankenstein. (Hammer/Warner Bros.-Seven Arts, 1957). Great Britain. Produced by Anthony Hinds. Directed by Terence Fisher. Script by James Sangster. Director of Photography, Jack Asher (Color). Production Designer, Ted Marshall. Music, James Bernard. Editor, James Needs. Starring Peter Cushing (Baron Victor Frankenstein), Christopher Lee (the Creature), Hazel Court (Elizabeth), Robert Urquhart (Paul Krempe), Valerie Gaunt (Justine), Noel Hood (Aunt Sophia), Paul Hardtmuth (Professor Bernstein). 83 minutes.

Dr. Frankenstein on Campus *(Flick).* (Agincourt/Astral, 1970). Canada. Produced by Bill Marshall. Directed by Gil Taylor. Script by David Cobb, B. Marshall, and G. Taylor. Director of Photography, Jackson Samuels (Color). Music, Paul Hoffert, Skip Prokop. Starring Robin Ward (Victor Frankenstein), Kathleen Sawyer, Austin Willis, Sean Sullivan, Ty Haller, Tony Moffat-Lynch. 81 minutes.

Dr. Hackenstein. (Vista St., 1989). USA. Produced by Megan Barnett and Reza Mizbani. Directed by Richard Clark. Script by Clark. Director of Photography, Jens Sturup (Color). Production Designer, Leon King. Starring David Muir, Stacey Travis, Phyllis Diller, Anne Ramsey, Catherine Fox, John Alexis. 90 minutes.

Drácula Contra Frankenstein *(The Screaming Dead; Dracula, Prisonnier*

de Frankenstein). (Ferrix/Comptoir Français du Film, 1972). Spain/France. Produced by Robert de Nesle and Arturo Marcos. Written and Directed by Jesus Franco. Director of Photography, José Climent (Color/Scope). Music, Daniel White and Bruno Nicolai. Starring Howard Vernon (Dracula), Dennis Price (Dr. Frankenstein), Alberto Dalbes, Britt Nichols, Anne Libert [Josiane Gibert], Mary Francis. 87 minutes.

Dracula vs. Frankenstein *(Blood of Frankenstein; Revenge of Dracula).* (Independent International, 1971). USA. Produced by Al Adamson and Samuel M. Sherman. Directed by Adamson. Script by William Pugsley and Sherman. Directors of Photography, Gary Graver, Paul Glickman (Color). Starring J. Carrol Naish (Dr. Frankenstein), Lon Chaney, Jr. (Groton, the Zombie), Zandor Vorkov [Roger Engel] (Dracula), Russ Tamblyn. 90 minutes.

The Evil of Frankenstein. (Hammer/Universal, 1964). Great Britain. Produced by Anthony Hinds. Directed by Freddie Francis. Script by John Elder [Anthony Hinds]. Director of Photography, John Wilcox (Color). Production Designer, Don Mingaye. Music, Don Banks. Editor, James Needs. Starring Peter Cushing (Baron Frankenstein), Peter Woodthorpe (Zoltan), Sandor Eles (Hans), Kiwi Kingston (Creature), Duncan Lamont (Chief of Police), Katy Wild (Beggar Girl), David Hutcheson (Burgomaster), Tony Arpino (Bodysnatcher). 84 minutes.

Les Experiences Érotiques de Frankenstein *(La Maldición de Frankenstein).*(Comptoir Français du Film/Fenix, 1972). France/Spain.

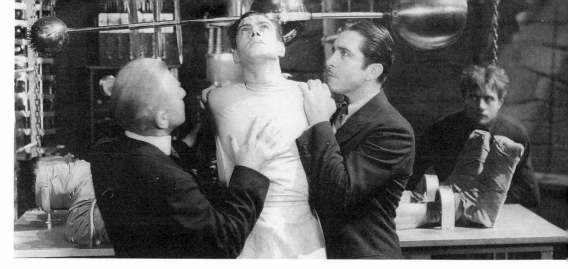

Above, Colin Clive as the obsessed Henry Frankenstein looks skyward while restrained by Dr. Waldman (Edward Van Sloan, left) and Victor Moritz (John Boles) as his assistant, Fritz (Dwight Frye), looks on apprehensively.

Produced by Victor de Costa and Arturo Marcos. Directed by Jesus Franco. Script by Franco. Directors of Photography, Raoul Artigot, Albert Prous (Color). Production Designer, Jean d'Eaubonne. Music, Daniel White. Editor, Roberto Fandino. Starring Howard Vernon (Cagliostro), Anne Libert [Josiane Gibert] (Melissa), Dennis Price (Dr. Frankenstein), Britt Nichols (Abigail), Alberto Dalbes (Dr. Seward), Luís Barboo (Caronte), Jesus Franco (Morpho) , Fred Harrison [Fernando Bilbao] (the Monster), Lina Romay [Rosa Maria Almirall] (Esmeralda). 90 minutes.

Fearless Frank. (Jericho/Trans-America, 1969). USA. Produced and Directed by Philip Kaufman. Script by Kaufman. Director of Photography, Bill Butler (Color). Music, Meyer Kupferman. Editors, Aram Boyajian, Luke Bennett. Starring Jon Voight (Frank), Monique Van Vooren (Plethora), Severn Darden (Doctor), Joan Darling (Lois), Lou Gilbert (Boss), David Steinberg (the Rat), Nelson Algren (Needles). 78 minutes.

La Figlia di Frankenstein (Lady Frankenstein). (Condor/New World,

1971).Italy. Produced and Directed by Ernst von Theumer [Mel Welles]. Script by Edward Di Lorenzo and Dick Randall. Director of Photography, R. Pallotini (Color). Production Designer, Francis Mellon. Music, Alessandro Alessandroni. Starring Joseph Cotten (Baron Frankenstein), Sara Bay [Rosalba Neri] (Tanya), Mickey Hargitay (Inspector Harris), Herbert Fux, Paul Muller. 99 minutes.

Frankenhooker. (Shapiro-Glickenhaus, 1990). USA. Produced by Edgar Ievins. Directed by Frank Henenlotter. Script by Robert Martin and Henenlotter. Director of Photography, Robert M. Baldwin (Color). Music, Joe Renzetti. Editor, Kevin Tent. Starring James Lorinz (Jeffrey Franken), Patty Mullen (Elizabeth), Charlotte Helmkamp (Honey), Shirley Stoler (Spike), Louise Lasser (Mom), Joseph Gonzalez (Zorro), Lia Chang (Crystal). 90 minutes.

Frankenstein. (Universal, 1931). USA. Produced by Carl Laemmle, Jr. Directed by James Whale. Script by Garrett Fort, Francis Edward Faragoh, and [uncredited] Robert Florey. Adapted by John L.

Balderston from the play by Peggy Webling. Director of Photography, Arthur Edeson. Production Designer, Charles D. Hall. Editor, Clarence Kolster. Starring Colin Clive (Henry Frankenstein), Mae Clark (Elizabeth), John Boles (Victor Moritz), Boris Karloff (the Monster), Edward Van Sloan (Dr. Waldman), Frederick Kerr (Baron Frankenstein), Dwight Frye (Fritz), Lionel Belmore (the Burgomaster). 71 minutes.

Frankenstein. (Curtis/ABC-TV. 1973). USA. Produced by Dan Curtis. Directed by Glenn Jordan. Script by Sam Hall, Richard Landau, and Curtis. Director of Photography, Ben Colman (Color). Production Designer, Trevor Williams. Music, Robert Cobert. Starring Robert Foxworth (Dr. Frankenstein), Susan Strasberg (Elizabeth), Bo Svenson (the Monster), Heidi Vaughn (Agatha),

Phillip Bourneuf (Alphonse), Robert Gentry (Henri), William Ames (William Frankenstein). 180 minutes.

Frankenstein. (Yorkshire TV, 1984). Great Britain. Produced by Bill Siegler. Directed by James Ormerod. Script by Ormerod. Director of Photography, Stuart Hinchliffe (Color). Production Designer, Jeremy Bear. Music, Alan Parker. Editor, Lance Tattersall, Mike Pearson. Starring Robert Powell (Dr. Frankenstein), Carrie Fisher (Elizabeth), Sir John Gielgud (De Lacey), David Warner (the Creature), Susan Wooldridge (Justine), Terence Alexander (Alphonse), Michael Cochrane (Henry). 81 minutes.

Frankenstein. (Turner Network Television, 1993). USA. Produced and Directed by David Wickes. Script by Wickes. Director of Photography,

Below, *Frankenstein* (1973): the Monster (Bo Svenson) listens to his maker (Robert Foxworth, right).

Above left, Peter Cushing as a still vigorous Frankenstein and his older assistant Dr. Hertz (Thorley Walters) prepare to operate in *Frankenstein Created Woman*; right, Cushing explains to the younger Dr. Helder (Shane Briant) that the same hands affected by age and misadventure can no longer perform delicate surgery in *Frankenstein and the Monster from Hell*.

Jack Conroy (Color). Production Designer, William Alexander. Music, John Cameron. Editor, John Grover. Starring Patrick Bergin (Dr. Frankenstein), Randy Quaid (the Creature), John Mills (De Lacey), Lambert Wilson (Clerval), Fiona Gillies (Elizabeth), Jacinta Mulcahy (Justine). 150 minutes.

Frankenstein all'Italiana. (Euro International, 1976). Italy. Produced by Filiberto Bandino. Directed by Armando Crispino. Script by Massimo Franciosa and Maria Luisa Montagnana. Director of Photography, Giuseppe Cipriani (Color). Music, S. Cipriani. Editor, Angela Cipriani. Starring Aldo Maccione (Monster), Gianricho Tedeschi (Dr. Frankenstein), Ninetto Davoli (Igor), Jenny Tamburi (Janet). 90 minutes.

Frankenstein and the Monster from Hell. (Hammer, 1973). Great Britain. Produced by Roy Skeggs. Directed by Terence Fisher. Script by John Elder [Anthony Hinds]. Director of Photography, Brian Probyn (Color). Production Designer, Scott MacGregor. Music, James Bernard.

Editor, James Needs. Starring Peter Cushing (Baron Frankenstein), Shane Briant (Dr. Simon Helder), Madeline Smith (Angel/Sarah), John Stratton (Director), Bernard Lee (Tarmut), Clifford Mollison (Judge), David Prowse (Monster). 99 minutes.

Frankenstein Created Woman. (Hammer/Warner Bros., 1966). Great Britain. Produced by Anthony Nelson Keys. Directed by Terence Fisher. Script by John Elder [Anthony Hinds]. Director of Photography, Arthur Grant (Color). Production Designer, Bernard Robinson. Music, James Bernard. Editor, Spencer Reeve. Starring Peter Cushing (Baron Frankenstein), Susan Denberg (Christina), Thorley Walters (Dr. Hertz), Robert Morris (Hans), Duncan Lamont (the Prisoner), Peter Blythe (Anton), Barry Warren (Karl), Derek Fowlds (Johann). 92 minutes.

Frankenstein General Hospital. (New Star, 1988). USA. Produced by Dimitri Villard. Directed by Deborah Roberts. Script by Michael Kelly and Robert Deel. Director of Photography, Tom Fraser (Color). Production Designer, Don Day. Music, John Ross. Editor, Ed Lotter. Starring Mark Blankfield (Dr. Frankenstein), Leslie Jordan (Iggy), Jonathan Farwell (Dr. Reutger), Kathy Shower (Dr. Singleton), Irwin Keyes (Monster), Hamilton Mitchell (Dr. Dixon). 92 minutes.

Frankenstein Meets the Wolf Man. (Universal, 1943). USA. Produced by George Waggner. Directed by Roy William Neill. Script by Curt Siodmak. Director of Photography, George Robinson. Production Designer, John B. Goodman. Music, Hans J. Salter. Editor, Edward Curtiss. Starring Lon Chaney, Jr. (Larry Talbot/Wolfman), Béla Lugosi (the Monster), Lionel Atwill (Mayor), Ilona Massey (Elsa Frankenstein), Patric Knowles (Dr. Mannering), Maria Ouspenskaya (Maleva). 72 minutes.

Frankenstein Must Be Destroyed. (Hammer/Warner Bros.-Seven Arts,

Below, Boris Karloff appearing as Baron Frankenstein in the low-budget *Frankenstein 1970.*

1969). Great Britain. Produced by Anthony Nelson Keys. Directed by Terence Fisher. Script by Anthony Nelson Keys and Bert Batt. Director of Photography, Arthur Grant (Color). Production Designer, Bernard Robinson. Music, James Bernard. Editor, Gordon Hales. Starring Peter Cushing (Baron Frankenstein), Veronica Carlson (Anna Spengler), Simon Ward (Karl), Freddie Jones (Prof. Richter), Thorley Walters (Inspector Frisch), Maxine Audley (Ella Brandt), George Pravda (Dr. Brandt). 97 minutes.

Frankenstein 1980 *(Frankenstein 1973).* (Mosaico, 1973). Italy. Produced by Benedetto Graziani. Directed by Mario Mancini. Script by Mancini and Ferdinando di Leoni. Director of Photography, Emilio Varriano (Color/Scope). Starring John Richardson, Renato Romano, Xiro Papas, Gordon Mitchell, Dalila Parker, Bob Fix. 96 minutes.

Frankenstein 1970. (Allied Artists, 1958). USA. Produced by Aubrey Schenck. Directed by Howard W. Koch. Script by Richard Landau and George W. Yates. Director of Photography, Carl E. Guthrie (Scope). Production Designer, Jack T. Collis. Music, Paul A. Dunlap. Editor, John A. Bushelman. Starring Boris Karloff (Baron Von Frankenstein), Tom Duggan (Mike), Jane Lund (Carolyn), Charlotte Austin (Judy), Don Barry (Douglas Row), Mike Lane. 83 minutes.

Frankenstein 90. (AMCF/A.J. Films/TFI, 1984). France. Produced and Directed by Alain Jessua. Script by Jessua and Paul Gegauff. Director of Photography, William Lubtchansky (Color). Production

Designer, Thierry Flamand, Christian Grossichard. Music, Armando Trovajoli. Editor, Héläne Plemiannikov. Starring Jean Rochefort (Frankenstein), Eddy Mitchell (Frank), Fiona Gelin (Elizabeth), Herma Vos (Adelaide), Ged Marlon (Inspector). 90 minutes.

Frankenstein, the College Years. (Fox Television, 1991). USA. Produced by Bob Engelman. Directed by Tom Shadyar. Script by Bryant Christ and John T. Wolff. Director of Photography, Steve Confer (Color). Production Designer, Mick Strawn. Music, Joel McNeely. Editor, David Garfield. Starring William Ragsdale (Mark), Christopher Daniel Barnes (Jay), Larry Miller (Prof. Loman), Andrea Elson (Andi), De Voreaux White (Kingston), Patrick Richmore (Blaine), Vincent Hammond (Frank). 97 minutes.

Frankenstein, the True Story. (Universal, 1973). Great Britain. Produced by Hunt Stromberg, Jr. Directed by Jack Smight. Script by Christopher Isherwood and Don Bachardy. Director of Photography, Arthur Ibbetson (Color). Production Designer, Wilfrid Shingleton. Music, Gil Mellé. Editor, Richard Marden. Starring James Mason (Dr. Polidori), Leonard Whiting (Victor Frankenstein), David McCallum (Henry Clerval), Jane Seymour (Agatha/Prima), Nicola Paget (Elizabeth), Michael Sarrazin (Monster), Michael Wilding (Sir Richard Fanshawe), Agnes Moorehead (Mrs. Blair), Sir John Gielgud (Chief Constable), Tom Baker (Sea Captain), Sir Ralph Richardson (Lacey). 180 minutes.

Frankenstein Unbound. (20th Century-Fox, 1990) USA. Produced by Roger Corman, Thom Mount, and Kobi Jaeger. Directed by Corman. Script by Corman, F.X. Feeney, and Ed Neumeier based on the novel by Brian Aldiss. Director of Photography, Armando Nannuzzi (Color). Production Designer, Enrico Tovaglieri. Editor, Jay Cassidy. Starring John Hurt (Dr. Buchanan), Raul Julia (Dr. Frankenstein), Bridget Fonda (Mary Shelley), Jason Patric (Byron), Michael Hutchence (Shelley), Nick Brimble (Monster), Catherine Rabett (Elizabeth). 86 minutes.

Frankenstein's Daughter. (Astor/Layton, 1958). USA. Produced by Marc Frederic. Directed by Dick Cunha. Script by H.E. Barrie. Director of Photography, Meredith Wilson. Music, Nicholas Carras. Editor, Everett Dodd. Starring John Ashley (Johnny Bruder), Sandra Knight (Trudy Morton), Donald Murphy (Oliver Frankenstein), Sally Todd (Suzy), Robert Dix, Harold Lloyd, Jr. 85 minutes.

Frankenstein's Great Aunt Tillie. (Filmier/Tillie Productions, 1985). Mexico. Produced and Directed by Myron J. Gold. Script by Gold. Director of Photography, Miguel Garzon (Color). Production Designer, Teresa Pecanins. Music, Ronald Stein. Editor, John Horger. Starring Donald Pleasance (Victor Frankenstein/ Baron Frankenstein), Yvonne Furneaux (Aunt Tillie), June Wilkinson (Randy Woonsock), Rod Colbin (Niederhangen), Garnett Smith (Schnitt). 93 minutes.

Ghost of Frankenstein. (Universal, 1942). USA. Directed by Erle C. Ken-

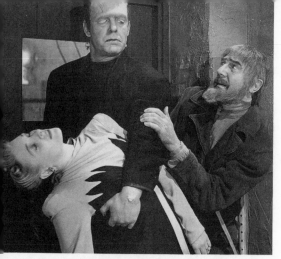

Mixing and matching at Universal: above, Bela Lugosi (normally Dracula) reprises Igor with Lon Chaney, Jr. (usually the Wolfman) as the Monster in *Ghost of Frankenstein*; below, Boris Karloff moves from Creature to Creator in *House of Frankenstein* with J. Carroll Naish.

Below, Kate O'Mara, Ralph Bates in Horror of Frankenstein.

ton. Script by W. Scott Darling, from a story by Eric Taylor. Directors of Photography, Milton Krasner and Woody Bredell. Production Designer, Jack Otterson. Music, Hans Salter. Editor, Ted Kent. Starring Cedric Hardwicke (Dr. Ludwig Frankenstein), Ralph Bellamy (Erik Ernst), Lionel Atwill (Dr. Theodore Bohmer), Béla Lugosi (Igor), Evelyn Ankers (Elsa), Lon Chaney, Jr. (Monster), Barton Yarborough (Dr. Kettering). 68 minutes.

Horror of Frankenstein. (Hammer, 1970). Great Britain. Produced and Directed by Jimmy Sangster. Script by Sangster and Jeremy Burnham. Director of Photography, Moray Grant (Color). Production Designer, Scott MacGregor. Music, James Bernard. Editor, Chris Barnes. Starring Ralph Bates (Victor Frankenstein), Kate O'Mara (Alys), Graham James (Wilhem), Veronica Carlson (Elizabeth), Bernard Archard (Elizabeth's Father), David Prowse (Monster). 95 minutes.

House of Dracula. (Universal, 1945). USA. Produced by Paul Malvern. Directed by Erle C. Kenton. Script by Edward T. Lowe. Director of Photography, George Robinson. Production Designer, John B. Goodman, Martin Obzina. Music, Edgar Fairchild. Editor, Russell Schoengarth. Starring John Carradine (Dracula/Baron Latoes), Lon Chaney, Jr. (Lawrence Talbot), Onslow Stevens (Dr. Edelman), Martha O'Driscoll (Miliza), Lionel Atwill (Inspector), Glenn Strange (the Monster), Jane Adams (Nina). 67 minutes.

House of Frankenstein. (Universal, 1944). USA. Produced by Paul Malvern. Directed by Erle C. Kenton. Script by Edward T. Lowe from a story by Curt Siodmak. Director of Photography, George Robinson. Production Designers, John B. Goodman, Martin Obzina. Music, H.J. Salter. Editor, Philip Cahn. Starring Boris Karloff (Dr. Niemann), J. Carrol Naish (Daniel), Lon Chaney, Jr. (Lawrence Talbot), John Carradine (Dracula), Anne Gwynne (Rita), Peter Coe (Carl), Lionel Atwill (Arnz). 70 minutes.

I Was a Teenage Frankenstein. (AIP/Santa Rosa, 1957). USA. Produced by Herman Cohen. Directed by Herbert L. Strock. Script by Kenneth Langtry. Director of Photography, Lothrop Worth. Production Designer, Leslie Thomas. Music, Paul Dunlap. Editor, Jerry Young. Starring Whit Bissell (Professor Frankenstein), Phyllis Coates (Margaret), Robert Burton (Karlton), George Lynn (Sgt. Burns), John Cliff (Sgt. McAfee), Gary Conway. 74 minutes.

Jesse James Meets Frankenstein's Daughter. (Circle/Embassy, 1966). USA. Produced by Carroll Case. Directed by William Beaudine. Script by Carl Hittleman. Director of Photography, Lothrop Worth. Production Designer, Paul Sylos. Music, Raoul Kraushaar. Editor, William Austin. Starring John Lupton (Jesse James), Narda Onyx (Maria Frankenstein), Cal Bolder (Hank Tracy/Igor), Jim Davis (Marshall), Estelita (Juanita), Felipe Turich (Manuel), Nestor Paiva. 82 minutes.

Life without Soul. (Ocean Films, 1915). USA. Produced by George De Carlton. Directed by Joseph W. Smiley. Script by Jesse J. Goldburg.

Starring Percy Standing (Monster), William A. Cohill, Jack Hopkins, Lucy Cotton, George De Carlton, Pauline Curley. 5 reels.

Mary Shelley's Frankenstein. (Tri-Star/American Zoetrope, 1994). USA/Great Britain. Produced by Francis Ford Coppola and James V. Hart. Directed by Kenneth Branagh. Script by Frank Darabont and Steph Lady. Starring Kenneth Branagh (Frankenstein), Robert De Niro (the Creature), Helena Bonham-Carter (Elizabeth), Tom Hulce (Henry), Aidan Quinn (Capt. Walton), John Cleese (Waldman).

The Monster Squad. (TriStar/Taft-Barish, 1987). USA. Produced by Jonathan A. Zimbert. Directed by Fred Dekker. Script by Shane Black and Dekker. Director of Photography, Bradford May (Color/Scope). Production Designer, Albert Brenner. Music, Bruce Broughton. Editor, James Mitchell. Starring Andre Gower (Sean), Robby Kiger (Patrick), Stephen Macht (Del Crenshaw), Duncan Regehr (Count Dracula), Tom Noonan (Frankenstein's Monster). 82 minutes.

Il Mostro di Frankenstein. (Albertini Films/VCI, 1920). Italy. Directed by Eugenio Testa. Script by Giovanni Drovetti. Director of Photography, De Simone. Starring Luciano Alberti, Umberto Guarracino.

Orlak, El Infierno de Frankenstein. (Columbia, 1960). Mexico. Produced and Directed by Baledón. Script by Alfredo Ruanova, Carlos E. Taboada. Director of Photography, Fernando Colín. Music, Fondo Jorge Perez. Starring Joaquin Cordero, Armando Calva.

Above, Boris Karloff as the tortured Monster mutely appealing to Basil Rathbone, the son of his creator in *Son of Frankenstein*.

The Revenge of Frankenstein. (Hammer/Columbia, 1958). Great Britain. Produced by Anthony Hinds. Directed by Terence Fisher. Script by James Sangster and H. Hurford Janes. Director of Photography, Jack Asher (Color). Production Designer, Bernard Robinson. Music, Leonard Salzedo. Editor, Alfred Cox. Starring Peter Cushing (Doctor Victor Stein), Michael Gwynn (Karl, the Monster), Francis Matthews (Doctor Hans Kleve), Eunice Gayson (Margaret), John Welsh (Bergman), Lionel Jeffries (Fritz), Oscar Quitak (the Dwarf), Michael Ripper (Kurt), John Stuart (Inspector). 91 minutes.

Son of Frankenstein. (Universal, 1939). USA. Produced by Rowland V. Lee. Directed by Lee. Script by Willis Cooper. Director of Photography, George Robinson. Production Designer, Jack Otterson and Richard Riedel. Music, Frank Skinner. Editor, Ted Kent. Starring Boris Karloff (the Monster), Béla Lugosi (Ygor), Basil Rathbone (Baron Wolf von Frankenstein), Lionel Atwill (Inspector Krough), Josephine Hutchinson (Elsa von Frankenstein), Edgar Norton (Benson), Donnie Dunagan (Peter von Frankenstein). 95 minutes.

Tres Eran Tres. (Cooperativa del Cinema/Victory, 1954). Spain. Directed by Eduardo G. Maroto. Script by Herranz Falquina, Antonio Lara, Tono, and Maroto [One episode is based on **Frankenstein**]. Director of Photography, Enrique Guerner Pahissa. Production Designer, Tadeo Villaba. Editor, Bienvenida Sanz. Starring Manolo Moran, Antonio Riquelme, Gustavo Re, Manuel Arbo.

Young Frankenstein. (Gruskoff/Venture/Crossbow/Jouer, 1974). USA. Produced by Michael Gruskoff. Directed by Mel Brooks. Script by Gene Wilder and Brooks. Director of Photography, Gerald Hirschfeld. Production Designer, Dale Hennesy. Music, John Morris. Editor, John Howard. Starring Gene Wilder (Dr. Frederick Frankenstein), Peter Boyle (Monster), Marty Feldman (Igor), Madeline Kahn (Elizabeth), Cloris Leachman (Frau Blücher), Teri Garr (Inga), Kenneth

Mars (Inspector), Gene Hackman (Blind Hermit). 107 minutes.

Bram Stoker

The Awakening. (Orion/Warner Bros., 1980). USA. Produced by Robert Solo, Andrew Scheinman, and Martin Schafer. Directed by Mike Newell. Script by Allan Scott, Bryant Christ, and Clive Exton, based on **The Jewel of Seven Stars** by Bram Stoker. Director of Photography, Jack Cardiff (Color). Production Designer, Michael Stringer. Music, Claude Bolling. Editor, Terry Rawlings. Starring Charlton Heston (Matthew Corbeck), Susannah York (Jane Turner), Jill Townsend (Anne Corbeck), Stephanie Zimbalist (Margaret Corbeck), Bruce Myers (Dr. Khalid). 102 minutes.

Blood from the Mummy's Tomb. (Hammer, 1972). Great Britain. Produced by Howard Brandy. Directed by Seth Holt and [uncredited] Michael Carreras. Script by Christopher Wicking, based on **The Jewel of Seven Stars** by Bram Stoker. Director of Photography, Arthur Grant (Color). Production Designer, Scott MacGregor. Music, Tristram Cary. Editor, Peter Weatherley. Starring Andrew Keir (Prof. Julian Fuchs), Valerie Leon (Margaret Fuchs/Queen Tera), James Villiers (Corbeck), Hugh Burden (Dandridge), George Coulouris (Berigan), Mark Edwards (Tod Browning), Rosalie Crutchley (Helen). 94 minutes.

The Lair of the White Worm. (Vestron, 1988). Great Britain. Produced and Directed by Ken Russell. Script by Russell, based on **The Lair of the White Worm** by Bram

Stoker. Director of Photography, Dick Bush (Color). Production Designer, Anne Tilby. Music, Stanislas Syrewicz. Editor, Peter Davies. Starring Amanda Donohoe (Lady Sylvia Marsh), Hugh Grant (Lord James D'-Ampton), Catherine Oxenberg (Eve Trent), Sammi Davis (Mary Trent), Peter Capaldi (Angus Flint), Stratford Johns (Peters), Paul Brooke (Constable), Chris Pitt (Kevin). 93 minutes.

Edgar Allan Poe

The Avenging Conscience. (Mutual, 1914). USA. Produced and Directed by D. W. Griffith. Script by Griffith based on "The Tell-Tale Heart" and "Annabel Lee" by Poe. Director of Photography, Billy Bitzer. Starring Henry B. Walthall (the Nephew), Blanche Sweet (Annabel, his Sweetheart), Spottiswoode Aiken (the Uncle), George Seigmann (the

Below, Margaret Fuchs (Valerie Leon) screams in *Blood from the Mummy's Tomb* either at the sight of her double in the sarcophagus or her coiffure on a truly bad hair day.

Italian), Ralph Lewis (the Detective), Mae Marsh (the Maid). 6 reels.

The Black Cat. (Universal, 1934). USA. Produced by Carl Laemmle, Jr. Directed by Edgar G. Ulmer. Script by Peter Ruric based on the story by Poe. Director of Photography, John Mescall. Music, Heinz Roemheld. Editor, Ray Curtiss. Starring Boris Karloff (Hjalmar Poelzig), Béla Lugosi (Dr. Vitus Verdegast), David Manners (Peter Alison), Jacqueline Wells (Joan Alison). 65 minutes.

The Black Cat. (Universal, 1941). USA. Produced by Burt Kelly. Directed by Albert S. Rogell. Script by Robert Lees, Fred Rinaldo, Eric Taylor, and Robert Neville based on the story by Poe. Director of Photography, Stanley Cortez. Production Designer, Jack Otterson. Music, Hans J. Salter. Editor, Ted Kent. Starring Basil Rathbone, Hugh Herbert, Broderick Crawford, Béla

Below, Boris Karloff as Poelzig in *The Black Cat*.

Lugosi, Gale Sondergaard, Anne Gwynne, Alan Ladd. 70 minutes.

The Black Cat. (Hemisphere/Falcon, 1970). USA. Produced and Directed by Harold P. Hoffman. Script by Hoffman based on the story by Poe. (Color). 72 minutes.

The Black Cat. (21st Century, 1989). USA. Produced by Lucio Lucidi. Directed by Lewis Coates. Script by Coates based on the story by Poe. Starring Florence Guerin, Urbano Barberini, Caroline Munro, Maurizio Fardo, Luis Maneri, Antonio Marsina. (Color).

Buried Alive. (21st Century/Breton, 1989). USA. Produced by Harry Alan Towers. Directed by Gerard Kikoine. Script by Jakes Clesi and Stuart Lee, from a story [uncredited] by Peter Walbeck, based on the stories of Poe. Director of Photography, Gerard Loubeau. Production Designer, Leonardo Coen. Music, Frederi Talgorn. Editor, Gilbert Kiko[i]ne. Starring Robert Vaughn (Dr. Gary), Donald Pleasance (Dr. Schaeffer), Karen Witter (Janet), Nia Long (Fingers), Ginger Lynn Allen (Debby), John Carradine. 91 minutes.

La Chute de la Maison Usher. (Epstein Films, 1928). France. Produced by Jean Epstein. Directed by Epstein. Script by Epstein based on "The Fall of the House of Usher" by Poe. Director of Photography, Georges Lucas, Jean Lucas. Production Designer, Pierre Keter. Starring Jean Debucourt (Roderick Usher), Marguerite Gance (Madeline Usher), Charles Lamy (the Visitor), Pierre Hot, Halma.

The Crime of Dr. Crespi. (Republic, 1935). USA. Produced and Directed by John H. Auer. Script by Auer based on "The Premature Burial" by Poe. Director of Photography, Larry Williams. Editor, Leonard Wheeler. Starring Eric Von Stroheim (Dr. Crespi), Dwight Frye (Dr. Thomas), Paul Guilfoyle (Dr. Arnold), Harriet Russel (Mrs. Ross), John Bohn (dead man). 63 minutes.

Due Occhi Diabolici *(Two Evil Eyes)*. (Artisti Associati/Bema/ADC, 1990). Italy. Produced by Achille Mazotti and Dario Argento. Directed by George Romero (First Episode) and Dario Argento (Second Episode). Script by Romero (First Episode); Argento and Franco Ferrini (Second Episode) based on "The Facts in the Case M. Valdemar" and "The Black Cat" by Poe. Director of Photography, Peter Reniers (Color). Production Designer, Cletus Anderson. Music, Pino Donaggio. Editor, Pat Buba. Starring Adrienne Barbeau (Jessica Valdemar), Bingo O'Malley (Ernest Valdemar), E.G. Marshall (Steven Pike), Harvey Keitel (Rod Usher), Madeline Potter (Annabel), Ramy Zada (Dr. Hoffman), Martin Balsam (Mr. B), Kim Hunter (Mrs. P). 105 minutes.

The Fall of the House of Usher. (Barnett Films, 1948). Great Britain. Produced and Directed by G. Ivan Barnett. Script by Kenneth Thompson, Dorothy Catt based on the story by Poe. Director of Photography, Barnett. Starring Kay Tendeter, Gwendoline Watford, Irving Steen. 70 minutes.

The Fall of the House of Usher. (Sunn Classics, 1980). USA. Produced by Charles E. Sellier. Directed by James L. Conway. Script by Stephen Lord based on the story

by Poe. Starring Martin Landau (Usher), Ray Walston (Thaddeus), Charlene Tilton (Jennifer), Dimitra Arliss (Madeline), Robert Hays (Jonathan). Color. 101 minutes.

Funf Unheimliche Geschichten *(Five Tales of Horror)*. (Oswald Films, 1919). Germany. Produced and Directed by Richard Oswald. Script by Oswald and Robert Liebmann based on "The Black Cat," "The System of Dr. Tarr and Professor Fether," by Poe and "The Suicide Club" by Robert Louis Stevenson. Director of Photography, Carl Hoffmann. Starring Conrad Veidt (Death), Anita Berber, Reinhold Schunzel (Devil), Hugo Doblin, Paul Morgan, Georg John. 112 minutes.

Funf Unheimliche Geschichten *(Five Tales of Horror, The Living Dead)*. (Hoffberg/Roto, 1933). Germany. Produced by Gabriel Pascal. Directed by Richard Oswald. Script by Heinz Goldberg and Eugen Szatmari based on "The Black Cat," "The System of Dr. Tarr and Professor Fether" by Poe and "The Suicide Club" by Robert Louis Stevenson. Director of Photography, Heinrich Gaertner. Starring Paul Wegener, Eugen Klopfer, Roma Bohn, Harold Paulsen. 89 minutes.

Il Gatto di Park Lane *(The Black Cat)*. (World Northal/Selenia, 1984). Italy. Produced by Giulio Sbarigia. Directed by Lucio Fulci. Script by Biagio Proietti, Fulci based on "The Black Cat" by Poe. Director of Photography, Sergio Salvati (Color/Scope). Music, Pino Donaggio. Editor, Vincenzo Tomassi. Starring Patrick Magee (Mr. Miles), Mimsy Farmer (Jill Travers), David Warbeck (Inspec-

tor Gorley), Al Cliver (Policeman). 91
minutes.

The Haunted Palace see entry
under **Lovecraft**

The Haunting Fear. (Troma, 1990).
USA. Produced by Diana Jaffe.
Directed by Fred Olen Ray. Script by
Sherman Scott based on "The Prema-
ture Burial" by Poe. Director of
Photography, Gary Graver (Color).
Music, Chuck Cirino. Editor, Chris
Roth. Starring Brinke Stevens, Jay
Richardson, Jan-Michael Vincent,
Delia Sheppard, Karen Black, Robert
Clark. 88 minutes.

The Haunting of Morella. (Con-
corde, 1990). USA. Produced by
Roger Corman. Directed by Jim
Wynorski. Script by R.J. Robertson
based on story "Morella" by Poe.
Director of Photography, Zoran
Hochstatten (Color). Production
Designer, Gary Randall. Music,
Fredric Teetsel, Chuck Cirino.
Editor, Diane Fingado. Starring
David McCallum (Gideon Locke),
Nicole Eggert (Morella/Lenora),
Maria Ford (Diane), Lana Clarkson
(Witch), Christopher Halsted (Guy),
Jonathan Farwell (Dr. Gault). 75
minutes.

Histoires Extraordinaires. (Orain,
1949). France. Directed by Jean
Faurez. Script by Faurez based on
"The Tell-Tale Heart" and "The Cask
of Amontillado" by Poe. Director of
Photography, Louis Page. Production
Designer, Rene Moulaert. Editor,
Suzanne De Trayes. Starring Jules
Berry, Fernand Ledoux, Suzy Car-
rier, Olivier Hussenot, Jandeline. 85
minutes.

Histoires Extraordinaires (Spirits
of the Dead). (Marceau/Cocinor/

Above, Terence Stamp as Toby Dammit in
Spirits of the Dead.

P.E.A., 1968). France/Italy. "Met-
zengerstein" Directed by Roger
Vadim. Script by Vadim and Pascal
Cousin based on the story by Poe.
Director of Photography, Claude
Renoir (Color). Production Designer,
Jean Forester. Music, Jean
Prodromides. Editor, Héläne Plemian-
Nikov. Starring Jane Fonda (Count-
ess Frederica), Peter Fonda (Baron
Wilhelm), Carla Marlier (Claude),
Francoise Prevost (Friend), James
Robertson Justice (Countess's Ad-
visor). "William Wilson" Directed by

Louis Malle. Script by Malle and Daniel Boulanger based on the story by Poe. Director of Photography, Tonino Delli Colli (Color). Production Designer, Ghislain Uhry and Carla Leva. Music, Diego Masson. Editor, Franco Arcalli and Suzanne Garon. Starring Brigitte Bardot (Giuseppina), Alain Delon (Wilson), Katia Cristina (Young Girl), Umberto D'-Orsi (Hans). "Never Bet the Devil Your Head" or "Toby Dammit" Directed by Federico Fellini. Script by Fellini and Bernardino Zapponi based on the story by Poe. Director of Photography, Giuseppe Rotunno (Color). Production Designer, Piero Tosi. Music, Nino Rota. Editor, Ruggero Mastroianni. Starring Terence Stamp (Toby Dammit), Salvo Randone (Priest), Fabrizio Angeli (1st Director), Ernesto Colli (2nd Director), Marina Yaru (Child), Anna Tonietti (TV Commentator). 123 minutes.

Horror *(The Blancheville Monster)*. (1963). Spain/Italy. Directed by Alberto de Martino. Script by Jean Grimaud and Gordon Wilson based on "The Fall of the House of Usher," "Berenice," and "The Premature Burial" by Poe. Director of Photography, Alejandro Ulloa. Music, Francis Clark. Starring Gerard Tichy, Leo Anchoriz, Joan Hills, Iran Eory, Helga Line.

House of Usher *(The Fall of the House of Usher)*. (Alta Vista/AIP, 1960). USA. Produced and Directed by Roger Corman. Script by Richard Matheson based on the story "The Fall of the House of Usher" by Poe. Director of Photography, Floyd Crosby (Color/Scope). Production Designer, Daniel Haller. Music, Les Baxter. Editor, Anthony Carras. Starring

Vincent Price (Roderick Usher), Mark Damon (Philip Winthrop), Myrna Fahey (Madeline Usher), Harry Ellerbe (Bristol), Bill Borzage. 85 minutes.

The House of Usher. (21st Century, 1989). USA. Produced by Harry Alan

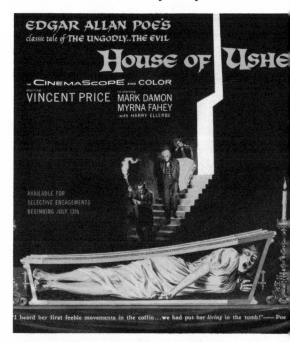

Below, Vincent Price as the effete Roderick Usher in *House of Usher.*

Above, the red-robed title character (seated) in *The Masque of the Red Death*.

Towers. Directed by Alan Birkinshaw. Script by Michael J. Murray based on story "The Fall of the House of Usher" by Poe. Starring Oliver Reed, Donald Pleasance, Romy Windsor. (Color). 92 minutes.

El Hundimiento de la Casa Usher *(The Fall of the House of Usher: Revenge in the House of Usher).* (Elite Films/Eurocine, 1983). Spain. Produced by Jesus Franco. Directed by Franco. Script by Franco based on the story by Poe. Director of Photography, Franco (Color/Scope). Music, Daniel White. Starring Howard Vernon (Usher), Lina Romay [Rosa Maria Almirall] (Usher's Mistress), Robert Foster [Antonio Mayans] (Dr. Alan Harker), Olivier Matho (Morpho), Dan Villiers [Daniel White] (Dr. Seward), Antonio Marin (Mathias). 90 minutes.

Legend of Horror. (General, 1972). USA. Produced by Ricky Torres Tudela. Directed by Bill Davies. Script by Davies, based on "The Tell-Tale Heart" by Poe. Starring Karin Field.

Manfish. (United Artists, 1956). USA. Produced and Directed by Lee Wilder. Script by Joel Murcott based on "The Tell-Tale Heart" and "The Gold Bug" by Poe. Director of Photography, Charles S. Wellborn. Music, Albert Elms. Editor, C. Turnley Smith. Starring John Bromfield, Lon

Chaney, Jr., Victor Jory, Barbara Nichols, Tessa Predergas, Eric Coverly, Vincent Chang. 76 minutes.

Maniac. (Roadshow, 1934). USA. Produced by Dwain Esper. Directed by Esper. Script by Hildegarde Stadie based on "The Black Cat" by Poe. Starring Bill Woods, Horace Carpenter.

La Mansión de la Locura (Dr. Tarr's Torture Dungeon). (Producciones Prisma, 1972). Mexico. Produced by Roberto Viskin. Directed by Juan Lopez Moctezuma. Script by Moctezuma, Carlos Illescas based on "The System of Dr. Tarr and Professor Fether" by Poe. Director of Photography, Rafael Corkidi (Color). Editor, F. Landeros. Starring Claudio Brook, Arturo Hanse, Ellen Sherman, Martin Lasalle, David Silva, Robert Dumont. 88 minutes.

The Masque of the Red Death. (Alta Vista/Anglo Amalgamated, 1964). Great Britain. Produced by George Willoughby. Directed by Roger Corman. Script by Charles Beaumont based on the story by Poe. Director of Photography, Nicolas Roeg (Color). Production Designer, Robert Jones. Music, David Lee. Editor, Ann Chegwidden. Starring Vincent Price (Prince Prospero), Hazel Court (Juliana), Jane Asher (Francesca), Skip Martin (Hop Toad), David Weston (Gino), Patrick Magee (Alfredo), Nigel Green (Ludovico), John Westbrook (Man in Red), Gay Brown (Senora Escobar). 86 minutes.

The Masque of the Red Death. (Concorde, 1989). USA. Produced by Roger Corman. Directed by Larry Brand. Script by Daryl Haney and Brand based on the story by Poe. Director of Photography, Edward Pei

(Color). Production Designer, Troy Meyers. Music, Mark Governor. Editor, Stephen Mark. Starring Patrick Macnee (Machiavel), Adrian Paul (Prospero), Clare Hoak (Julietta), Jeff Osterhage (Claudio), Tracy Reiner (Lucretia). 85 minutes.

The Masque of the Red Death. (21st Century/Breton, 1992). USA. Produced by Harry Alan Towers. Directed by Alan Birkinshaw. Script by Michael J. Murray based on the story by Poe. Director of Photography, Jossi Wein (Color). Production Designer, Leith Ridley. Music, Coby Recht. Editor, Jason Krasucki. Starring Herbert Lom, Frank Stallone, Brenda Vaccaro, Christine Lunde, Michelle Hoey. 90 minutes.

The Oblong Box. (AIP, 1969). Great Britain. Produced and Directed by Gordon Hessler. Script by Lawrence Huntingdon and Christopher Wicking based on the story by Poe. Director of Photography, John Coquillon (Color). Production Designer, George Provis. Music, Harry Robinson. Editor, Max Benedict. Starring Vincent Price (Julian Markham), Christopher Lee (Dr. Newhart), Alastair Williamson (Sir Edward Markham), Hilar Dwyer (Elizabeth), Peter Arne (Samuel Trench), Harry Baird (N'-Balo), Carl Rigg (Mark). 95 minutes.

Obras Maestras del Terror (Master of Horror). (Sono, 1960). Argentina. Produced by Nicolas Carreras. Directed by Enrique Carreras. Script by Luis Penafiel based on "The Facts in the Case of M. Valdemar," "The Cask of Amontillado," "The Tell-Tale Heart" by Poe. Director of Photography, Americo Hoss. Production Designer, Mario Vanarelli. Music, Victor Schlichter. Editor, Jose Gal-

lego. Starring Narciso Ibanez
Menta, Inez Moreno, Carlos Estrada,
Narcisco Ibanez Serradór, Mercedes
Carreras. 115 minutes.

The Pit and the Pendulum. (Alta
Vista/AIP, 1961). USA. Produced by
Roger Corman. Directed by Corman.
Script by Richard Matheson based
on the story by Poe. Director of
Photography, Floyd Crosby
(Color/Scope). Production Designer,
Daniel Haller. Music, Les Baxter.
Editor, Anthony Carras. Starring Vin-
cent Price (Nicholas Medina), John
Kerr (Francis Barnard), Barbara
Steele (Elizabeth Medina), Luana
Anders (Catherine Medina), Anthony
Carbone (Dr. Leon). 95 minutes.

The Pit and the Pendulum. (Full
Moon, 1991). USA. Produced by Albert Band. Directed by Stuart Gor-

don. Script by Dennis Paoli based on
the story by Poe. Director of Photog-
raphy, Adolfo Bartoli (Color). Produc-
tion Designer, Giovanni Muratori.
Music, Richard Band. Editor, Andy
Horvitch. Starring Lance Henriksen
(Torquemada), Rona De Ricci
(Maria), Jonathan Fuller (Antonio),
Jeffrey Combs (Francisco), Tom
Towles (Don Carlos), Oliver Reed (the
Cardinal). 96 minutes.

The Premature Burial.
(Filmgroup/AIP, 1962). USA.
Produced and Directed by Roger Cor-
man. Script by Charles Beaumont
and Ray Russell based on the story
by Poe. Director of Photography,
Floyd Crosby (Color/Scope). Produc-
tion Designer, Daniel Haller. Music,
Ronald Stein. Editor, Ronald
Sinclair. Starring Ray Milland (Guy
Carrell), Hazel Court (Emily Gault),

Below, Nicholas Medina (Vincent Price) adjusts his blade in *The Pit and the Pendulum.*

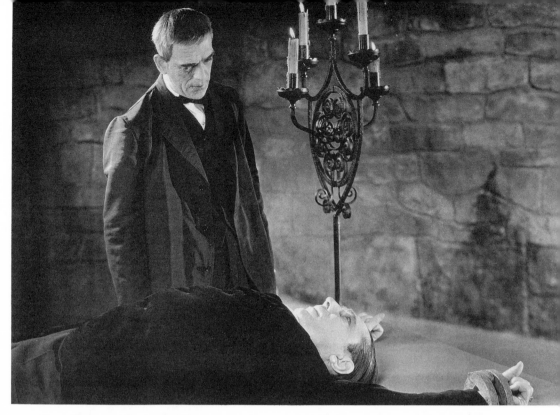

Above, Bateman (Boris Karloff) gives Dr. Vollin (Béla Lugosi) a stretch in *The Raven* (1935).

Richard Ney (Miles Archer), Heather Angel (Kate Carrell), Alan Napier (Dr. Gideon Gault), John Dierkes (Sweeney), Richard Miller (Mole). 81 minutes.

The Raven. (Universal, 1935). USA. Produced by David Diamond. Directed by Louis Friedlander [aka Lew Landers]. Script by David Boehm and Jim Tully based on the poem by Poe. Director of Photography, Charles Stumar. Production Designer, Albert S. D'Agostino, Music, Gilbert Kurland. Editor, Alfred Akst. Starring Boris Karloff (Bateman), Béla Lugosi (Dr. Vollin), Irene Ware (Jean Thatcher), Lester Matthews (Dr. Jerry Halden), Samuel Hinds (Judge Thatcher), Inez Courtney, Ian Wolfe. 61 minutes.

The Raven. (Alta Vista/AIP, 1963). USA. Produced and Directed by Roger Corman. Script by Richard Matheson based on the poem by Poe. Director of Photography, Floyd Crosby (Color/Scope). Production Designer, Daniel Haller. Music, Les Baxter. Editor, Ronald Sinclair. Starring Vincent Price (Dr. Erasmus Craven), Peter Lorre (Dr. Bedlo), Boris Karloff (Dr. Scarabus), Hazel Court (Lenore Craven), Olive Sturgess, William Baskin (Grimes). 86 minutes.

Die Schlangengrube und das Pendel *(The Snake Pit and the Pendulum; The Blood Demon; The Curse of the Walking Dead; The Torture Chamber of Dr. Sadism; Le Vampire et Le Sang des Vierges).* (Constantin, 1967). West Germany. Produced by Wolfgang Kuehnlenz. Directed by Harald Reinl. Script by Manfred R. Kohler, based on "The Pit and the Pendulum" by Poe. Director of Photography, Ernst W. Kalinke, Dieter Liphardt (Color/Scope). Production Designer, Gabriel Pellon.

Above, Leiona Gage and Vincent Price in *Tales of Terror*.

W.M. Achtmann. Music, Peter Thomas. Editor, Hermann Heller. Starring Christopher Lee, Lex Barker, Karin Dor, Carl Lange. 85 minutes.

Tales of Terror. (AIP, 1962). USA. Produced and Directed by Roger Corman. Script by Richard Matheson based on "Morella," "The Black Cat," "The Facts in the Case of M. Valdemar" by Poe. Director of Photography, Floyd Crosby (Color/Scope). Production Designer, Daniel Haller. Music, Les Baxter. Editor, Anthony Carras. Starring Vincent Price (Locke/Fortunato/Valdemar), Peter Lorre (Montresor), Basil Rathbone (Carmichael), Debra Paget (Helene), Maggie Pierce (Leonora), Leiona Gage (Morella), Joyce Jameson (Annabel). 90 minutes.

The Tell-Tale Heart. (Barber, 1927). USA. Produced by Maurice Barber. Directed by Charles F. Klein. Script by Klein based on the story by Poe. Director of Photography, Leon Shamroy. Starring Otto Matiesen, Herford de Fuerberg, Darvas.

The Tell-Tale Heart (*Bucket of Blood*). (Clifton-Hurst, 1934). Great Britain. Produced by Harry Clifton.

Directed by Brian Desmond Hurst. Script by David Plunkett Greene based on the story by Poe. Starring Norman Dryden, John Kelt, Yolande Terrell, Thomas Shenton, James Fleck, Colonel Cameron. 52 minutes.

The Tell-Tale Heart (*The Hidden Room of 1000 Horrors*). (The Danzigers, 1960). Great Britain. Produced by Edward J. and Harry Lee Danziger. Directed by Ernest Morris. Script by Brian Clemens and Eldon Howard based on the story by Poe. Director of Photography, Jimmy Wilson. Production Designer, Norman Arnold. Music, Tony Crombie, Bill Le Sage. Editor, Derek Parsons. Starring Laurence Payne (Edgar), Adrienne Corri (Betty), Dermot Walsh (Carl), Selma Vaz Dias (Mrs. Vine), John Scott (Inspector), John Martin (Police Sergeant), Annette Carell (Landlady), David Lander (Jeweller). 81 minutes.

The Tomb of Ligeia. (Alta Vista/AIP, 1964). Great Britain/USA. Produced by Pat Green. Directed by Roger Corman. Script by Robert Towne from the story by Poe. Director of Photography, Arthur Grant (Color). Production Designer, Colin Southcott. Music, Kenneth V. Jones. Editor,

Below, Elizabeth Shepherd as Rowena and Vincent Price as Fell in *The Tomb of Ligeia*.

Alfred Cox. Starring Vincent Price (Verden Fell), Elizabeth Shepherd (Rowena/Ligeia), John Westbrook (Christopher Gough), Oliver Johnston (Kenrick), Derek Francis (Lord Trevanion), Richard Vernon (Dr. Vivian), Ronald Adam (Parson). 81 minutes.

H.P. Lovecraft

Bride of the Re-Animator. (Troma, 1991). USA. Produced by Brian Yuzna and Michael Muscal. Directed by Yuzna. Script by Woody Keith, Rick Fry based on "Herbert West— Reanimator" by Lovecraft. Director of Photography, Rick Fichter (Color). Production Designer, Philip Duffin. Music, Richard Band. Editor, Peter Teschner. Starring Bruce Abbott (Dan Cain), Jeffrey Combs (Herbert West), Kathleen Kinmont (Gloria), Claude Earl Jones (Lt. Chapman), Fabiana Udenio (Francesca), David Gale (Dr. Carl Hill). 95 minutes.

Cthulhu Mansion. (Filmagic/Golden, 1992). USA/Spain. Produced by Juan Piquer. Directed by J.P. Simon [Juan Piquer]. Script by Piquer based on the writings of Lovecraft. Director of Photography, Julio Bragado (Color). Editor, Paul Aviles. Starring Frank Finlay, Marcia Layton, Melanie Shatner. 92 minutes.

The Curse. (Trans World, 1987). USA. Produced by Ovidio G. Assonitis. Directed by David Keith. Script by David Chaskin based on "The Colour out of Space" by Lovecraft. Director of Photography, Robert D. Forges (Color). Production Designer, Frank Vanorio. Music, John Debney. Editor, Claude Kutry. Starring Wil Wheaton (Zachary), Claude Akins (Nathan Hayes), Kath-

leen Jordan Gregory (Frances), Steve Davis (Mike), Amy Wheaton (Alice), Malcolm Danare (Cyrus). 100 minutes.

Curse of the Crimson Cult *(The Crimson Cult).* (Tigon/AIP, 1968). Great Britain. Produced by Louis M. Heyward. Directed by Vernon Sewell. Script by Mervyn Haisman, Henry Lincoln, and Gerry Levy based on "The Dreams in the Witch-House" by Lovecraft. Director of Photography, John Coquillon (Color). Production Designer, Derek Barrington. Editor, Howard Banning. Starring Boris Karloff (Prof. Marsh), Christopher Lee (Morely), Mark Eden (Robert Manning), Virginia Wetherell (Eve), Barbara Steele (Lavinia), Rupert Davies (Vicar), Michael Gough (Elder), Rosemarie Reede (Esther), Derek Tansley (Judge). 89 minutes.

The Dunwich Horror. (AIP, 1969). USA. Produced by James H. Nicholson, Samuel Z. Arkoff. Directed by Daniel Haller. Script by Curtis Lee Hanson, Henry Rosenbaum, Ronald Silkosky based on the writings of Lovecraft. Director of Photography, Richard C. Glouner (Color). Production Designer, Paul Sylos. Music, Les Baxter. Editor, Fred Feitshans, Jr.,

Below, Wilbur Whateley (Dean Stockwell) prepares to sacrifice Nancy (Sandra Dee) in *The Dunwich Horror.*

Christopher Holmes. Starring Sandra Dee (Nancy Walker), Dean Stockwell (Wilbur Whateley), Ed Begley, Sr. (Dr. Henry Armitage), Sam Jaffe (Old Whateley), Donna Baccala (Elizabeth), Lloyd Bochner (Dr. Cory), Joanna Moore Jordan (Lavinia), Talia Coppola (Cora), Barboura Morris (Mrs. Cole). 90 minutes.

H.P. Lovecraft's Necronomicon. (Necronomicon Films, 1994). USA. Produced by Samuel Hadida and Brian Yuzna. Directed by Christophe Gans, Shusuke Kaneko, and Brian Yuzna (Three Episodes). Script by Brent V. Friedman based on the writings of Lovecraft. Directors of Photography, Gerry Lively, Russ Brandt (Color). Production Designer, Anthony Tremblay. Starring David Warner, Millie Perkins, Dennis Christopher, Bess Meyer, Don Calfa, Gary Graham. 92 minutes.

The Haunted Palace. (AIP, 1964). USA. Produced and Directed by Roger Corman. Script by Charles Beaumont based on the poem by Poe and **The Case of Charles Dexter Ward** by Lovecraft. Director of Photography, Floyd Crosby (Color/Scope). Production Designer, Daniel Haller. Music, Ronald Stein. Editor, Ronald Sinclair. Starring Vincent Price (Charles Dexter Ward/Curwen), Debra Paget (Ann Ward), Lon Chaney (Simon Orne), Frank Maxwell (Dr. Willet), Leo Gordon (Edgar Weeden), Elisha Cook (Peter Smith), John Dierkes (Jacob West), Harry Ellerbe (Minister). 85 minutes.

Monster of Terror *(Die, Monster, Die).* (Alta Vista/AIP, 1965). Great Britain. Produced by Pat Green. Directed by Daniel Haller. Script by Harry Sohl based on "The Colour Out of Space" by Lovecraft. Director of Photography, Paul Beeson (Color/Scope). Production Designer, Colin Southcott. Music, Don Banks. Editor, Alfred Cox. Starring Boris Karloff (Nahum Witley), Nick Adams (Stephen Reinhart), Suzan Farmer (Susan Witley), Freda Jackson (Letitia Witley), Terence de Marney (Merwyn), Patrick Magee (Dr. Henderson), Paul Farrell (Jason). 81 minutes.

Re-Animator. (Empire, 1985). USA. Produced by Brian Yuzna. Directed by Stuart Gordon. Script by Dennis Paoli, William J. Norris, and Gordon based on "Herbert West— Reanimator" by Lovecraft. Director of Photography, Mac Ahlberg (Color). Production Designer, Robert A. Burns. Music, Richard Band. Editor, Lee Percy. Starring Jeffrey Combs (Herbert West), Bruce Abbott (Daniel Cain), Barbara Crampton (Megan Halsey), Robert Sampson (Dr. Alan

Below, crumbled remains at the end of *Monster of Terror.*

Halsey), David Gale (Dr. Hill), Gerry Black (Mace). 86 minutes.

The Resurrected. (Scotti Bros./Borde/Raich, 1992). USA. Produced by Mark Borde and Ken Raich. Directed by Dan O'Bannon. Script by Brent V. Friedman based on **The Case of Charles Dexter Ward** by Lovecraft. Director of Photography, Irv Goodnoff (Color). Production Designer, Brent Thomas. Music, Richard Band. Editor, Russell Livingstone. Starring John Terry (John March), Jane Sibbett (Claire Ward), Chris Sarandon (Charles Dexter Ward), Robert Romanus (Detective). 108 minutes.

The Shuttered Room. (Troy/Schenck, 1966). Great Britain. Produced by Phillip Hazelton. Directed by David Greene and [uncredited] Ken Russell. Script by D.B. Ledrov and Nathaniel Tanchuck based on **The Shuttered Room** by Lovecraft and August Derleth. Director of Photography, Ken Hodges (Color). Production Designer, Brian Eatwell. Music, Basil Kirchin. Editor, Brian Smedley-Aston. Starring Carol Lynley (Susannah Kelton/Sarah), Gig Young (Mike Kelton), Oliver Reed (Ethan), Flora Robson (Aunt Agatha), William Devlin (Zebulon Whateley), Bernard Kay (Tait), Judith Arthy (Emma), Robert Cawdron (Luther Whateley). 99 minutes.

The Unnamable. (K.P./Yankee Classics, 1987). USA. Produced by Dean Ramser and Jean-Paul Ouellette. Directed by Ouellette. Script by Ouellette based on "The Unnamable" by Lovecraft. Director of Photography, Tom Fraser, Greg Gardiner (Color). Production Designer, Gene Abel. Music, David Bergeaud. Editor,

Wendy J. Plump. Starring Charles King (Howard Damon), Mark Kinsey Stephenson (Randolph Carter), Alexandra Durrell (Tanya), Laura Albert (Wendy Barnes), Eben Ham (Bruce Weeks), Blane Wheatley (John Babcock). 87 minutes.

The Unnamable II. (Prism/Yankee Classics/New Age, 1992). USA. Produced and Directed by Jean-Paul Ouellette. Script by Ouellette based on "The Unnamable" by Lovecraft. Director of Photography, Greg Gardiner (Color). Music: David Bergeaud. Editor, Bill Williams. Starring John Rhys-Davies, David Warner, Mark Kinsey Stephenson, Charles Klausmeyer, Maria Ford, Peter Breck, Julie Strain.

Robert Louis Stevenson

NOTE: All the scripts in this section are based on Robert Louis Stevenson's novella, **The Strange Case of Dr. Jekyll and Mr. Hyde,** or the characters contained therein. Other stories, novels, or plays noted below are similarly based.

Dr. Black, Mr. Hyde. (Dimension, 1976). USA. Produced by Charles Walker. Directed by William Crain. Script by Larry LeBron. Director of Photography, Tak Fujimoto (Color). Music, Johnny Pate. Editor, Jack Horger. Starring Bernie Casey (Dr. Pride/Hyde), Rosalind Cash (Dr. Billie Worth), Marie O'Henry (Linda), Ji-Tu Cumbuka (Lt. Jackson), Milt Korgan, Stu Gillam. 87 minutes.

Dr. Heckyll and Mr. Hype. (Cannon, 1980). USA. Produced by Menahem Golan and Yoram Globus. Directed by Charles B. Griffith. Script by Griffith. Director of Photography, Robert Carras (Color). Production Designer, Maxwell Mendes. Music, Richard Band. Editor, Skip Schoolnik. Starring Oliver Reed (Heckyll/Hype), Sunny Johnson (Coral Careen), Maia Danziger (Miss Finebum), Mel Welles (Dr. Hinkle), Virgil Frye ("Il Topo"). 99 minutes.

Dr. Jekyll and Mr. Hyde. (Pioneer, 1920). USA. Produced by Louis B. Mayer. Directed by Charles J. Hayden. Script by Hayden. Starring Sheldon Lewis (Dr. Jekyll/Hyde), Alexander Shannon, Dora Mill Adams, Gladys Field, Harold Forshay, Leslie Austin. 40 minutes.

Dr. Jekyll and Mr. Hyde. (Famous Players-Lasky, 1920). USA. Produced by Adolph Zukor. Directed by John S. Robertson. Script by Clara S. Beranger. Directors of Photography, Karl Struss, Roy Overbaugh. Starring John Barrymore (Jekyll/Hyde),

Below, Barrymore as Jekyll.

Martha Mansfield (Millicent), Nita Naldi (Gina), Louis Wolheim, Brandon Hurst. 63 minutes.

Dr. Jekyll and Mr. Hyde. (Paramount, 1931). USA. Produced and Directed by Rouben Mamoulian. Script by Samuel Hoffenstein, and Percy Heath. Director of Photography, Karl Struss. Production Designer, Hans Dreier. Editor, William Shea. Starring Fredric March (Dr. Jekyll/Hyde), Miriam Hopkins (Ivy Parsons), Rose Hobart (Muriel Carew), Holmes Herbert (Dr. Lanyon), Halliwell Hobbes (General Carew), Edgar Norton (Poole), Arnold Lucy (Utterson). 98 minutes.

Dr. Jekyll and Mr. Hyde. (MGM, 1941). USA. Produced and Directed by Victor Fleming. Script by John Lee Mahin. Director of Photography, Joseph Ruttenberg. Production Designer, Cedric Gibbons. Music, Franz Waxman. Editor, Harold F. Kress. Starring Spencer Tracy (Dr. Jekyll/Hyde), Ingrid Bergman (Ivy Peterson), Lana Turner (Beatrix), Donald Crisp (Sir Charles Emery), Ian Hunter (Dr. Lanyon), Barton MacLane (Sam Higgins), C. Aubrey Smith (the Bishop), Peter Godfrey (Poole), Sara Allgood (Mrs. Higgins). 127 minutes.

Dr. Jekyll and Mr. Hyde. (NBC-TV, 1973). USA. Produced by Burt Rosen. Directed by David Winters. Script by Sherman Yellen. Music and Lyrics by Mel Mandell and Norman Sachs. Starring Kirk Douglas (Dr. Jekyll/Hyde), Michael Redgrave (Gen. Danvers), Susan Hampshire (Isabel), Susan George (Annie), Donald Pleasance (Smudge), Stanley Holloway (Poole).

Dr. Jekyll and Sister Hyde. (Hammer/EBI, 1971). Great Britain. Produced by Albert Fennell and Brian Clemens. Directed by Roy Ward Baker. Script by Clemens. Director of Photography, Norman Warwick (Color). Production Designer, Robert Jones. Music, David Whitaker. Editor, James Needs. Starring Ralph Bates (Dr. Jekyll), Martine Beswick (Sister Hyde), Gerald Sim (Prof. Robertson), Lewis Fiander (Howard), Dorothy Alison (Mrs. Spencer), Neil Wilson (Policeman), Ivor Dean (Burke), Susan Brodrick (Susan), Paul Whitsum-Jones (Sgt. Danvers), Tony Calvin (Hare). 97 minutes.

Dr. Jekyll y el Hombre Lobo *(Dr. Jeckill y el Hombre Lobo).* (Gonzalez, 1971). Spain. Produced by Arturo Gonzalez. Directed by Leon Klimovsky. Script by Jacinto Molina. Director of Photography, Francisco Fraile (Color/Scope). Starring Paul Naschy [Jacinto Molina], Shirley C-Orrigan, Mirtha Miller, Barta Barri, Luis Induni. 96 minutes.

Dr. Jekyll's Dungeon of Death. (New American/Rochelle/Hyde, 1982). USA. Produced and Directed by James Wood. Script by James Mathers. Director of Photography, Wood (Color). Music, Marty Allen. Editor, Wood. Starring James Mathers, John Kearney, Tom Nicholson, Dawn Carver, Nadine Kalmes. 88 minutes.

Dottor Jekyll e Gentile Signora *(Dr. and Mrs. Jekyll; Dr. Jekyll, Jr.).* (Medusa, 1979). Italy. Produced by F. Poccioni. Directed by Steno [Stefano Vanzina]. Script by Steno, Leo Benvenuti, Piero de Bernardi, and Giovanni Manganelli. Directors

of Photography, Ennio Guarnieri, Sergio Salvati (Color). Starring Paolo Villaggio, Edwige Fenech, Gianrico

Above, Fredric March as Jekyll and Hyde in the 1931 version; below, Spencer Tracy as Jekyll in 1941.

Tedeschi, Gordon Mitchell. 99 minutes.

Edge of Sanity. (Millimeter, 1989). Great Britain/Hungary. Produced by Harry Alan Towers and Edward Simons. Directed by Gerard Kikoine. Script by J.P. Felix, amd Ron Raley. Director of Photography, Tony Spratling (Color). Production Designer, Jean Charles Dédieu. Music, Frederic Talgorn. Editor, Malcolm Cooke. Starring Anthony Perkins (Jekyll/Hyde), Glynis Barber (Elisabeth), Sarah Maur-Thorp (Susannah), David Lodge (Underwood), Ben Cole (Johnny), Ray Jewers (Newcomen). 90 minutes.

Funf Unheimliche Geschichten see entry under **Poe**

El Hombre y la Bestia. (Sono/Azteca, 1951). Argentina. Directed by Mario Soffici. Script by Ulises Petit de Murat, Soffici, and Carlos Marin. Directors of Photography, Gori Munoz, Antonio Merayo. Music, Silvio Vernazza. Editor, Jorge Garate. Starring Mario Soffici, Ana Maria Campoy, Olga Zubarry, Jose Cibrian, Rafael Frontura. 80 minutes.

Horror High *(Twisted Brain)*, (Crown International, 1974). USA. Produced by James P. Graham. Directed by Larry Stouffer. Script by Jake Fowler. Director of Photography, John Valenbergs (Color). Production Designer, Joe Thompkins. Editor, Travis Rhodes. Starring Pat Cardi, Rosie Holotik, John Nilano, Austin Stoker, Joye Hash, Mike McHenry. 85 minutes.

I, Monster. (Amicus, 1970). Great Britain. Produced by Max J. Rosenberg and Milton Subotsky. Directed by Stephen Weeks. Script by Subotsky. Director of Photography, Moray Grant (Color). Production Designer, Tony Curtis. Music, Carl Davis. Editor, Peter Tanner. Starring Christopher Lee (Dr. Marlowe/Edward Blake), Peter Cushing (Utterson), Mike Raven (Enfield), Richard Hurndall (Lanyon), George Merritt (Poole). 75 minutes.

Der Januskopf. (Decla Bioscop/Lipow, 1920). Germany. Directed by F. W. Murnau. Script by Hans Janowitz. Directors of Photography, Karl Freund, Carl Hoffmann. Production Designer, Heinrich Richter. Starring Conrad Veidt (Dr. Warren/Mr. O'Connor), Margarete Schlegel (Grace), Willy Kayser-Heyl, Margarete Kupfer, Gustav Botz, Jaro Furth. 83 minutes (2,300 meters).

Jekyll and Hyde. (London Weekend Television, 1989). Great Britain. Produced by Patricia Carr. Written and Directed by David Wickes. Director of Photography, Norman Langley (Color). Production Designer, William Alexander. Music, John Cameron. Editor, John Shirley. Starring Michael Caine (Jekyll/Hyde), Cheryl Ladd (Sara), Joss Ackland (Dr. Lanyon), Kevin McNally (Sgt. Hornsby). 92 minutes.

Jekyll and Hyde...Together Again. (Paramount, 1982). USA. Produced by Lawrence Gordon. Directed by Jerry Belson. Script by Monica Johnson, Harvey Miller, Michael Leeson, and Belson. Director of Photography, Philip Lathrop (Color). Production Designer, Peter Wooley. Editor, Billy Weber. Starring Mark Blankfield (Jekyll/Hyde), Bess Armstrong (Mary), Krista Errickson (Ivy), Tim Thomerson (Dr. Lanyon),

Michael McGuire (Dr. Carew), Neil Hunt (Queen). 87 minutes.

The Man with Two Heads. (Constitution/Mishkin, 1971). USA/Great Britain. Produced by William Mishkin. Directed by Andy Milligan. Script by Milligan. Director of Photography, Milligan (Color). Starring Denis DeMarne, Julia Stratton, Gay Feld, Jacqueline Lawrence, Berwick Kaler, Bryan Southcombe. 81 minutes.

The Nutty Professor. (Lewis Productions/Paramount, 1963). USA. Produced by Ernest D. Glucksman. Directed by Jerry Lewis. Script by Lewis and Bill Richmond. Director of Photography, W. Wallace Kelley (Color). Production Designers, Hal Pereira, Walter Tyler. Music, Walter Scharf. Editor, John Woodcock. Starring Jerry Lewis (Julius Kelp/Buddy Love), Stella Stevens (Stella Purdy), Del Moore (Dr. Warfield), Kathleen Freeman (Millie), Ned Flory (Football Player), Norman Alden (Football Player), Howard Morris (Father Kelp), Buddy Lester (Bartender). 107 minutes.

Pacto Diabolico. (Vergara, 1968). Mexico. Produced by Luís Enrique Vergara. Directed by Jaime Salvador. Script by Ramon Obón, Jr. and Aldolfo Torres Portillo. Director of Photography, Alfredo Uribe (Color). Production Designers, Octavio Ocampo, José Mendez. Music, Gustavo Cesar Carreon. Editor, Juan Jose Munguia. Starring John Carradine, Angel Alvarez, Regina Torne, Isela Vega, Andres Garcia, Guillermo Zetina. 78 minutes.

Ein Seltsamer Fall. (Vitascope, 1914). Germany. Directed by Max Mack. Script by Richard Oswald.

Starring Alwin Neuss, Hanni Weisse, Lotte Neumann.

Shado Kalo. (1953). India. Produced by Basu Mitra. Directed by Amal Bose. Director of Photography, Dibyenda Ghose. Starring Sipra, Sisir, Gurudas, Pahari Sanyal, Biren Chatterjee.

Son of Dr. Jekyll. (Columbia, 1951). USA. Directed by Seymour Friedman. Script by Mortimer Braus and Jack Pollexfen. Director of Photography, Henry Freulich. Music, Paul Sawtell. Editor, Gene Havlick. Starring Louis Hayward (Edward), Jody Lawrence (Lynn), Alexander Knox (Curtis Lanyon), Lester Matthews (Utterson), Gavin Muir (Richard Daniels), Paul Cavanagh (Inspector). 77 minutes.

The Strange Case of Dr. Jekyll and Miss Osbourn (Dr. Jekyll et les Femmes; Bloodlust). (Whodunit/Allegro, 1981). France. Directed by Walerian Borowczyk (Color). Starring Udo Kier, Patrick Magee, Marina Pierro. Color.

The Strange Case of Dr. Jekyll and Mr. Hyde. (CBC/ABC-TV, 1968). USA/Canada. Produced by Dan Curtis. Directed by Charles Jarrott. Script by Ian McLellan Hunter.

Right, Hyde (Jack Palance) lashes out in anger in *The Strange Case of Dr. Jekyll and Mr. Hyde.*

Production Designer, Trevor Williams (Color). Music, Robert Cobert. Starring Jack Palance (Jekyll/Hyde), Denholm Elliott (Devlin), Torin Thatcher (Sir John Turnbull), Billie Whitelaw (Gwynn), Tessie O'Shea (Tessie), Leo Fenwick (Poole), Oscar Homolka (Stryker). Color 150 minutes.

The Strange Case of Dr. Jekyll and Mr. Hyde. (Showtime/Think, 1989). USA. Produced by Bridget Terry. Directed by Michael Lindsay-Hogg. Script by Michael Straczynski. Director of Photography, Ron Vargas (Color). Production Designer, Jane Osmann. Music, Stephen Barber. Editor, Roy Watts. Starring Anthony Andrews (Dr. Jekyll/Hyde), Laura Dern (Rebecca), Nicholas Guest, George Murdock, Gregory Cooke. 60 minutes.

Strannayar Istoriyar Doktora Dzhekila I Mistera Khaida *(The Stange Case of Dr. Jekyll and Mr. Hyde).* (Mosfilm, 1987). USSR. Directed by Alexander Orlov. Script by Orlov and Georgy Kapralov. Director of Photography, Valery Shuvalov (Color). Production Designer, Igor Lemeshev. Music, E. Artemyev. Starring Innokenti Smoktunovsky (Dr. Jekyll), Alexander Feklistov (Hyde), Anatoly Adoskin (Utterson), A. Lazarev (Lanyon). 89 minutes.

Le Testament du Dr. Cordelier. (RTF/Sofirad/Compagnie Renoir, 1959). France. Produced by Albert Hollebecke. Directed by Jean Renoir. Script by Renoir. Director of Photography, Georges Leclerc. Production Designer, Marcel-Louis Dieulot. Music, Joseph Kosma. Editor, Renée Lichtig. Starring Jean-Louis Barrault (Dr. Cordelier/Opale), Teddy Billis (Joly), Michel Vitold (Dr. Severin), Jean Topart (Desire, the butler), Micheline Gary (Marguerite), Jacques Dannoville (Commissaire Lardout). 95 minutes.

The Two Faces of Dr. Jekyll *(Jekyll's Inferno; House of Fright).* (Hammer, 1960). Great Britain. Produced by Michael Carreras.

Below, another debonair Hyde (Paul Massie) in Terence Fisher's *The Two Faces of Dr. Jekyll.*

Directed by Terence Fisher. Script by Wolf Mankowitz. Director of Photography, Jack Asher (Color/Scope). Production Designers, Bernard Robinson, Don Mingaye. Music, Monty Norman, David Heneker. Editor, James Needs, Eric Boyd-Perkins. Starring Paul Massie (Jekyll/Hyde), Dawn Addams (Kitty), Christopher Lee (Paul Allen), David Kossoff (Litauer), Francis De Wolff (Inspector), Norma Marla (Maria), Magda Miller (Sphinx Girl), William Kendall (Clubman). 89 minutes.

The Ugly Duckling. (Hammer/Columbia, 1959). Great Britain. Produced by Michael Carreras. Directed by Lance Comfort. Script by Sid Colin and Jack Davies. Director of Photography, Michael Reed. Production Designer, Bernard Robinson. Music, Douglas Gamley. Editor, James Needs, John Dunsford. Starring Bernard Bresslaw (Jekyll/Hyde), Reginald Beckwith (Reginald), Jon Pertwee (Victor Jekyll), Maudie Edwards (Henrietta). 84 minutes.

Oscar Wilde

NOTE: All the scripts in this section are based on Oscar Wilde's novel, **The Picture of Dorian Gray,** or the characters contained therein. Other stories, novels, or plays noted below are similarly based.

Das Bildnis der Dorian Gray *(The Picture of Dorian Gray).* (Oswald Films, 1917). Germany. Written, Produced, and Directed by Richard Oswald. Director of Photography, Max Fassbender. Starring Bernd Aldor, Lupu Pick, Ernst Pittaschau, Andreas Van Horn, Lea Lara, Ernst Ludwig. 80 minutes.

Az Élet Kiralya *(The Royal Life).* (1917). Hungary. Directed by Alfred Deesy. Starring Béla Lugosi, Norbert Dan, Gustav Twian, Ila Loth, Annie Goth, Richard Kornai, Carmilla Hollay.

The Picture of Dorian Gray. (Barker/Neptune, 1916). Great Britain. Directed by Fred W. Durrant. Script by Rowland Talbot. Starring Henry Victor, Pat O'Malley, Jack Jordan, Sydney Bland, A.B. Imeson, Douglas Cox. 77 minutes (5,752 feet).

The Picture of Dorian Gray. (MGM, 1945). USA. Produced by Pandro S. Berman. Directed by Albert Lewin. Script by Lewin. Director of Photography, Harry Stradling. Production Designer, Cedric Gibbons, Hans Peters. Music, Herbert Stothart. Editor, Ferris Webster. Starring George Sanders (Lord Henry Wotton), Hurd Hatfield (Dorian Gray), Donna Reed (Gladys Hallward), Angela Lansbury (Sibyl Vane), Peter Lawford (David Stone), Lowell Gilmore (Basil Hallward), Richard Fraser (James Vane), Douglas Walton (Allen Campbell), Morton Lowry (Adrian Aingleton). 110 minutes.

The Picture of Dorian Gray. (Susskind/CBS-TV, 1961). USA. Produced by Jacqueline Babbin. Directed by Paul Bogart. Script by Babbin and Audrey Gellen. Starring John Fraser, George C. Scott, Susan Oliver, Louis Hayward, Margaret Phillips, Robert Goodier. 60 minutes.

The Picture of Dorian Gray. (Curtis/ABC-TV, 1973). USA. Produced by Dan Curtis. Directed by Glenn Jordan. Script by John Tomerlin. Director of Photography, Ben Colman (Color). Music, Robert Cobert. Editor, Dennis Virkler. Starring

Shane Briant (Dorian Gray), Nigel Davenport (Sir Henry Wotton), Charles Aidman (Basil Hallward), Fionnuala Flanagan (Felicia), Linda Kelsey (Beatrice), Vanessa Howard (Sybil). 144 minutes.

Portret Doriana Greya *(The Picture of Dorian Gray).* (1915). Russia. Directed by Vsevolod Meyerhold. Script by Meyerhold. Director of Photography, Alexander Levitsky. Production Designer, Vladimir Yegorov. Starring Varvara Yanova, V. Meyerhold. 89 minutes (6,694 feet).

The Secret of Dorian Gray *(Dorian Gray).* (Towers of London/Commonwealth United, 1972). Great Britain/Italy. Produced by Harry Alan Towers. Directed by Massimo Dallamo. Script by Marcello Coscia and Dallamo. Director of Photography, Otello Spila (Color). Production Designer, Maria Ambrosino. Editor, Nicholas Wentworth. Starring Helmut Berger (Dorian Gray), Richard Todd (Basil), Herbert Lom (Henry Wotten), Marie Liljedahl (Sybil), Margaret Lee (Gwendolyn), Maria Rohm (Alice), Isa Miranda (Mrs. Ruxton), Eleonora Rossi Drago (Esther). 93 minutes.

The Sins of Dorian Gray.
(Rankin/Bass/ABC-TV, 1983). USA. Produced by Jules Bass. Directed by Tony Maylam. Script by Ken August and Peter Lawrence. Director of Photography, Zale Madger (Color). Production Designer, Karen Bromley. Music, Bernard Hoffer. Editor, Ron

Below, Hurd Hatfield as Dorian Gray and Lowell Gilmore as Basil Hallward.

Wisman. Starring Anthony Perkins (Henry Lord), Belinda Bauer (Dorian Gray), Joseph Bottoms (Stuart Vane), Olga Karlatos (Sofia Lord), Michael Ironside (Alan Campbell). 95 minutes.

M. R. James

Night of the Demon (Curse of the Demon). (Sabre/Columbia, 1957). Great Britain. Produced by Frank Bevis. Directed by Jacques Tourneur. Script by Charles Bennett and Hal E. Chester based on "Casting the Runes" by M.R. James. Director of Photography, Ted Scaife. Production Designer, Ken Adam. Music, Clifton Parker. Editor, Michael Gordon. Starring Dana Andrews (John Holden), Peggy Cummins (Joanna Harrington), Niall MacGinnis (Dr. Karswell), Maurice Denham (Prof. Harrington), Athene Seyler (Mrs. Karswell), Liam Redmond (Mark O'-Brien), Reginald Beckwith (Mr. Meek). 95 minutes.

Henry James

The Innocents. (Achilles/20th Century-Fox, 1961). Great Britain. Produced and Directed by Jack Clayton. Script by William Archibald and Truman Capote, based on the play by Archibald, adapted from **The Turn of the Screw** by James. Director of Photography, Freddie Francis (Scope). Production Designer, Wilfred Shingleton. Music, Georges Auric. Editor, James Clark. Starring Deborah Kerr (Miss Giddens), Megs Jenkins (Mrs. Grose), Martin Stephens (Miles), Pamela Franklin (Flora), Peter Wyngarde (Peter Quint), Isla Cameron (Anna), Clytie

Jessop (Miss Jessel), Michael Redgrave (the Uncle). 99 minutes.

The Nightcomers. (Scimitar/Kastner-Kanter-Ladd, 1971). Great Britain. Produced and Directed by Michael Winner. Script by Michael Hastings, based on characters in **The Turn of the Screw** by James. Director of Photography, Robert Paynter (Color). Production Designer, Herbert Westbrook. Music, Jerry Fielding. Editor, Frederick Wilson. Starring Marlon Brando (Peter Quint), Stephanie Beacham (Miss Jessel), Thora Hird (Mrs. Grose), Harry Andrews (Master of the House), Verna Harvey (Flora), Christopher Ellis (Miles), Anna Palk (Governess). 96 minutes.

Otra Vuelta de Tuerca (The Turn of the Screw). (1985). Spain. Directed by Eloy de la Iglesia (Color). Based on **The Turn of the Screw** by James. Starring Maria Sanchez, Queta Claver, Asier Hernandez Landa.

The Turn of the Screw. (NBC-TV/Ford Startime, 1959). USA. Produced by Hubbell Robinson. Directed by John Frankenheimer. Script by James Costigan, based on **The Turn of the Screw** by James. Music, David Amram. Starring Ingrid Bergman, Isobel Elsom, Heywood Morse, Alexandra Wager, Laurinda Barrett, Paul Stevens. 90 minutes.

The Turn of the Screw. (ABC-TV, 1974). USA. Produced and Directed by Dan Curtis. Script by William F. Nolan, based on **The Turn of the Screw** by James. Director of Photography, Ben Colman (Color). Production Designer, Trevor Williams. Music, Robert Cobert. Editor, Dennis Virkler. Starring Lynn Redgrave

(Jane Cubberly), Jasper Jacobs (Miles), Eva Griffith (Flora), Megs Jenkins (Mrs. Grose), John Barton (Mr. F.), Anthony Langdon (Luke), Benedict Taylor (Timothy). 180 minutes.

The Turn of the Screw. (Showtime/Think Entertainment, 1979). Produced by Bridget Terry. Directed by Graeme Clifford. Script by James M. Miller and Robert Hutchinson, based on **The Turn of the Screw** by James. Director of Photography, Ron Vargas (Color). Production Designer, Jane Osmann. Music, J. Peter Robinson. Editor, Conrad Gonzales. Starring Amy Irving (the Governess), David Hemmings (Mr. Harley), Balthazar Getty (Miles), Nicole Mercurio (Flora), Irina Cashen (Mrs. Grose). 60 minutes.

The Turn of the Screw. (Unitel, 1982). Great Britain/West Germany/Czechoslovakia. Produced by Zdenek Oves and Hans-Günter Herbertz. Directed by Petr Weigl. Script by Melanie Némecková, based on opera libretto by Myfawny Piper, adapted from **The Turn of the Screw** by James. Director of Photography, Jiri Kadanka (Color). Production Designer, Miloš Cervinka. Music: Benjamin Britten, performed by the Royal Opera House Orchestra, Covent Garden under the direction of Sir Colin Davis. Editor, Karel Kohout. Starring Magdalena Vásáryová [sung by Helen Donath] (Governess), Dana Medrická [sung by Ava June] (Mrs. Grose), Juraj Kukura [sung by Robert Tear] (Quint), Emilia Vásáryová [sung by Heather Harper] (Miss Jessel), Beata Blazicková [sung by Lilian Watson] (Flora), Michael Gulyás [sung by Michael Ginn] (Miles), Vladimir

Müller (Guardian), Philip Langridge (Narrator). 116 minutes.

The Turn of the Screw. (Electric Pictures/White, 1992). Great Britain/France. Produced by Staffan Ahrenberg and Nicole Seguin. Directed by Rusty Lemorande. Script by Lemorande, based on **The Turn of the Screw** by James. Director of Photography, Witold Stok (Color). Production Designer, Max Gottlieb. Music, Simon Boswell. Editor, John Victor Smith. Starring Patsy Kensit (Jenny Gooding), Stephane Audran (Mrs. Grose), Julian Sands (Mr. Cooper), Marianne Faithfull (Narrator), Claire Szekeres (Flora), Joseph England (Miles), Olivier Dubray (Quint), Bryony Brind (Miss Jessel). 95 minutes.

Fritz Leiber

Night of the Eagle (Burn, Witch, Burn). (Independent Pictures/AIP, 1961). Great Britain. Produced by Albert Fennell. Directed by Sidney Hayes. Script by Richard Matheson, Charles Beaumont, and George Baxt based on **Conjure Wife** by Fritz Leiber. Director of Photography, Reginald Wyer. Production Designers, Jack Shampan, Peter Lamont. Music, William Alwyn. Editor, Ralph Sheldon. Starring Peter Wyngarde (Prof. Norman Taylor), Janet Blair (Tansy Taylor), Colin Cordon (Prof. Carr), Margaret Johnston (Flora Carr), Judith Scott (Margaret Abbott), Bill Mitchell (Fred Jennings). 89 minutes.

Weird Woman. (Universal, 1944). USA. Produced by Oliver Drake. Directed by Reginald Le Borg. Script by Brenda Weisberg and W. Scott Darling based on **Conjure Wife** by Fritz Leiber. Director of Photography, Virgil Miller. Production Designers, Richard Reidel, John Goodman. Music, Paul Sawtell. Editor, Milton Carruth. Starring Lon Chaney, Jr. (Prof. Norman Reed), Anne Gwynne (Paula Reed), Evelyn Ankers (Ilona Carr), Ralph Morgan (Prof. Sawtelle), Elisabeth Risdon (Grace Gunnison), Lois Collier (Margaret Mercer). 63 minutes.

Witches' Brew. (Lightman, 1985). USA. Produced by Donna Ashbrook. Directed by Richard Shorr and Her-bert L. Strock. Script by Syd Dutton and Shorr based on [uncredited] **Conjure Wife** by Fritz Leiber. Directors of Photography, Norman Gerard, Joao Fernandes (Color). Production Designer, Marie Kordus. Music, John Parker. Editor, Strock. Starring Richard Benjamin (Joshua Lightman), Teri Garr (Margaret Lightman), Lana Turner (Vivian Cross), Kathryn Leigh Scott (Susan Carey), James Winkler (Linus Cross), Bill Sorrels (Nick Carey). 98 minutes.

Below, Norman Saylor (Peter Wyngarde) prepares the ceremony to recall his wife, Tansy, in Night of the Eagle,

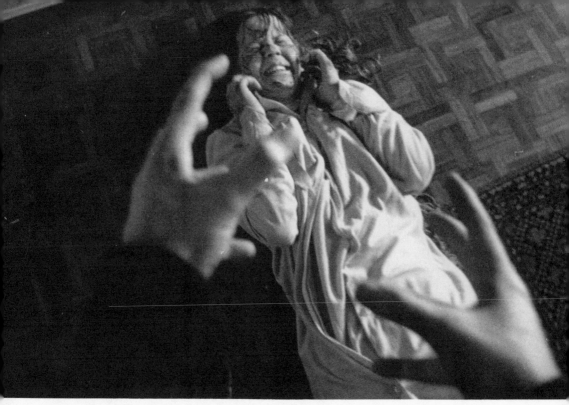

Above, the hands of *The Exorcist* reach out for the possessed Regan (Linda Blair).

Shirley Jackson

The Haunting. (MGM, 1963). USA.
Produced and Directed by Robert
Wise. Script by Nelson Gidding
based on **The Haunting of Hill
House** by Shirley Jackson. Director
of Photography, Davis Boulton
(Scope). Production Designer, Elliott
Scott. Music, Humphrey Searle.
Editor, Ernest Walter. Starring Julie
Harris (Eleanor), Claire Bloom
(Theo), Richard Johnson (Dr.
Markway), Russ Tamblyn (Luke), Fay
Compton (Mrs. Sannerson), Rosalie
Crutchley (Mrs. Dudley), Lois Max-
well (Grace Markway). 112 minutes.

Stephen Vincent Benet

The Devil and Daniel Webster
*(Here Is a Man; All That Money Can
Buy).* (RKO, 1941). USA. Produced
by William Dieterle. Directed by
Dieterle. Script by Daniel Totheroh
and Stephen Vincent Benet based on
the story by Benet. Director of
Photography, Joseph August. Music,
Bernard Herrmann. Editor, Robert
Wise. Starring Edward Arnold
(Daniel Webster), Walter Huston (Mr.
Scratch), Jane Darwell (Mrs. Stone),
James Craig (Jabez Stone), Simone
Simon (Belle), Gene Lockhart (Squire
Slossum), John Qualen (Miser
Stevens). Ann Shirley (Mary Stone).
100 minutes.

The Devil and Daniel Webster.
(NBC-TV, 1960). USA. Produced by
David Susskind. Directed by Tom
Donovan. Script by Phil Reisman,
Jr., based on the story by Benet.
Starring Edward G. Robinson, David
Wayne, Tim O'Connor, Betty Lou Hol-
land, Royal Beal, Stuart Germain. 60
minutes.

Ira Levin

Rosemary's Baby.
(Paramount/Castle, 1968). USA.
Produced by William Castle. Directed
by Roman Polanski. Script by
Polanski based the novel by Ira
Levin. Director of Photography, William Fraker (Color). Production
Designer, Richard Sylbert, Hal
Pereira. Music, Krzysztof Komeda.
Editor, Sam O'Steen, Bob Wyman.
Starring Mia Farrow (Rosemary
Woodhouse), John Cassavetes (Guy
Woodhouse), Ruth Gordon (Minnie
Castavet), Sidney Blackmer (Roman
Castavet), Maurice Evans (Hutch),
Ralph Bellamy (Dr. Sapirstein), Angela Dorian (Terry), Patsy Kelly
(Laura), Elisha Cook (Mr. Nicklas).
137 minutes.

William Peter Blatty

The Exorcist. (Hoya/Warner Bros.,
1973). USA. Produced by William
Peter Blatty. Directed by William
Friedkin. Script by Blatty based on
his novel. Directors of Photography,
Owen Roizman, Billy Williams
(Color). Production Designer, Bill
Malley. Music, Jack Nitzsche.
Editor, Evan Lottman, Norman
Gray, Bud Smith. Starring Ellen
Burstyn (Chris MacNeil), Max von
Sydow (Father Merrin), Lee J. Cobb
(Lt. William Kinderman), Kitty Winn
(Sharon Spencer), Linda Blair
(Regan MacNeil), Jason Miller
(Father Damien Karras), William O'-
Malley (Father Dyer), Barton
Heyman (Dr. Klein), Jack Mac-
Gowran (Burke). 122 minutes.

Stephen King

The Dead Zone. (Paramount/De
Laurentiis, 1983). USA. Produced by
Debra Hill. Directed by David
Cronenberg. Script by Jeffrey Boam
based on the novel by Stephen King.
Director of Photography, Mark Irwin
(Color). Production Designer, Carol
Spier. Music, Michael Kamen.
Editor, Ronald Sanders. Starring
Christopher Walken (Johnny Smith),
Brooke Adams (Sarah Bracknell),
Tom Skerritt (Sheriff Bannerman),
Herbert Lom (Dr. Weizak), Anthony
Zerbe (Roger Stuart), Colleen
Dewhurst (Henrietta Dodd), Martin
Sheen (Greg Stillson). 102 minutes.

Below, Rosemary (Mia Farrow) and
Roman Castevet (Sidney Blackmer)
by the crib of *Rosemary's Baby.*

Stephen King
THE
DEAD
ZONE

Above, cover art from the First Edition of Stephen King's **The Dead Zone** with the lettering style used in the main titles of David Cronenberg's film adaptation.

Bibliography

Barclay, Glen St. John. **The Masters of Occult Fiction.** London: Weidenfeld and Nicholson, 1978.

Bedford, Michael and Dettman, Bruce. **The Horror Factory: The Horror Films of Universal, 1931-1955.** New York: Gordon, 1976.

Birkhead, Edith. **The Tale of Terror.** London: Constable, 1921.

Bleiler, E.F. **The Checklist of Science-Fiction and Supernatural Fiction.** New Jersey: Firebell, 1978.

_____. **Supernatural Fiction Writers: Fantasy and Horror.** New York: Scribner's, 1985.

Bonaparte, Marie. **The Life and Works of Edgar Allan Poe.** London: Imago Publishing, 1949.

Bourgoin, Stephane. **Terence Fisher.** Paris: Édilig, 1986.

Briggs, Julia. **Night Visitors: The Rise and Fall of the English Ghost Story.** London: Faber and Faber, 1977.

Brunas, Michael, Brunas, John and Weaver, Tom. **Universal Horrors: The Studio's Classic Films.** Jefferson, North Carolina/London: McFarland, 1990.

Buckley, J.H. **The Victorian Temper.** New York: Vintage, 1964.

Butler, Ivan. **Horror in the Cinema.** London: Tantivy, 1967.

Clarens, Carlos. **An Illustrated History of the Horror Film.** New York: G.P. Putnam, 1967.

Daniels, Les. **Living in Fear: A History of Horror in Mass Media.** New York: Charles Scribner's, 1975.

Davis, Richard, ed. **The Octopus Encyclopedia of Horror.** London: Octopus, 1981.

Day, William Patrick. **In the Circles of Fear and Desire: A Study of Gothic Fantasy.** Chicago: University of Chicago Press, 1985.

De Camp, L. Sprague. **Lovecraft: A Biography.** New York: Doubleday, 1975.

Del Vecchio, Deborah and Johnson, Tom. **Peter Cushing.** Jefferson, North Carolina/London: McFarland, 1992.

Derry, Charles. **Dark Dreams: A Psychological History of the Modern Horror Film.** Cranbury, New Jersey: A.S. Barnes and Co., 1977.

Dixon, Wheeler Winston. **The Charm of Evil: The Life and Times of Terence Fisher.** Metuchen, New Jersey: Scarecrow, 1993.

Eisner, Lotte. **The Haunted Screen.** Berkeley: University of California, 1969.

Everson, William K. **Classics of the Horror Film.** Secaucus, New Jersey: Citadel, 1974.

Eyles, Allen, ed. **The House of Horror, the Story of Hammer Films.** London: Lorrimer, 1973.

Florescu, Radu. **In Search of Frankenstein.** Boston: New York Graphic Society, 1975.

Frank, Alan G. **Horror Movies, Tales of Terror in the Cinema.** London: Octopus, 1974.

Geary, Robert F. **The Supernatural in Gothic Fiction.** New York: Edwin Mellen, 1992.

Geduld, Harry M., ed. **The Definitive Dr. Jekyll and Mr. Hyde Companion.** New York: Garland, 1983.

Grant, Barry Keith, ed. **Planks of Reason: Essays on the Horror Film.** Metuchen, New Jersey: Scarecrow, 1984.

Glut, Donald F. **The Frankenstein Legend.** Metuchen, New Jersey: Scarecrow, 1973.

Haggerty, George E. **Gothic Fiction/Gothic Form.** Pennsylvania: Pennsylvania State University, 1989

Hanke, Ken. **A Critical Guide to Horror Film Series.** New York: Garland, 1991.

Hardy, Phil. **The Encyclopedia of Horror Movies.** New York: Harper and Row, 1986.

Hays, H.R. **The Dangerous Sex.** New York: Pocket, 1972.

Hearn, Lafcadio. **Interpretations in Literature.** New York: Dodd, Mead, 1916.

Heller, Terry. **The Delights of Terror: An Aesthetics of the Tale of Terror.** Chicago: University of Illinois, 1987.

Hillyer, Robert. Introduction to **Tales of Horror and the Supernatural** by Arthur Machen. New York: Knopf, 1948.

Hogan, David J. **Dark Romance: Sexuality in the Horror Film.** Jefferson, North Carolina/London: McFarland, 1986.

_____. **Who's Who of the Horrors and Other Fantasy Films.** Cranbury, New Jersey: A.S. Barnes, 1980.

Hutchings, Peter. **Hammer and Beyond: the British Horror Film.** Manchester: Manchester University Press, 1993.

Hutchinson, Tom. **Horror and Fanstasy in the Movies.** New York: Crescent, 1974.

Jensen, Paul M. **Boris Karloff and His Films.** South Brunswick and New York: A.S. Barnes and Co., 1974.

Jones, Ernest. **On the Nightmare.** New York: Liveright, 1971.

Joshi, S.T. **The Weird Tale: Machen, Dunsany, Blackwood, M.R. James, Bierce, Lovecraft.** Austin, Texas: University of Texas Press, 1990.

Klein, Michael and Parker, Gillian, eds. **The English Novel and the Movies**. New York: Frederick Ungar, 1981.

Kimbrough, Robert, ed. **Turn of the Screw: Backgrounds and Sources.** New York: Norton Critical, 1966.

King, Stephen. **Danse Macabre.** New York: Everest House, 1981.

Knoepflmacher, U.C. and Levine, George, eds. **The Endurance of Frankenstein: Essays on Mary Shelley's Novel.** Berkeley: University of California, 1987.

Kyrou, Ado. **Le Surrealisme au Cinéma.** Paris: Le Terrain Vague, 1963.

Lee, Walt. **Reference Guide to Fantastic Films.** California: Walt Lee, 1972 (three volumes).

Lenne, Gerard. **Le Cinéma Fantastique et Ses Mythologies.** Paris: Éditions du Cert, 1970.

Lentz, Harris M. **Science Fiction, Horror and Fantasy Film and Television Credits**. Jefferson, North Carolina/London: McFarland, Volume I: 1983, Volume II: 1989, Supplement: 1989.

London, Rose. **The Cinema of Mystery.** London: Lorrimer, 1975.

_____. **Zombie, the Living Dead**. New York: Bounty, 1976.

Lovecraft, H.P. Essay on "Supernatural Horror in Literature" in **Dagon**. New York: Panther, 1969.

Lucas, Tim. **The Video Watchdog Book.** Cincinnati, Ohio: Video Watchdog, 1992.

Milne, Tom and Willemen, Paul. **The Encyclopedia of Horror Movies.** New York: Harper and Row, 1986.

Naha, Ed. **Horrors from Screen to Scream, an Encyclopedic Guide to the Greatest Horror and Fantasy Films of All Time.** New York: Avon, 1975.

Newman, Kim. **Nightmare Movies: A Critical History of the Horror Film Since 1968.** New York: Proteus, 1984.

Pearsall, Ronald. **The Worm in the Bud: The World of Victorian Sexuality.** London: Penguin, 1983.

Penzoldt, Peter. **Supernatural in Fiction.** New York: Humanities Press, 1965.

Praz, Mario. **The Romantic Agony.** London and New York: Oxford University, 1970.

Predal, Rene. **Le Cinéma Fantastique.** Paris: Seghers, 1970.

Rabkin, Eric S. **The Fantastic in Literature.** Princeton, New Jersey: Princeton University Press, 1976.

Rottensteiner, Franz. **The Fantasy Book: The Ghostly, the Gothic, the Magical, the Unreal.** London: Thames and Hudson, 1978.

Scarborough, Dorothy. **The Supernatural in Modern English Fiction.** New York: Humanitas Press, 1965.

Senn, Bryan and Johnson, John. **Fantastic Cinema Subject Guide**. Jefferson, North Carolina/London: McFarland, 1992.

Soren, David. **The Rise and Fall of the Horror Film: An Art Historical Approach to Fantasy Cinema.** Columbia, Missouri: Lucas Bros., 1977.

Sullivan, Jack. **Elegant Nightmares: The English Ghost Story.** Columbus, Ohio: Ohio State University Press, 1978.

_____. **The Penguin Encyclopedia of Horror and the Supernatural.** New York: Viking-Penguin, 1986.

Sweetser, Wesley D. **Arthur Machen.** New York: Twayne Publishers, 1964.

Todorov, Tzvetan. **The Fantastic: A Structural Approach to a Literary Genre**. Ithaca: Cornell University Press, 1975.

Tropp, Martin. **Images of Fear: How Horror Stories Helped Shape Modern Culture.** Jefferson, North Carolina/London: McFarland, 1990.

Twitchell, James B. **Dreadful Pleasures: An Anatomy of Modern Horror.** New York/Oxford: Oxford University, 1985.

Willis, Donald C. **Horror and Science Fiction Films: A Checklist.** Metuchen, New Jersey: Scarecrow, 1972.

_____. **Horror and Science Fiction Films II.** Metuchen, New Jersey: Scarecrow, 1982.

_____. **Horror and Science Fiction Films III.** Metuchen, New Jersey: Scarecrow, 1984.

Tymn, Marshall B. **Horror Literature: A Core Collection and Reference Guide.** New York: R.R. Bowker, 1981.

Varnado, S.L. **Haunted Presence: the Numinous in Gothic Fiction.** Tuscaloosa, Alabama: University of Alabama, 1987.

Wagenknecht, Edward. **Seven Masters of Supernatural Fiction.** New York: Greenwood Press, 1991.

Will, David and Willamen, Paul, eds. **Roger Corman: the Millenic Vision**. Edinburgh: Edinburgh Film Festival/*Cinema* Magazine, 1970.

Willen, Gerald, ed. **A Casebook on Henry James's The Turn of the Screw.** New York, Crowell, 1969.

Wilson, Edmund. Essay on "The Ambiguity of Henry James" in **The Triple Thinkers**. New York: Oxford University Press, 1948.

Wolf, Leonard. **The Annotated Frankenstein.** New York: Clarkson N. Potter, 1977.

_____. **Horror: A Connoisseur's Guide to Literature and Film.** New York: Facts on File, 1989.

Index

As in the main text, italics are used to indicate film titles, including television movies and shorts, and boldface for books, novels, and other long form fiction. Plays, short stories, etc. are enclosed within quotation marks. Parenthetical annotations provide additional information; in the case of persons who have several occupations, the most relevant one is given. Films with the same title are distinguished first by year of release, then by country of origin. In an instance where this fails to distinguish them, as with the two American adaptations of *Dr. Jekyll and Mr. Hyde* released in 1920, the lead actor is used.

Page numbers in italics indicate illustrations. References to pages in the filmography appear after the semi-colon.

211